Noviter Non Nova

The development of doctrine and the Church of England debate about marriage and sexuality

Martin Davie

GILEAD BOOKS PUBLISHING

This book is dedicated with gratitude to the memory of those past generations of Christian scholars whose development of Christian doctrine still benefits us today.

We see further because we stand on the shoulders of giants.

GileadBooksPublishing.com

First published in Great Britain, January 2026
2 4 6 8 10 9 7 5 3 1

Copyright ©Martin Davie 2026
British Library Cataloguing-in-Publication Data:
A catalogue record for this book is available from the British Library.

ISBN: 978-1-8381828-6-1

All rights reserved.
No part of this publication may be reproduced, stored in a retrieval system or transmitted in any form or by any means, electronic, mechanical, photocopying, recording or otherwise, without the prior permission of the publisher.

Unless otherwise stated scripture quotations are from the Revised Standard Version of the Bible, Copyright © 1946, 1952, and 1971 the Division of Christian Education of the National Council of the Churches of Christ in the United States of America. Used by permission. All rights reserved.

Indexer: Lyndsay Marshall
Cover design: Nathan Ward

Contents

Introduction		4
Chapter 1	What is doctrine?	12
Chapter 2	The evidence for the development of doctrine	46
Chapter 3	*Noviter non nova* - The Commonitory of Vincent of Lerins	93
Chapter 4	To be perfect is to have changed often – John Henry Newman on the development of doctrine	129
Chapter 5	Schleiermacher's ghost – Maurice Wiles on the Making and Remaking Of Christian Doctrine	178
Chapter 6	The development of doctrine and the Church of England debate about marriage and sexuality	228
Bibliography		281
Subject index		291
Scripture and ancient sources index		302

Introduction
The Theseus Paradox and Prayers of Love and Faith

In Greek legend, Theseus, the King of Athens, rescued the children of Athens from King Minos of Crete after slaying the Minotaur. He then escaped from Crete on a ship heading to Delos. This ship was subsequently preserved at Athens and taken on an annual pilgrimage to Delos to honour Apollos.

As time went on, more and more bits of the original ship were replaced as they decayed, and this raised a question among ancient philosophers which has come to be known as the 'Theseus paradox.' If a stage was reached when all the pieces of the original ship were thus replaced was the current ship still the Ship of Theseus? If not, at what point did the original ship cease to exist?

The discussion about this issue was first noted by the Greek historian and philosopher Plutarch in his *Life of Theseus*. Plutarch writes:

> The ship on which Theseus sailed with the youths and returned in safety, the thirty-oared galley, was preserved by the Athenians down to the time of Demetrius Phalereus. They took away the old timbers from time to time, and put new and sound ones in their places, so that the vessel became a standing illustration for the philosophers in the mooted question of growth, some declaring that it remained the same, others that it was not the same vessel.[1]

A modern version of the Theseus Paradox is raised by Admiral Nelson's flagship HMS Victory which is preserved in dry dock in Portsmouth. As the conservation log for HMS Victory compiled by the National Museum of the Royal Navy makes clear, although there are

---

[1] Plutarch, 'Life of Theseus' 23:1, in *Plutarch's Lives,* Vol I (Harvard and London: Harvard University Press/William Heinemann, 1917), p.49.

some original parts of the ship left, a very large proportion of the ship has been replaced since it was launched in 1765 and took part in the Battle of Trafalgar in 1805.[2] This raises the question, is the HMS Victory we see today sufficiently original that we can still say that it is Nelson's flagship, and, if this is the case, if pieces continue to be replaced in the future will it at some point cease to be Nelson's flagship?

The issue raised by the Ship of Theseus and by HMS Victory is that of continuity in the face of change. How much can something change and still retain its identity? Philosophers differ on this point, but the answer seems to be that identity can be said to persist in the face of change if there is some essential form of continuity. Thus, in the case of the two ships we have mentioned, the fact of their having a continuous history even while a growing number of parts are replaced means that they can be said to be the same ships. In a similar way a human being remains the same person although billions of cells in their bodies are replaced every day.[3]

However, if some form of essential continuity does not persist, then identity cannot be said to be maintained. For example, if the decision was taken to scrap HMS Victory entirely and to replace her at Portsmouth with the World War II battleship HMS Belfast, currently moored in the Thames in the Pool of London, it would generally be agreed that the ship in Portsmouth was not now the same ship as HMS Victory, even if HMS Belfast was renamed HMS Victory by the Royal Navy. In the same way, if someone takes someone else's name, whether by agreement or in some form of identity theft, this would not make them that person. In both cases the necessary element of continuity would be generally agreed to be missing.

[2] *HMS Victory – Conservation Log*, at https://www.nmrn.org.uk/hms-victory-conservation-log
[3] See Mark Fischetti & Jen Christiansen, 'Our Bodies Replace Billions of Cells Every Day', *Scientific American*, April 1, 2021, at: https://www.scientificamerican.com/article/our-bodies-replace-billions-of-cells-every-day/

The issue of continuity and change raised by the examples we have just considered is also raised by the *Prayers of Love and Faith* process that is currently taking place in the Church of England.

The legal basis of this process is a motion that was passed by the Church of England's General Synod on 9 February 2023. This motion runs as follows:

> 'That this Synod, recognising the commitment to learning and deep listening to God and to each other of the Living in Love and Faith process, and desiring with God's help to journey together while acknowledging the different deeply held convictions within the Church:
>
> a) lament and repent of the failure of the Church to be welcoming to LGBTQI+ people and the harm that LGBTQI+ people have experienced and continue to experience in the life of the Church;
>
> b) recommit to our shared witness to God's love for and acceptance of every person by continuing to embed the Pastoral Principles in our life together locally and nationally;
>
> c) commend the continued learning together enabled by the Living in Love and Faith process and resources in relation to identity, sexuality, relationships and marriage;
>
> d) welcome the decision of the House of Bishops to replace Issues in Human Sexuality with new pastoral guidance;
>
> e) welcome the response from the College of Bishops and look forward to the House of Bishops further refining, commending and issuing the Prayers of Love and Faith described in GS 2289 and its Annexes;
>
> f) invite the House of Bishops to monitor the Church's use of and response to the Prayers of Love and Faith, once they have been commended and published, and to report back to Synod in five years' time;

g) endorse the decision of the College and House of Bishops not to propose any change to the doctrine of marriage, and their intention that the final version of the Prayers of Love and Faith should not be contrary to or indicative of a departure from the doctrine of the Church of England.'[4]

The key clause in the motion is clause (g). This is because it constrains the House on Bishops from changing the Church of England's existing doctrine of marriage and from including anything in the forms of prayer contained in the Prayers of Love and Faith material that involved any departure from the Church of England's doctrine concerning sexual ethics. It also means in relation to clause (d) of the motion that any new pastoral guidance to replace *Issues in Human Sexuality* will need to conform to the Church's existing doctrine both in respect of the Church's teaching with regard to marriage and sexual ethics, and the requirement that members of the clergy live lives that are in accordance with this teaching.

Since the Synod motion was passed, the House of Bishops has commended a set of prayers that can be used in the case of same-sex couples, including those who have entered same-sex marriages[5]. It is also currently proposing the introduction of standalone services for those who have entered same-sex civil marriages or civil partnerships, as well as working on proposals for new 'pastoral guidance' to replace *Issues in Human Sexuality* which would permit the ordination of those in civil same-sex marriages.[6]

---

[4] The Church of England, 'Prayers for God's blessing for same-sex couples take step forward after Synod Debate' at
https://www.churchofengland.org/media/press-releases/prayers-gods-blessing-same-sex-couples-take-step-forward-after-synod-debate
[5] The Church of England, *Prayers of Love and Faith* at:
https://www.churchofengland.org/sites/default/files/2023-12/prayers-of-love-and-faith.pdf
[6] See GS 2358, *LLF: Moving Forward as One Church* at:
https://www.churchofengland.org/sites/default/files/2024-06/gs-2358-living-in-love-and-faith.pdf and GS Misc 1407, *A part report of the Episcopal Reference*

Currently there are no proposals for formally changing the Church of England's doctrine of marriage, or for permitting the solemnisation of same-sex marriages to take place in Church of England churches. However, if the Church of England decides that such marriages can be marked by standalone services in church and are compatible with the holiness of life required of ordained ministers, it is difficult to see how the Church of England would still be able to maintain that it does not view such marriages as marriages and therefore capable of being solemnised in church. A formal change in the Church's doctrine of marriage would thus seem almost inevitable in the medium to long term once that point is reached.

If we ask on what basis the House of Bishops proposes to move forward with standalone services and the replacement of *Issues in Human Sexuality* along the lines just described, the answer lies in the concept of the development of doctrine. What the bishops are arguing is that what they are proposing is a development of, rather than a departure from, the doctrine of the Church of England and thus not in conflict with clause (g) of the 2023 Synod motion.

In paragraph 44 of GS 2358, *LLF: Moving Forward as One Church,* the bishops explain that theological work will be undertaken to 'to provide clarity around how doctrine can develop or change within the Church of England'[7] and in GS Misc 1407, *A part report of the Episcopal Reference Group of the Faith and Order Commission: Living in Love and Faith and the Doctrine of Marriage* the bishops review the history of the doctrine of marriage in the Church of England since the Reformation and then declare:

The story of the doctrine of marriage in the Church of England over the last five hundred years, therefore, is one of a high degree of consistency and stability, and yet with some significant developments

---

Group of the Faith and Order Commission: Living in Love and Faith and the Doctrine of Marriage, at: https://www.churchofengland.org/sites/default/files/2025-01/gs-misc-1407-part-report-from-episcopal-reference-group.pdf.
[7] GS 2358, p.10.

in understanding and emphasis within the envelope of continuity reflected in Canon B30 and the Prayer Book tradition.

The ERG, in consultation with FAOC and the Liturgical Commission, intend next to consider whether and how that doctrinal 'envelope' has been altered or enlarged with the commendation of the PLF; whether it is now already a big enough envelope to accommodate some of the other changes that are sought by many within the Church (such as the use of the PLF in bespoke services and a change in discipline regarding clergy and same-sex marriage) or whether the Church would need an explicitly bigger doctrinal envelope for them; and to begin to consider what kind of size and shape 'envelope' could be created if the Church discerned and resolved that it wanted same-sex marriage to be included therein also. It ought to be acknowledged at this juncture that the great majority of those within the Church of England who would like the doctrine and discipline of the Church to expand in such a way that it can accommodate same-sex marriage do not deny nor wish to dilute or overturn the doctrine of marriage thus expressed in the nine theses above, but to adjust certain aspects of it to be inclusive of same-sex unions. It would not be fair or accurate, therefore, to cast the Church's current disagreement as simply a binary contest between those who wish to defend the Church's doctrine of marriage and those who disbelieve it. Rather, the dispute concerns whether the Church's doctrine of marriage is already, or may legitimately become, spacious enough to include same-sex couples in its ambit. Some believe the necessary adjustment to be modest and to be following and flowing organically from an established trajectory in the Church's moral, pastoral, and theological treatment of marriage over the last century or so; others believe such an 'adjustment' would in fact be to tear the 'envelope' of a God-given institution.[8]

The bishops do not state in these paragraphs that they believe that 'the Church's doctrine of marriage is already, or may legitimately

---

[8] GS Misc 1407, p.16.

become, spacious enough to include same-sex couples in its ambit.' However, they are setting out this issue as the ground on which they think the issue of standalone, or 'bespoke,' PLF services and the ordination of those in same-sex marriages must be determined.

In the remainder of this book, I shall argue that the bishops are entirely right to identify the issue of the development of doctrine as the key issue that needs to be decided in relation to what the House of Bishops are proposing. However, I shall also argue that a proper theological understanding of the development of doctrine rules out the kind of changes that the bishops are suggesting might take place. Continuity of doctrine would not be maintained. To return to the examples given at the beginning of this introduction, it would be like replacing HMS Victory with HMS Belfast or one person taking the identity of another.

I shall argue this case in four parts.

First, in chapter 1 I shall set out what is meant by the term doctrine and why traditional Christian doctrine remains relevant today.

Secondly, in chapter 2 I shall explain why the historical evidence we possess shows that doctrine is not static but is something that develops over time.

Thirdly, in chapters 3-5 I shall consider three representative accounts of how to understand the development of doctrine and how to distinguish between legitimate and illegitimate forms of development. These accounts are the Patristic account given by Vincent of Lerins in the fifth century in his *Commonitory*, the account given by John Newman in the middle of the nineteenth century in his *Essay on the Development of Doctrine* to justify his conversion from Anglicanism to Roman Catholicism, and the Liberal Anglican account given in the second half of the twentieth century by Maurice Wiles in his two books *The Making of Christian Doctrine* and *The Remaking of Christian Doctrine*. In each case I shall explain what I think we can learn from the work(s) in question either about how we should rightly understand the development of doctrine, or about errors we should avoid when thinking about this issue.

Fourthly, in chapter 6 I shall then apply the lessons learned in the previous chapters to the specific case of the Church of England's doctrine of marriage and the view of sexual ethics that goes with it. I shall argue that a move in the direction that the House of Bishops is proposing would involve not a development of, but a departure from, the traditional doctrine of the Church of England and of the Christian Church as whole, a departure that would amount to what the Church has traditionally called heresy. To use the bishops' terminology, the doctrinal envelope is not big enough to accommodate the changes they propose.

Chapter 1
What is doctrine?

The nature of doctrine

A helpful place to start thinking about the nature of Christian doctrine is the statement by Alister McGrath in his book *The Nature of Christian Doctrine* that '…doctrine can be seen as a gateway to and articulation of the life-giving and life-changing realities that lie at the heart of the Christian community of faith.' As such, doctrine has '…the capacity to illuminate reality, create meaning, elicit joy and wonder, and bring hope in a darkening world.' [9]

The basic point that McGrath is making in these two quotations is that doctrine is something that has the power to change lives for the better.

At the heart of Christianity is the knowledge that Christians possess of the action of God in Jesus Christ, knowledge which makes it possible for them to begin new life with God and transforms the way that they live their lives in this world. What McGrath is saying is that doctrine is the way that the Christian community gives expression to this knowledge, thereby enabling those inside the community to grow in their appreciation of it, and those outside the community to share in it. When this happens reality is illuminated, meaning is created, joy and wonder are elicited, and hope is born.

The question that McGrath's account of Christian doctrine raises is how Christians have access to the knowledge of the action of God in Jesus Christ and its life changing implications. We can begin to answer this question if we consider the alternative definition of Christian Doctrine offered by J I Packer in his book *Taking God Seriously*.

---

[9] Alister McGrath, *The Nature of Christian Doctrine* (Oxford: OUP, 2024), Kindle edition, p.166.

Packer writes that:

> Doctrine is the revealed truth of God as defined and taught in the church, by the church, for the church, and for the world.
>
> Our word *doctrine* is from the Latin *doctrina*, which means teaching. The corresponding word in the Greek New Testament is *didache*, which has the same meaning. The New Testament church appears as a community of learners, some of whom become teachers as well, but all of whom are called to the lifelong task of taking in, digesting, and living out, which includes giving out, the good news of Jesus Christ that the apostles expounded to them. *Disciple* translates a Greek word that means learner; the church is seen as a fellowship of disciples, and any congregation that did not consist of persons labouring to learn more about Christ than they know as yet would hardly count as a church by New Testament standards.[10]

Packer further explains that:

> Doctrine is taught not only by sermons, catechisms, and instructional talks, by printed books and audio-visual devices, but also by worship patterns (liturgies, both written and unwritten; hymns and songs) and by creeds, confessions, and declarations of councils and synods. It is learned by attending to these and buttressing them with personal and group Bible study. By all these means Christians and congregations seek to assimilate, articulate, and apply what the apostles taught the first churches in Christ's name. Faithfulness to this heritage is the mark of sound doctrine - doctrine, that is, that promotes spiritual health. Deviations from the heritage constitute false doctrine, which will at least stunt growth and at worst ruin souls completely. Christian doctrine is

---

[10] J I Packer, *Taking God Seriously* ((Wheaton: Crossway, 2013), Kindle edition, p.33

thus serious business, as serious as anything with which the church ever deals. [11]

If we unpack Packer's definition of doctrine, we find that what he is saying is that the subject matter of Christian doctrine is the revealed truth of God, and the source of doctrine is the teaching of the apostles which the Christian Church passes on to those inside and outside the Church in various different ways. It is by this means that Christians have knowledge of the action of God in Jesus Christ.

This understanding of doctrine then raises two further questions. First, what is the connection between the revealed truth of God and the teaching of the apostles? Secondly, how does the Christian Church have access to the teaching of the apostles, given that they are all now dead?

The answer to the first question is given in the words of Jesus recorded in John 14:9 'He who has seen me has seen the Father.' The point that Jesus is making in these words is that because he is God the Father's eternal Son, who shares the Father's nature and always perfectly does the Father's will, what is perfectly revealed in his person, words and actions is the nature, will and action of God himself.

At this point a potential problem arises. Jesus Christ reveals the nature, will and action of God within a life lived on earth. This earthly life came to an end at his ascension when he was taken up into heaven, where he will remain until he comes in glory at the end of time (Acts 1:9-11). How then does God continue to be revealed through him? The solution to this problem is set out in Acts 1:8 in which Jesus says to the apostles: 'But you shall receive power when the Holy Spirit has come upon you; and you shall be my witnesses in Jerusalem and in all Judaea and Samaria and to the end of the earth.' God will continue to be revealed through Jesus, even after the

---

[11] Packer, p.33.

ascension through the Spirit empowered witness of the apostles, a reality which the Book of Acts then goes on to describe.

This brings us on to the question of how the Church now has access to the witness of the apostles. The answer to this question is that the witness of the apostles was preserved in the books of the New Testament, which were written either by the apostles themselves or those like Mark, Luke or James, who were the companions, or the appointees, of the apostles, and faithfully reflected their witness. These books build on the witness to Jesus borne in advance by the writers of the Old Testament (Luke 24:26-27, 44-45) and the books of the Old and Testaments together constitute the Bible, one witness to Jesus in two parts. [12]

What this means is that we can expand Packer's account of the nature of doctrine by saying that the basis of doctrine is the truth concerning the nature, will and action of God revealed by Jesus Christ and made known to us by the record of the Spirit inspired witness of the apostles contained in the books of the New Testament, a witness which supplements and completes the previous witness to Jesus borne by the writers of the Old Testament. It is this truth 'as defined and taught in the church, by the church, for the church, and for the world,' that constitutes Christian doctrine.

The reason the truth about God's nature, will and action needs to be defined as well as taught is that if the Church is going to teach this truth on the basis of the apostolic witness it has to decide precisely how this truth needs to be understood and expressed. Defining doctrine means making this decision.

---

[12] For a detailed exposition and defence of what is said in this paragraph see Andreas Kostenberger and Michael Kruger, *The Heresy of Orthodoxy* (Nottingham: Apollos, 2010) and Bruce Metzger, *The Canon of the New Testament* (Oxford: Clarendon Press, 1997).

Five additional facts relating to doctrine

What we have said so far in the chapter gives us a basic definition of Christian doctrine. However, to understand the nature of doctrine more fully, there are five additional facts relating to doctrine that also need to be taken into account.

1. The importance of words

If we look at Packer's list of ways that doctrine is communicated - sermons, catechisms, instructional talks, printed books and audio-visual devices, worship patterns (liturgies, both written and unwritten; hymns and songs) creeds, confessions, and declarations of councils and synods plus personal and group Bible study - we find that they all involve the use of words. This is not an accident, but reflects what the Bible teaches us about the importance of words.

To quote Carl Trueman in his book *Crisis of Confidence*:

> ...the Bible not only presents us with a picture of God's relationship to creation and to his people in which words are absolutely crucial means of his presence and his revelation, and are, by obvious implication, completely adequate for such purposes; it also shows us that words are a vital means of communicating the message of God from person to person. Moses preached; Elijah breached; the prophets, major and minor, preached; Christ preached; Paul and Paul preached. All used words to impress the nature and claims of God upon people. Words are clearly the main means of so doing. Thus, any theology that claims to take the Bible as its authority must take the teaching of the Bible about words, and indeed the verbal form of the Bible itself, without utmost seriousness and thus see words as a normative and normal part of Christianity.[13]

It is because of the importance of words for the reasons just described that Christian doctrine has been formulated and communicated down the centuries in verbal forms, both oral and written, and it is also why

---

[13] Carl Trueman, *Crisis of Confidence* (Wheaton: Crossway, 2024), Kindle edition pp.75-76.

Christians have traditionally taken great pains to try to ensure that the words used are the right ones (the process of defining truth previously mentioned). If the truth of the Christian message is to be communicated in words, then these words have to be as adequate as possible in order to ensure that the truth is properly communicated.

For example, in the fourth century there was a major dispute between those who wanted to say that God the Son was 'like' (in Greek *homoiousios*) the Father and those who wanted to say that he was of 'one substance' with the Father (in Greek *homoousios*) What the latter group rightly understood was that if you say the Son is 'like' the Father you are necessarily implying that he is in some way different from him, whereas if you say that he is of 'one substance' with the Father you do justice to the biblical witness that the one divine nature is as fully possessed by the Son as it is by the Father (and thus protect biblical monotheism by avoiding any notion that Christians believe in two slightly different gods). [14]

The use of the word *homoousios* in the way just described points us to the further fact that one aspect of the Church's concern for the importance of words in the communication of Christian truth has been the development of a specialised theological vocabulary in which specific words are used to convey specific aspects of Christian truth. Alongside homoousios other examples are words like trinity, person, incarnation, atonement, grace, total depravity, election, justification, sanctification and so forth. Understanding Christian doctrine involves understanding the meaning of such key theological terms.

---

[14] For this point see Michael Thompson, 'Arianism: Is Jesus Christ divine and eternal or was he created?' in Ben Quash and Michael Ward (eds), *Heresies and how to avoid them* (London: SPCK, 2007), pp.15-23 and A I C Heron, 'Homoousios with the Father' in Thomas F Torrance (ed), *The incarnation – Ecumenical Studies in the Nicene-Constantinoplian Creed A.D. 381* (Edinburgh: The Handsel Press, 1981), pp. 58-87.

For example, it means understanding that the term 'trinity' (short for tri-unity) expresses the truth that the one creator God exists eternally as Father, Son and Holy Spirit, and that the term 'total depravity' does not mean that all human beings are as bad as they possibly could be, but is used to point to the truth that our sinfulness affects every party of our existence. In the words of the contemporary Reformed theologian Michael Horton:

> The stain of sin [has corrupted] us physically, emotionally, psychologically, mentally, morally, and spiritually. That doesn't mean ...we are all brute savages who always carry out every possible evil; it does mean that there is no island of purity from which we might mount a campaign to save ourselves.[15]

2. The importance of tradition

The fact that the Church began to produce doctrine from the time of the apostles and has continued to do so to the present day has meant that doctrine has been passed on from one generation of Christians to the next. The technical term that is used for the handing of doctrine in this way is 'tradition' (from the Latin verb *tradere* meaning to deliver, hand over, or hand down) a term that is used to refer both to the process of handing doctrine down from one generation to another and to the content of what is handed down in this way.

There are Protestant Christians, influenced by the criticism of the tradition of the Scribes and the Pharisees by Jesus as recorded in the Gospels (Matthew 15:1-20) and the criticism of the teaching and practice of the medieval Church by the Protestant reformers, who are wary of tradition, seeing it as at best superfluous or at worst misleading. However, as Trueman notes, the letters of Paul to the churches in Thessalonica and Corinth show that the importance of tradition was emphasised by the apostles and has its roots in the very nature of the Christian gospel. As Trueman explains:

---

[15] Michael Horton quoted in Timothy Paul Jones, 'Martin Luther on Beards and Human Depravity' *Proof* 31 October 2014 at:
https://www.timothypauljones.com/proof-what-we-did-and-what-we-deserve/

...In 2 Thessalonians 2:15, Paul says, 'So then, brothers, stand firm and hold the traditions that you were taught by us, either by our spoken word or by our letter.' Again, the verbal emphasis is clear: these traditions were taught by words spoken or written; and they are to be the norm of life and teaching in church in Thessalonica. Similar statements can be found in 1 Corinthians 11:2 and 2 Thessalonians 2:6, where Paul makes conformity to the tradition of his teaching a condition for fellowship.

The content of the gospel is thus to be handed on from generation to generation. In today's the society that is in some senses a strange notion. Traditions, say, of computer programming are not passed on. If they were, I would not be typing on my notebook but would be sitting in a room full of machines with spinning spools of tape. There are continuities in technology, but they are often less substantial than the dramatic discontinuities that scientific and technological breakthroughs bring in their wake. Not so with Paul's gospel. This is truly traditional: it has a stable content and is passed on from generation to generation. Indeed, for Paul, the fact that something was not taught in the past and not passed on as a tradition would presumably have dramatically increased the chances that it was false.

This notion of tradition, of the need to hand on the gospel, is deeply imbedded in the nature of the gospel itself. The historical particularity of the history of Israel and of Jesus Christ means that if the gospel, the meaning and significance of these things, is not passed on from generation to generation then it remains in a sense trapped in the past. God's saving actions require interpretation and proclamation in order for later generations to have access by faith to them. This tradition is to be regulated by Scripture as the sole authoritative source of knowledge of God's actions; but it is not formally identical with Scripture. It uses forms of sound words - sermons, hymns, and prayers, among other things - in order to pass the message on from one generation to another.[16]

As Trueman acknowledges, Scripture has a unique authority for Christian doctrine, for the reasons explained earlier in this chapter. However. this does not exclude the importance of extra-biblical traditions as a subordinate doctrinal norm. To use the conventional theological language on this point, Scripture is the '*norma normans*' or 'norming norm.' that which is the norm for everything else, whereas tradition is '*norma normata*' or 'normed norm' the form of doctrinal authority that is itself governed by the higher authority of Scripture.

This distinction between Scripture and extra-biblical tradition is helpfully explained by the nineteenth century English high churchman Edward Pusey. In his words, tradition:

> ...it is not a supplementary, not an independent source of truth, but a concurrent interpretive, definitive, and harmonising witness of one and the same truth. They are not separate truths, apart from Holy Scripture, but the same body of truth which is in it; not to supply anything wanting to Holy Scripture, but to explain what is in it; not to add to our knowledge, but to prevent our misunderstanding it, or failing to understand the depth of the words which God the Holy Ghost spake.[17]

As Trueman has noted, tradition takes a variety of different forms, of which the following are generally seen as among the most important.

---

[16] Trueman, pp.96-97. The reference to 'forms of sound words' is a deliberate reference to the further words of Paul in 2 Timothy 1:13, 'Follow the pattern of the sound words which you have heard from me.'

[17] Edward Pusey, *The Rule of Faith as Maintained by the Fathers and the Church of England* (Oxford: John Henry Parker, 1851), p.15. For further helpful discussions of the relation of Scripture to tradition see also Stephen Holmes, *Listening to the Past* (Carlisle and Grand Rapids: Paternoster/Baker Academic, 2002) and *Edith Humphrey, Scripture and Tradition* (Grand Rapids: Baker Academic, 2013).

- The teaching of the Fathers, or Fathers of the Church, those people who have come to be recognised as the most significant teachers of the apostolic faith during the early centuries of the Church's existence and whose theology helped to establish the basis for the Church's subsequent doctrinal activity. There is no definitive list of the Fathers, but examples of those generally recognised as among the Fathers would be Irenaeus, Tertullian, Cyprian, Athanasius, Ambrose, Augustine, Jerome, Basil of Caesarea, Gregory the Great and John of Damascus. [18]

- The four great creedal statements produced during the early centuries, the Apostles,' Nicene, and Athanasian Creeds and the Chalcedonian Confession.[19]

- The decisions of what are known as the six General, or Ecumenical, Councils of the first seven centuries, the First Council of Nicaea (325), the First Council of Constantinople (381), the First Council of Ephesus (431), the Council of Chalcedon (451), the Second Council of Constantinople (553) and the Third Council of Constantinople (680).[20]

- The Confessions of Faith produced by specific churches at the Reformation and subsequently such as the Lutheran Augsburg Confession (1530), the Thirty-Nine Articles of the Church of England (1571), the Reformed Westminster Confession (1646), the Barmen Declaration of the German Confessing

---

[18] For helpful introductions to the Fathers see F L Cross *The Early Christian Fathers* (London: Duckworth 1960) and Tony Lane, *The Lion Book of Christian Thought* (Oxford: Lion, 1984), Parts 1-2.

[19] The text of these Creeds can be found in Justin Holcomb, *Know the Creeds and Councils* (Grand Rapids: Zondervan 2014).

[20] These decisions can be found in *The Nicene and Post Nicene Fathers*, 2nd series, Vol XIV (Edinburgh and Grand Rapids: T&T Clark/Eerdmans, 1997)

Church (1934) and the Documents of the Second Vatican Council of the Roman Catholic Church (1962-1965). [21]

- The writings of those theologians since the time of the Fathers who are regarded either formally or informally[22] as Doctors of the Church, that is to say particularly important teachers of Christian doctrine. As with the Fathers, there is no definitive list, but examples of those who would generally be regarded as coming into this category would include the Venerable Bede, Anselm, Peter Lombard, Thomas Aquinas, Catherine of Siena, Martin Luther, John Calvin, Teresa of Avila, Thomas Cranmer, Richard Hooker, John Owen, Jonathan Edwards, Benjamin Warfield, Karl Barth and Dietrich Bonhoeffer. [23]

- The liturgies produced by the various churches down the centuries which have both reflected and shaped how people have understood the Christian faith. The importance of liturgy in this regard is often summarised by the use of the Latin tag *lex orandi, lex credendi* ('the law of praying is the law of believing') the principle that how the Church prays helps to establish what the Church believes (both in the sense that it witnesses to it and in the sense that it helps to determine it as people take part in the liturgy on a regular basis).

If it is asked why Christians today should bother to read Christian writings from the past, such as those just listed, three helpful answers are provided by C S Lewis in his introduction to a new English

---

[21] The Protestant Confessions can be found in John Leith, *Creeds of the Churches* revd ed (Oxford: Blackwells, 1973) and the documents of Vatican II can be found in Walter Abbott (The Documents of Vatican II (London: Geoffrey Chapman, 1967).

[22] The Roman Catholic Church has a formal list of Catholic Doctors of the Church, but others outside the Roman Catholic Church would be informally regarded as having similar status by other churches.

[23] A good introduction to many of these doctors can be found in Lane.

translation of Athanasius' fourth century treatise *On the Incarnation of the Word*.

His first answer is that reading Christian writings from the past (such as the works of Athanasius) gives you the ability to properly understand and assess Christian writings from the present. In Lewis's words:

> [The] mistaken preference for the modern books and this shyness of the old ones is nowhere more rampant than in theology. Wherever you find a little study circle of Christian laity you can be almost certain that they are studying not St. Luke or St. Paul or St. Augustine or Thomas Aquinas or Hooker or Butler, but M. Berdyaev or M. Maritain or M. Niebuhr or Miss Sayers or even myself.

> Now this seems to me topsy-turvy. Naturally, since I myself am a writer, I do not wish the ordinary reader to read no modern books. But if he must read only the new or only the old, I would advise him to read the old. And I would give him this advice precisely because he is an amateur and therefore much less protected than the expert against the dangers of an exclusive contemporary diet.

> A new book is still on its trial and the amateur is not in a position to judge it. It has to be tested against the great body of Christian thought down the ages, and all its hidden implications (often unsuspected by the author himself) have to be brought to light.

> Often it cannot be fully understood without the knowledge of a good many other modern books. If you join at eleven o'clock a conversation which began at eight you will often not see the real bearing of what is said. Remarks which seem to you very ordinary will produce laughter or irritation and you will not see why—the reason, of course, being that the earlier stages of the conversation have given them a special point.

> In the same way sentences in a modern book which look quite ordinary may be directed at some other book; in this way you may

be led to accept what you would have indignantly rejected if you knew its real significance. The only safety is to have a standard of plain, central Christianity ('mere Christianity' as Baxter called it) which puts the controversies of the moment in their proper perspective. Such a standard can be acquired only from the old books.[24]

His second answer is that we can only avoid the characteristic outlook (and therefore mistakes) of modern thought by reading writings from the past. As Lewis puts it:

> Every age has its own outlook. It is specially good at seeing certain truths and specially liable to make certain mistakes. We all, therefore, need the books that will correct the characteristic mistakes of our own period. And that means the old books.
>
> All contemporary writers share to some extent the contemporary outlook—even those, like myself, who seem most opposed to it. Nothing strikes me more when I read the controversies of past ages than the fact that both sides were usually assuming without question a good deal which we should now absolutely deny. They thought that they were as completely opposed as two sides could be, but in fact they were all the time secretly united—united with each other and against earlier and later ages—by a great mass of common assumptions.
>
> We may be sure that the characteristic blindness of the twentieth century—the blindness about which posterity will ask, 'But how could they have thought that?'—lies where we have never suspected it, and concerns something about which there is untroubled agreement between Hitler and President Roosevelt or between Mr. H. G. Wells and Karl Barth. None of us can fully escape this blindness, but we shall certainly increase it, and weaken our guard against it, if we read only modern books. Where they are

---

[24] C S Lewis in *St Athanasius, The Incarnation of the World of God* (London: Geoffrey Bless, 1944), pp.5-6

true they will give us truths which we half knew already. Where they are false they will aggravate the error with which we are already dangerously ill.

The only palliative is to keep the clean sea breeze of the centuries blowing through our minds, and this can be done only by reading old books. Not, of course, that there is any magic about the past. People were no cleverer then than they are now; they made as many mistakes as we. But not the same mistakes. They will not flatter us in the errors we are already committing; and their own errors, being now open and palpable, will not endanger us. Two heads are better than one, not because either is infallible, but because they are unlikely to go wrong in the same direction. To be sure, the books of the future would be just as good a corrective as the books of the past, but unfortunately we cannot get at them.[25]

His third answer is that a study of Christian writings from the past reveals that, despite the divisions that have existed between Christians, the orthodox Christian tradition has had a definite and distinctive content. 'Christianity' has historically meant something specific. To quote Lewis again:

I myself was first led into reading the Christian classics, almost accidentally, as a result of my English studies. Some, such as Hooker, Herbert, Traherne, Taylor and Bunyan, I read because they are themselves great English writers; others, such as Boethius, St. Augustine, Thomas Aquinas and Dante, because they were "influences." George Macdonald I had found for myself at the age of sixteen and never wavered in my allegiance, though I tried for a long time to ignore his Christianity.

They are, you will note, a mixed bag, representative of many Churches, climates and ages. And that brings me to yet another reason for reading them. The divisions of Christendom are undeniable and are by some of these writers most fiercely

[25] Lewis, pp.6-7.

expressed. But if any man is tempted to think—as one might be tempted who read only con- temporaries—that "Christianity" is a word of so many meanings that it means nothing at all, he can learn beyond all doubt, by stepping out of his own century, that this is not so.

Measured against the ages "mere Christianity" turns out to be no insipid interdenominational transparency, but something positive, self-consistent, and inexhaustible. I know it, indeed, to my cost. In the days when I still hated Christianity, I learned to recognise, like some all too familiar smell, that almost unvarying something which met me, now in Puritan Bunyan, now in Anglican Hooker, now in Thomist Dante. It was there (honeyed and floral) in Francois de Sales; it was there (grave and homely) in Spenser and Walton; it was there (grim but manful) in Pascal and Johnson; there again, with a mild, frightening, Paradisial flavour, in Vaughan and Boehme and Traherne.

In the urban sobriety of the eighteenth century one was not safe— Law and Butler were two lions in the path. The supposed "Paganism" of the Elizabethans could not keep it out; it lay in wait where a man might have supposed himself safest, in the very centre of The Faerie Queene and the Arcadia. It was, of course, varied; and yet—after all—so unmistakably the same; recognisable, not to be evaded, the odour which is death to us until we allow it to become life:

> an air that kills
> From yon far country blows.

We are all rightly distressed, and ashamed also, at the divisions of Christendom. But those who have always lived within the Christian fold may be too easily dispirited by them. They are bad, but such people do not know what it looks like from without. Seen from there, what is left intact despite all the divisions, still appears (as it truly is) an immensely formidable unity. I know, for I saw it; and well our enemies know it. That unity any of us can find by going out of his own age.

It is not enough, but it is more than you had thought till then. Once you are well soaked in it, if you then venture to speak, you will have an amusing experience. You will be thought a Papist when you are actually reproducing Bunyan, a Pantheist when you are quoting Aquinas, and so forth. For you have now got on to the great level viaduct which crosses the ages and which looks so high from the valleys, so low from the mountains, so narrow compared with the swamps, and so broad compared with the sheep-tracks.[26]

For these three reasons given by Lewis, Christians today need to continue to read Christians writings from the past. If they fail to do so their understanding of Christianity will be impoverished.

3. The unchanging nature of God and humanity

One key reason why people today are reluctant to read books from the past is because the world we live in today has been profoundly shaped by the scientific discoveries and technological achievements that have taken place since the Renaissance, and which seem to be continuing at an increasing rate. This fact leads many people in our culture to be sceptical about the possible relevance of the historic Christian doctrinal tradition. They ask how theological statements produced hundreds, and sometimes thousands, of years ago can possibly claim authority today, given that in all areas of thought new discoveries have constantly overthrown previously accepted views of the world and human life within it.

There are two answers to this question.

The first reason why theological statements from the past do not become outdated is that God himself does not change. In the words of Malachi 3:6 'I the Lord do not change.'

---

[26] Lewis, pp.8-9.

As the seventeenth century Puritan theologian Stephen Charnock explains in his lectures on *The Existence and Attributes of God*, God's changelessness or immutability can be understood in four ways.

First, God is immutable in his essence:

> He is an unalterably fixed in his being, so that not a particle of it can be lost from it, not a mite added it to it. If a man continue in being as long as Methuselah, nine hundred and sixty-nine years; yet there is not a day, nay an hour, where in there is not some alteration in his substance. Though no substantial part is wanting, yet there is an addition to him by his food, a diminution of something by his labour; he is always making some acquisition, or suffering some loss; but in God there can be no alteration by the accession of anything to make his substance greater or better, or by diminution to make it less or worse. He who hath not being from another, cannot but be always what he is: God is the first Being, an independent Being; He was not produced of himself, or of any other, but by nature always hath been, and, therefore, cannot by himself, or any other, be changed from what he is in his own nature. [27]

Secondly, God is immutable in his regard to his knowledge:

> God has known from all eternity all that which he can know, so that nothing is hid from him. He knows not at present anymore then he hath known from eternity and that which he knows now he always knows: 'all things are open and naked before him (Hebrews 4:13). [28]

Thirdly, God is immutable in regard to his will and purpose:

> A change in his purpose is, when a man determines to do that now which before he determined not to do, or to do the contrary; when

---

[27] Stephen Charnock, *The Existence and Attributes of God* (New York: Robert Carter and Brothers, 1874), Kindle edition, p.328. edition, p. 328.
[28] Charnock, p.330.

> a man hates that thing which he loved, or begins to love that which he before hated; When the will is changed, a man begins to will that which he willed not before, and ceaseth to will that which he willed before. But whatsoever God has decreed, is immutable; whatsoever God hath promised, shall be accomplished; 'The word that goes forth off his mouth shall not return to him void, but shall accomplish that which he pleaseth (Isaiah 55:11); Whatsoever 'he purposeth, he will do' (Isaiah 46:11, Numbers 23:19); his decrees are therefore called 'mountains of brass' (Zechariah 6:1): brass as having substance and solidity; mountains, as being immovable, not only by any creature, but by himself; because they stand upon the basis of infallible wisdom, and are supported by uncontrollable power. [29]

Fourthly, God is immutable in terms of place:

> As God is unchangeable in regard of essence, knowledge, purpose, so he is unchangeable in regard of place. He cannot be changed in time, because he is eternity; so he cannot be changed in place, because he hath ubiquity: he is eternal, therefore cannot be changed in time; he is omnipresent, therefore cannot be changed in place. He does not begin to be in one place wherein he was not before, or cease to be in a place wherein he was before. He that fills every place in heaven and earth, cannot change place; he cannot leave one and possess another, that is equally, in regard of his essence, in all: 'He fills heaven and earth' (Jeremiah 23:24). [30]

The fact that God is immutable in these four ways means that anything that is truthfully said about God by Christian doctrine must always be true. It can never be out of date.

This argument might be challenged on the grounds that God has done new things such as, for example, saving Noah from the flood, making a covenant with Abram, rescuing Israel from Egypt, sending his people

---

[29] Charnock, p.333.
[30] Charnock, p.337.

into exile in Babylon and becoming incarnate as Jesus Christ. The argument would be that God changed when he did new these things, and therefore he might change again by doing something else new and thus make existing doctrine out of date.

The problem with this argument is that the actions of God in time do not involve any change in God himself. Charnock explains this point in relation to the creation of the world. He writes:

> There was no change in God when he began to create the world in time. The creation was a real change, but the change was not subjectively in God, but in the creature; the creature began to be what it was not before. Creation is considered as active or passive. Active creation is the will and power of God to create. This is from eternity, because God willed from eternity to create in time; This never had beginning for God never began in time to understand anything, to will anything, or to be able to do anything; but he always understood and always willed those things which he determined from eternity to produce in time.[31]

When God does something in the world it involves a change of some sort within the created order. However, it does not involve any change in God. Rather it is a manifestation in time of God's eternal and unchanging understanding, will and power.

What has just been said also applies to God's repentance, and to his abrogating some aspects of Old Testament law under the new covenant (such as the requirement to be circumcised, or the prohibition on eating certain kinds of food).

There are biblical verses in which God is said to have repented. Thus, in Jonah 3:10 we are told that after the people of Nineveh repented in sackcloth and ashes: 'When God saw what they did, how they turned from their evil way, God repented of the evil which he had said he would do to them and did not do it.' This might seem at first sight to

---

[31] Charnock, p.346.

indicate that a change took place in God. However, this is not the case. To quote Charnock again:

> God is said to repent when he changes the disposition of affairs without himself; as men, when they repent, alter the course of their actions, so God alters things, *extra se*, or without himself, but changes nothing of his own purpose within himself. It rather notes the action he is about to do, than anything in his own nature, or any change in his eternal purpose. [32]

With regard to the abrogation of parts of the Old Testament law, the point again is that there is no change in God, but only an enactment in time of what he has eternally decreed. To quote Charnock one final time:

> A change of laws by God argues no change in God, when God abrogate some laws which he had settled in the church and enacts others… God commanded one thing to the Jews, when the church was in an infant state; and removed those laws when the church came to some growth… When God changed the ceremonial law, there was no change in the divine will, but an execution of his well; for when God commanded the observance of the law he intended not the perpetuity of it; nay in the prophets he declares the cessation of it; he decreed to command it, but he decreed to command it only for such a time; so that the abrogation of it was no less an execution of his decree, then his establishment of it for a season was; the commanding of it was pursuant to his decree for the appointing of it, and the nulling of it was pursuant to his decree of continuing it only for such a season; that in all this there was no change in the will of God.[33]

---

[32] Charnock, p.351.
[33] Charnock, p.355. For a helpful discussion of the relationship between the laws in the Old and New Testaments see John Richardson, *What God has made clean* (Epsom: Good Book Company, 2013).

If it were to be suggested that just as God decreed a change in the law between the Old and New Testaments so he might have decreed that the law should change again today, the problem would be that such a suggestion fails to take into account that, unlike the old covenant, the new covenant established by Christ will be in force until the end of time and therefore so also will be the laws which it contains.

In response to these objections. we can therefore still say that God does not change and therefore doctrine is on secure ground when it describes God in unchanging ways. What God was, God is, and God will be, and doctrine is correct when it reflects this fact.

The second reason why doctrinal statements from the past do not become outdated is the fact that not only does God not change, but human nature does not change either. This point is emphasised by Trueman who writes as follows:

> Human nature is something that is more basic than gender, class, culture, location, or time. It cannot be reduced to or contained within a specific context such as to isolate it from all else. This is not to deny that context has a huge impact on who we are and how we think; it is simply to say that all these particulars that make individuals unique and allow us to differentiate one person from another are relativized by the universal reality of human nature that binds us all together.

> Human beings remain essentially the same in terms of their basic nature as those made in God's image and addressed by his word even as we move from place to place and from generation to generation. God remains the same; his image remains the same; his address to us remains the same. The clear inference is that the basic categories that define the relationship between the two (creation in his image, the fall, redemption in Christ, etc) remind hardy perennials, unaffected at their core by the comparatively trivial accidents of time and space that separate one person from another. Modern culture, for all its often drab uniformity, prides itself on difference and on kaleidoscopic variety. Whatever the

truth of this may be, it does not affect the essential core of identity that binds me together with human beings in modern China and with people in ancient Rome: we are all made in God's image, and he addresses his all through his word.

In short, a biblical understanding of human nature as a universal will temper any talk that seeks to dismiss theological statements from the past on the simplistic grounds that we have nothing in common with the people who wrote them...All human beings are partakers of a common human nature. All are addressed by the same revelation of the same God, and all are called to respond to that revelation.[34]

In summary, God does not change and neither does human nature. Because doctrine is concerned with how God relates to those who possess human nature, what it says, providing it is said truthfully, will never become outdated. The passage of time will not affect its relevance.

4. Doctrine and ethics

If you look at textbooks on the history of Christian doctrine such as James Orr's *The Progress of Dogma*,[35] John Kelly's *Early Christian Doctrines*, or Roger Olson's *The Story of Christian Theology* you will find that they say nothing about Christian ethics. This fact reflects a distinction between doctrine and ethics (or in Roman Catholic terminology doctrine and moral theology) that goes back to the immediate post-reformation period in which, as Sean Lau writes:

Catholic and Protestant churches wanted to impress their moral teachings more forcefully on their respective populations. Moral

---

[34] Trueman, p.79.
[35] James Orr, *The Progress of Dogma* (Cambridge: James Clarke 2002), John Kelly, *Early Christian Doctrines* 5th ed (London: A&C Black, 1977) and Roger Olson, *The Story of Christian Theology* (Leicester: Apollos 1999)

theology and Christian ethics developed because they were pedagogically useful for that task.[36]

To put it simply, what both Catholics and Protestants felt was needed was teaching material that focussed on right Christian behaviour and a separate academic discipline of ethics/moral theology developed to meet this need.

As Lau further notes, the theoretical basis for the distinction between doctrine and ethics was a distinction between theory and practice which goes back to Book VI of Aristotle's *Nicomachean Ethics* and which entered Christian thought through the Scholastic theologians of the later Middle Ages.[37] As he further notes, this distinction remains crucial for justifying the existence of ethics as an academic discipline in its own right.[38] Doctrine is seen as having to do with theoretical questions about the nature of God and humanity while ethics has to do with practical questions about human behaviour.

However, there are two problems with this distinction.

First, one cannot separate questions about how human beings should behave from questions about the nature of God and of humanity. It is because God is the all wise and all good creator and human beings are his creatures, that it makes sense to say, as Christians always have, that human beings should live in obedience to God. If there was no God, or if God was not all good and all wise, or if human beings were not his creatures, then the foundations of Christians ethics (and arguably of ethics as such) would collapse.[39]

---

[36] Sean Lau, 'The Distinction between Theology and Ethics: A critical history,' *The Journal of Religious Ethics*, Vol.52, Issue 2, June 2024, p,215 at: https://onlinelibrary.wiley.com/doi/epdf/10.1111/jore.12468.
[37] Lau, p.214.
[38] Lau, p.215.
[39] For this point see David Baggett and Jerry Walls, *Good God – The theistic foundations of morality* (Oxford: OUP, 2011).

Secondly, if one accept Packer's definition of doctrine as 'the revealed truth of God as defined and taught in the church, by the church, for the church, and for the world' then Christian ethics has to be seen as an integral part of doctrine, since a major part of what has been revealed by God in Scripture and subsequently been defined and taught by the Church has been instruction on how God's human creatures should behave.

The classic illustration of the way in which ethics have formed an integral part of Christian doctrine is provided by the Ten Commandments, or 'Decalogue,' found in Exodus 20:2-17.

According to both Exodus 20:1 and Deuteronomy 5:5, the Ten Commandments were given to Israel by God himself at Mount Sinai to provide them with foundational instruction about how they should live as his people, and the traditional Christian view has been that they are also given to us as Christians to provide the guidance we need in order to live in filial obedience to God the Father and thus bear witness to him among the nations of the earth. We can live in this way because Jesus's perfect fulfilment of the Commandments is being reproduced in us through the Holy Spirit. We therefore need to allow our consciences to be formed by an awareness of what is required of us in the Ten Commandments and then begin to live accordingly, seeking the assistance of God through the Spirit to enables us to do so.

Because Christians have traditionally viewed the Ten Commandments in this way, the Commandments have formed a central part of Christian catechesis alongside the Apostles' Creed and the Lord's Prayer and in each succeeding generation Christians have continued to teach the Commandments and sought to define their meaning as a guide for Christian conduct.

Two examples of this fact are provided by the expositions of the Ten Commandments contained in Martin Luther's *Small Catechism* of 1529 and in the Catechism in the Church of England's 1662 *Book of Common Prayer*.

Luther's exposition runs as follows:

The First
'You shall have no other gods.'

What does this mean?

Answer: We should fear, love, and trust in God above all things.

The Second
'You shall not take the name of the Lord, your God, in vain.'

What does this mean?

Answer: We should fear and love God that we may not curse, swear, use witchcraft, lie, or deceive by His name, but call upon it in every trouble, pray, praise, and give thanks.

The Third
'Remember the Sabbath day, to keep it holy.'

What does this mean?

Answer: We should fear and love God and so we should not despise his Word and the preaching of the same, but deem it sacred, and gladly hear and learn it.

The Fourth
'Honor your father and your mother.'

What does this mean?

Answer: We should fear and love God, and so we should not despise nor anger our parents or superiors, but honor, serve, obey, love and esteem them.

The Fifth
'You shall not kill.'

What does this mean?

Answer: We should fear and love God and so we should not endanger our neighbours' life, nor cause him any harm, but help and befriend him in every necessity of life.

The Sixth
'You shall not commit adultery.'

What does this mean?

Answer: We should fear and love God, and so we should lead a chaste and pure life in word and deeds, and each one loving and honouring his wife or her husband.

The Seventh
'You shall not steal.'

What does this mean?

Answer: We should fear and love God, and so we should not rob our neighbour of his money or his property, nor Bring them into my possession by dishonest trade or by dealing in shoddy wares, but help him to improve and protect his income and property.

The Eighth
'You shall not bear false witness against you neighbour.'

What does this mean

Answer: We should fear and love God and so we should not tell lies about our neighbour, nor betray, slander, or defame him, but apologize for him, speak well of him, and interpret charitably all that he does.

The Ninth
'You shall not covet you neighbour's house.

What does this mean?

Answer: We should fear and love God and so we should not seek by craftiness to gain possession of our neighbour's inheritance or home, nor to obtain them under pretext of legal right, but be of service and help to him so that he may keep what is his.

The Tenth
'You shall not covet your neighbour's wife, or his manservant, or his ox, or his ass, or anything that is your neighbour's.

What does this mean?

Answer: We should fear and love God and so we should not abduct, estrange, or entice away our neighbour's wife, servants, or cattle, but encourage them to stay and discharge their duty to him.

[Conclusion]
What Does God declare concerning all of these Commandments?

Answer: He says, 'I the Lord, thy God, am a jealous God, visiting the iniquity of the fathers upon the children unto the third and fourth generation of those who hate me, but showing steadfast love to thousands of those who love me and keep my commandments.

What does this mean?

Answer: God threatens to punish all who transgress these commandments. We should therefore fear his wrath and not disobey these commandments. On the other hand, he promised his grace and every blessing to all who keep them. We should therefore love him, trust in him, and cheerfully do what he has commanded. [40]

The Prayer Book Exposition, which was written by Alexander Nowell, runs as follows:

---

[40] 'Martin Luther's Small Catechism, 1529' in Mark Noll (ed), *Confessions and Catechisms of the Reformation* (Vancouver: Regent College Publishing 2004), pp. 65-68.

You said that your Godfathers and Godmothers did promise for you, that you should keep God's Commandments. Tell me how many there be?

Answer. Ten.

Question. Which be they?

Answer. The same which God spake in the twentieth chapter of Exodus, saying, I am the Lord thy God, who brought thee out of the land of Egypt, out of the house of bondage.

I. Thou shalt have none other gods but me.

II. Thou shalt not make to thyself any graven image, nor the likeness of any thing that is in heaven above, or in the earth beneath, or in the water under the earth. Thou shalt not bow down to them, nor worship them. For I the Lord thy God am a jealous God, and visit the sins of the fathers upon the children unto the third and fourth generation of them that hate me, and shew mercy unto thousands in them that love me and keep my commandments.

III. Thou shalt not take the Name of the Lord thy God in vain: for the Lord will not hold him guiltless, that taketh his Name in vain.

IV. Remember that thou keep holy the Sabbath day. Six days shalt thou labour, and do all that thou hast to do; but the seventh day is the Sabbath of the Lord thy God. In it thou shalt do no manner of work, thou, and thy son, and thy daughter, thy man-servant, and thy maid-servant, thy cattle, and the stranger that is within thy gates. For in six days the Lord made heaven and earth, the sea, and all that in them is, and rested the seventh day: wherefore the Lord blessed the seventh day, and hallowed it.

V. Honour thy father and thy mother; that thy days may be long in the land which the Lord thy God giveth thee.

VI. Thou shalt do no murder.

VII. Thou shalt not commit adultery.

VIII. Thou shalt not steal.

IX. Thou shalt not bear false witness against thy neighbour.

X. Thou shalt not covet thy neighbour's house, thou shalt not covet thy neighbour's wife, nor his servant, nor his maid, nor his ox, nor his ass, nor any thing that is his.

Question. What dost thou chiefly learn by these Commandments?

Answer. I learn two things: my duty towards God, and my duty towards my Neighbour.

Question. What is thy duty towards God?

Answer. My duty towards God is to believe in him, to fear him, and to love him, with all my heart, with all my mind, with all my soul, and with all my strength; to worship him, to give him thanks, to put my whole trust in him, to call upon him, to honour his holy Name and his Word, and to serve him truly all the days of my life.

Question. What is thy duty towards thy Neighbour?

Answer. My duty towards my Neighbour is to love him as myself, and to do to all men as I would they should do unto me: To love, honour, and succour my father and mother: To honour and obey the King, and all that are put in authority under him: To submit myself to all my governors, teachers, spiritual pastors and masters: To order myself lowly and reverently to all my betters: To hurt nobody by word nor deed: To be true and just in all my dealing: To bear no malice nor hatred in my heart: To keep my hands from picking and stealing, and my tongue from evil-speaking, lying, and slandering: To keep my body in temperance, soberness, and chastity: Not to covet nor desire other men's goods; but to learn and labour truly to get mine own living, and to do my duty in that state of life, unto which it shall please God to call me.

These two expositions by Luther and Nowell, and other similar expositions of the Ten Commandments down the centuries, are pieces of doctrine concerning ethics. Similar forms of doctrine relating to ethics have been produced in every century of the history of the Church. Ethics has always been a part of the Church's doctrine.

5. Doctrine and the threefold order of ministry

A fifth and final fact concerning Christian doctrine is that Christian doctrine and the Church's traditional threefold structure of ordained ministry consisting of the three orders of bishops, priests (also called presbyters or elders) and deacons go together in two ways.

First, historically most Christians have regarded a belief in the God given nature of the three orders of ministry as an integral part of orthodox Christian doctrine. It has been seen as part of the body of Christian tradition handed down from the time of the apostles.

For example, in his *Apology of the Church of England* the sixteenth century English reformer John Jewel gives a list of those beliefs of the Church of England that are in accordance with the teaching of Christ, the apostles, and the Fathers and as part of this list he writes:

> We believe that but there is one Church of God, and that the same is not shut up (as in past time among the Jews) into some one corner or kingdom, but that it is Catholic and universal, and dispersed throughout the whole world; so there is now no nation which can truly complain that they be shut forth, and may not be one of the church and people of God; and that this church is the kingdom, the body, and the spouse of Christ; and that Christ alone is the prince of this Kingdom; that Christ alone is the head of this body; and that Christ alone is the bridegroom of this spouse.
>
> Furthermore, that there be divers degrees of ministers in the church; whereof some be deacons, some priests, some bishops; to

whom is committed the office to instruct the people, and the whole charge and setting forth of religion. [41]

Secondly, in accordance with the instructions given to Titus by Paul as the first bishop of Crete[42] to 'teach what befits sound doctrine' (Titus 2:1) and to appoint elders who 'hold firm to the sure word as taught, so that he may be able to give instruction in sound doctrine and also to confute those who contradict it' (Titus 1:9) it has also historically been held that a particular responsibility of bishops and priests is to 'instruct the people' both by teaching orthodox doctrine derived from the teaching of Scripture, and by refuting heresy. [43]

This understanding of the responsibilities of bishops and priests is illustrated, for instance, in the Church of England's *Ordinal* of 1662. In this Ordinal, which remains normative for the Church of England's understanding of the ordained ministry, the rite for the consecration of bishops contains the following set of question and answers:

The Archbishop

Are you persuaded that the holy Scriptures contain sufficiently all doctrine required of necessity for eternal salvation through faith in Jesus Christ? And are you determined out of the same holy Scriptures to instruct the people committed to your charge, and to teach or maintain nothing as required of necessity to eternal salvation, but that which you shall be persuaded may be concluded and proved by the same?

Answer. I am so persuaded and determined, by God's grace.

---

[41] John Jewel, 'An apology of the Church of England' in John Ayre (ed) *The Works of John Jewel, The Third Portion* (Cambridge: Parker Society/CUP, 1848), p.59.
[42] For the evidence for Titus as first bishop of Crete see Martin Davie, *Bishops Past, Present and Future* (Malton: Gilead Books, 2022), pp.54-63.
[43] Historically deacons have been permitted to preach and give instruction in the faith, but the primary responsibility for teaching doctrine and countering heresy has been seen to lie with bishops and priests.

The Archbishop.

Will you then faithfully exercise yourself in the same holy Scriptures, and call upon God by prayer, for the true understanding of the same; so as ye may be able by them to teach and exhort with wholesome doctrine, and to withstand and convince the gainsayers?

Answer. I will so do, by the help of God.

The Archbishop.

Be you ready, with all faithful diligence, to banish and drive away all erroneous and strange doctrine contrary to God's Word; and both privately and openly to call upon and encourage others to the same?

Answer. I am ready, the Lord being my helper.

The rite for the ordering of priests contains a similar set of questions and answers:

The Bishop.

Are you persuaded that the holy Scriptures contain sufficiently all doctrine required of necessity for eternal salvation through faith in Jesus Christ? And are you determined out of the said Scriptures to instruct the people committed to your charge, and to teach nothing (as required of necessity to eternal salvation) but that which you shall be persuaded may be concluded and proved by the Scripture?

Answer. I am so persuaded, and have so determined by God's grace.

The Bishop.

Will you then give your faithful diligence always so to minister the doctrine and sacraments, and the discipline of Christ, as the Lord hath commanded, and as this Church and Realm hath received the same, according to the commandments of God; so that you may teach the people committed to your cure and charge with all diligence to keep and observe the same?

Answer. I will so do, by the help of the Lord.

The Bishop.

Will you be ready, with all faithful diligence, to banish and drive away all erroneous and strange doctrines contrary to God's Word; and to use both publick and private monitions and exhortations, as well to the sick as to the whole, within your cures, as need shall require, and occasion shall be given?

Answer. I will, the Lord being my helper.

What is clear from these two sets of questions and answers is that like the other mainstream Protestant reformers the English reformers saw Scripture as the primary and sufficient source of Christian doctrine. As the Church of England's homily *A fruitful exhortation to the reading and knowledge of Holy Scripture* puts it, they believed that:

> ...in holy Scripture is fully contained, what we ought to do, and what to eschew, what to believe, what to love, and what to look for at God's hands at length.[44]

However, also like the other mainstream Protestant reformers, the English reformers did not believe that Scripture was the sole source of doctrine. As their writings make clear, they also viewed the creeds, councils and Fathers of the Early Church as having secondary doctrinal authority because they faithfully summarised and expounded the teaching of Scripture, an approach which also opens up the possibility of later writings (such as the writings of the

---

[44] *A fruitful exhortation to the reading and knowledge of Holy Scripture*, in Ian Robinson (ed), The Homilies (Bishopstone: The Brynmill Press/Preservation Press, 2006), p.5.

reformers themselves) being viewed as having doctrinal authority on the same basis.

In this chapter we have looked at the nature of Christian doctrine and the reasons why the historic Christian doctrinal tradition has continuing relevance for people today. In the next chapter we shall go on to explore the issue of whether Christian doctrine can be said to develop.

Chapter 2
The evidence for the development of doctrine

1. Why doctrinal development isn't always wrong

The French Roman Catholic theologian Jacques Bossuet (1627-1704) was a staunch opponent of the concept of doctrinal change. As he once put it:

> The Church's doctrine is always the same...The Gospel is never different from what it was before. Hence, if at any time someone says that the faith includes something which yesterday was not said to be of the faith, it is always *heterodoxy*, which is any doctrine different from *orthodoxy*. There is no difficulty about recognising false doctrine: there is no argument about it: it is recognised at once, whenever it appears, merely because it is new.[45]

Although Bossuet is writing from a Roman Catholic perspective, many Protestant and Orthodox Christians would agree with what he says in this quotation. Where they would disagree with him is that they would think that it is Protestantism or Orthodoxy that has maintained Christian doctrine unchanged while it is the other branches of Christianity that have introduced doctrinal novelty and have therefore fallen into heresy.

The starting point for this view of the impossibility of legitimate doctrinal change is a correct one. The Gospel, the good news of the saving action of God in Jesus Christ that was first taught by Jesus himself and subsequently witnessed to by the writers of the New Testament, is indeed never different from what it was before. Its content is fixed and unchanging. Just as Jesus is 'the same yesterday and today and forever' (Hebrews 13:8) so is the good news concerning him.

---

[45] Jacques Bossuet quoted in Owen Chadwick, *From Bossuet to Newman*, 2ed (Cambridge: CUP, 1987), p.17.

What follows from this is that if it is claimed that something that was not previously part of the Gospel now forms part of the Gospel, then that claim must be wrong. Conversely, if it is claimed that something that was part of the Gospel is no longer part of the Gospel then that claim also must be wrong. As Bossuet rightly declares: 'The Gospel is never different from what it was before.'

What also follows is that because the content of the Christian faith is the Gospel it is also the case that the Christian faith is likewise not subject to change. 'The faith which was once for all delivered to the saints' (Jude 1:3), precisely because it was delivered 'once for all,' remains the same in all generations.

However, the fact that the Gospel, and therefore also the faith, always remain the same does not mean that doctrine is likewise immutable. We can see this if we consider Packer's definition of doctrine that we looked at in chapter 1.

As we noted, Packer's definition of doctrine is 'the revealed truth of God as defined and taught in the church, by the church, for the church, and for the world.' The revealed truth of God that is defined and taught by Christian doctrine will always be unchanging because this revealed truth is 'the faith which was once for all delivered to the saints.' However, the point that is not covered by Bossuet's argument is that the linguistic form by means of which the revealed truth of God is defined and taught can rightly be subject to change. The same faith can be expressed using different language, and it may need to be expressed using different language, in order that it may be understood by new groups of people, or in new situations.

It is because this is the case that doctrine has constantly developed throughout the history of the Christian Church. The development of doctrine is the way in which Christians in every generation have sought to find new ways to express the unchanging truth of the Christian faith as time has gone on. It is too simplistic to say with Bossuet that doctrine is false simply because it is new. A new form of doctrine may be false, but if it is false, it is because it has defined and taught the Christian faith in a misleading way, not simply because it has defined and taught it in a new way.

In the remainder of this chapter, I shall give evidence to illustrate this point from four points in Church history, First, the writing of the New Testament, secondly, the production of the Creeds and the Chalcedonian confession in the Patristic period, thirdly, the production of confessional documents at the time of the Reformation and fourthly the production of new doctrinal statement statements in the twentieth and twenty-first centuries. What this evidence shows us is that forms of doctrine which are widely, or in the case of the New Testament documents, universally, regarded as orthodox were new developments of doctrine at the time when they were first produced.

2. The New Testament writings

When thinking about Christian doctrine there is a tendency to see the New Testament writings as being the old compared with which all subsequent forms of Christian teaching are new. There is truth in this way of looking at the matter. The New Testament writing are the oldest examples of Christian teaching that we possess and so compared with them all other forms of Christian teaching are indeed new.

However, looking at the matter in this way can cause us to overlook the fact that at the time when they were written the New Testament writings were new developments of Christian teaching. At the time when they were written there was already Christian teaching in existence, and they were intended to be new additions to this existing body of teaching.

The four gospels

A study of the contents of the four gospels shows that they have certain things in common.

First, they are all examples of a common literary genre from the Greco-Roman world of the first century, that of biography. They each tell the story of the life of Jesus Christ. [46]

Secondly, they are all biographies of Jesus Christ that draw on eyewitness testimony. In the words of the introduction to Luke's gospel they tell the story of Jesus based on the testimony of those 'who from the beginning were eyewitnesses and ministers of the word' (Luke 1:2).[47]

Thirdly, they all have the dual purpose of testifying to the fact that in Jesus Christ the God who created the world and revealed himself to the people of Isreal has come into the world in person to keep his promise to deliver the world from the power of sin and death, and indicating what it means to respond appropriately to this fact in terms of Christian belief and behaviour.

However, although they have these three elements in common, the four gospels are all different. Each of the gospel writers tells the story of the life of Jesus in a different way to fulfil the two purposes just mentioned[48] and in each case this difference was the result of a deliberate decision to write something new.

There is a long-standing debate amongst New Testament scholars about the literary connections between the first three gospels (what is known as the synoptic problem), but as John Wenham has argued, a close study of the gospels seems to indicate that they were written in the traditional canonical order of Matthew, Mark, Luke. Furthermore, it also suggests that:

---

[46] For the gospels as biographies see Craig Keener, *Christobiography* (Grand Rapids: Eerdmans, 2019).
[47] For this point see Richard Bauckham, *Jesus and the Eyewitnesses* (Grand Rapids: Eerdmans, 2006).
[48] For this point see for example, Richard Burridge, *Four Gospels, one Jesus?* (London: SPCK, 1994), Peter Leithart, *The Four – A Survey of the Gospels* (Moscow: Canon Press, 2010) and Richard Hays, *Reading Backwards* (London: SPCK, 2014).

a) Matthew was written for a Jewish audience, probably in Jerusalem.

b) The writer of Mark was aware of the contents of Matthew, but decided to tell the story of Jesus differently, in line with the way that Peter told the story to predominantly Gentile audiences in Rome.

c) The writer of Luke made use of the material contained in the existing gospels of Matthew and Mark, plus additional material derived from eyewitnesses, to produce his own distinctive account of the life of Jesus. [49]

In addition, it seems probable that although Matthew may have been the first gospel to have been written it was not the first written record of Jesus' life and teaching. As Peter Davids puts it:

> The apostles may not have been learned in the Jewish law (so Acts 4:13), but due to the prevalence of education in Jewish communities many, if not most, of them must have been literate. We should not therefore be surprised if at least a minimal account of the *testimonia*, narratives, and teaching which found their way into the gospels was recorded in writing before or soon after Easter...The pre-Easter Sitz-im-Leben of such material was the mission of the twelve and the need to be behind teaching as the itinerant band travelled. The post-Easter setting was the teaching needs of the growing church and especially the mission outside Jerusalem. [50]

What was new about Matthew was that its author appears to have been the first person to produce a full-length biography of Jesus, a 'gospel,' a model which Mark and Luke then followed.

---

[49] John Wenham, *Redating Matthew, Mark and Luke* (London: Hodder and Stoughton, 1991).
[50] Peter Davids, 'The Gospels and Jewish Tradition' in R T France and David Wenham (eds), *Studies of History and Tradition in the Four Gospels* (Sheffield: JSOT, 1980), pp.87 and 98.

In the case of John's gospel, the evidence suggests that its author knew the other three gospels and decided to produce his own new biography of Jesus as a supplement to them. As Donald Guthrie explains, a number of considerations support this idea:

> The large amount of material in John, which is absent from the Synoptics, would be well accounted for if John was filling in the gaps. Moreover, John often avoids unnecessary duplication, so that it would seem he assumes his readers will be acquainted with the Synoptic records. Since the Gospel as a whole, with its concentration upon the ministry in Judaea and Jerusalem and its greater quantity of discourse material, was evidently conceived on a different pattern from that of the Synoptics it is reasonable to suppose that it was composed with the others in mind. It should be noted that this view is tenable even if it be maintained that John did not use the Synoptic Gospels as a source. But it does, of course, presuppose some knowledge of the content of those Gospels by both author and his readers. [51]

To put it another way, the author of John seems to have felt that he had something to add to what had already been written in Matthew, Mark and Luke, just as Matthew felt that he had something new to add to the existing written records about Jesus, Mark felt he had something to say in addition to what was in Matthew, and Luke felt he had something to say in addition to what was in Matthew and Mark. In all four cases the result was a development of doctrine, a development of the Church's teaching concerning the revealed truth about the being and action of God and how Christians should live in the light of this.

Acts
As well as producing his own distinctive account of the life of Jesus, Luke also developed Christian doctrine by writing the Book of Acts as

---

[51] Donald Guthrie, *New Testament Introduction* (Leicester: Inter-Varsity Press, 1970), p.298.

an account of what Jesus continued to do and teach through his apostles following his ascension.

In Acts 1:1-2 Luke writes as follows:

> In the first book, O Theophilus, I have dealt with all that Jesus began to do and teach, until the day when he was taken up, after he had given commandment through the Holy Spirit to the apostles whom he had chosen.

The first book Luke mentions here is his gospel, which recorded 'all that Jesus began to do and teach' and in the words of John Stott what he is saying to Theophilus is that in this second book: 'he will write about what Jesus continued to do and teach after his ascension, especially through the apostles whose sermons and authenticating 'signs and wonders' Luke will faithfully record.' [52]

What is not generally appreciated is that in writing about the activity of Jesus through the apostles in this way Luke was building on pre-existent Christian practice. In his essay 'The Problem of Traditions in Acts,' Jacob Jervell notes that traditions about the activity of the apostles were a regular part of Christian teaching before Luke wrote Acts. Drawing on the evidence of the New Testament epistles, he declares:

> There was preaching about the apostles. The report of the establishment of a congregation played an important part in the missionary proclamation. Stories of the life in faith of a congregation were used in paraclesis and parenesis. A remarkable amount of information about the Jerusalem congregation was available. All this was important to the other congregations. [53]

What Luke was doing in Acts was developing this existing element of Christian teaching in a fresh way, producing teaching about the work

---

[52] John Stott, The Message of Acts (Leicester: Inter-Varsity Press, 1990) p.32.
[53] Jacob Jervell, The Problem of Traditions in Acts in *Luke and the People of God* (Minneapolis: Augsburg, 1972), p.33.

of Jesus through his apostles that was more coherent and more comprehensive than previous teaching about this subject had been.

The Letters
The majority of the New Testament is made up of twenty-one letters. If we accept the traditional view of their authorship they were written by the apostles Paul, Peter and John and by those associated with the apostles, namely Jesus' brothers James and Jude and the author of the letter to the Hebrews.

One of the things that is striking about these letters is their diversity. Although they can be seen to reflect a common theology and a common code of ethics, each of them is different from all the others in the way that this common understanding of Christian belief and behaviour is expressed and applied to the particular situations which the letters address. Even letters written by the same author can be very different from one another as can be seen, for example, by comparing Romans with Philemon or 1 John and 3 John.

The combination of a common understanding of Christian belief and behaviour and diversity in the way this finds expressions means that each of the twenty-one letters can be seen as an example of the development of doctrine. What is taught in each of the letters is the same basic Christian doctrine, but this doctrine is expressed in a fresh new way each time.

Revelation
The final book of the New Testament canon, Revelation, can be seen to share a common view of theology and ethics with the rest of the New Testament. However, the way it gives expression to Chrisian theology and ethics in the introductory vision of the risen Christ (Revelation 1:1-20), in the letters to the angels of the seven churches of Asia (Revelation 2:1-3.22), and in the symbolic visions of the events leading up to the establishment of the new heaven and the new earth 4:1-22:21) is novel.

For example, nowhere else in the New Testament do we read about the opening of the scroll containing God's plan for the redemption of the world, or the universal worship of the lion of the tribe of Judah who is also the lamb sacrificed to provide salvation for people from all nations, as described in Revelation 5:

> And I saw in the right hand of him who was seated on the throne a scroll written within and on the back, sealed with seven seals; and I saw a strong angel proclaiming with a loud voice, 'Who is worthy to open the scroll and break its seals?' And no one in heaven or on earth or under the earth was able to open the scroll or to look into it, and I wept much that no one was found worthy to open the scroll or to look into it. Then one of the elders said to me, 'Weep not; lo, the Lion of the tribe of Judah, the Root of David, has conquered, so that he can open the scroll and its seven seals.'
>
> And between the throne and the four living creatures and among the elders, I saw a Lamb standing, as though it had been slain, with seven horns and with seven eyes, which are the seven spirits of God sent out into all the earth; and he went and took the scroll from the right hand of him who was seated on the throne. And when he had taken the scroll, the four living creatures and the twenty-four elders fell down before the Lamb, each holding a harp, and with golden bowls full of incense, which are the prayers of the saints; and they sang a new song, saying,
>
> 'Worthy art thou to take the scroll and to open its seals, for thou wast slain and by thy blood didst ransom men for God from every tribe and tongue and people and nation, and hast made them a kingdom and priests to our God, and they shall reign on earth.'
>
> Then I looked, and I heard around the throne and the living creatures and the elders the voice of many angels, numbering myriads of myriads and thousands of thousands, saying with a loud voice, 'Worthy is the Lamb who was slain, to receive power and wealth and wisdom and might and honour and glory and blessing!' And I heard every creature in heaven and on earth and

under the earth and in the sea, and all therein, saying, 'To him who sits upon the throne and to the Lamb be blessing and honour and glory and might for ever and ever!' And the four living creatures said, 'Amen!' and the elders fell down and worshiped.

As commentaries on Revelation explain, the symbolic language used in Revelation 5 can be seen to be drawn from a variety of Old Testament sources and also echoes theological ideas that can be found elsewhere in the New Testament,[54] but the combination of symbols and the juxtaposition of ideas that is found in Revelation 5 is something that is without precedent. As in the case of the Gospels, Acts and the New Testament letters, what we see in Revelation 5 (and in Revelation as a whole) is thus doctrinal development, the Christian faith being taught and defined in a new way.

3. The Creeds and the Chalcedonian Confession

The Apostles', Nicene and Athanasian Creeds and the Chalcedonian Confession are key statements of Christian doctrine. Whether or not churches and individuals are willing to accept the doctrine they contain has historically been seen as a litmus test of their theological orthodoxy.

They are also clear examples of the development of Christian doctrine. We shall see this as we look at each of them in turn.

The Apostles' Creed

The Apostles' Creed has historically been seen as a prime example of the immutability of doctrine. This is because, in the words of John Kelly: 'For more than half of the Church's history…it was confidently assumed that the twelve Apostles had themselves composed and authorized the first summary of belief.'[55]

---

[54] See for example George Caird, *The Revelation of St John the Divine* (London A&C Black 1984) and Ian Paul, *Revelation – An introduction and commentary* (London, Inter-Varsity Press, 2018).
[55] John Kelly, *Early Christian Creeds,* 3ed (Harlow: Longmans, 1972), p.1.

A good illustration of this belief can be found in an introduction to a commentary on the Creed written by Rufinus of Aquileia in about 404 AD. In this introduction Rufinus declares:

> Our forefathers have handed down to us the tradition, that, after the Lord's ascension when, through the coming of the Holy Ghost, tongues of flame had settled upon each of the Apostles, that they might speak diverse languages, so that no race however foreign, no tongue however barbarous, might be inaccessible to them and beyond their reach, they were commanded by the Lord to go severally to the several nations to preach the word of God. Being on the eve therefore of departing from one another, they first mutually agreed upon a standard of their future preaching, lest haply, when separated, they might in any instance vary in the statements which they should make to those whom they should invite to believe in Christ. Being all therefore met together, and being filled with the Holy Ghost, they composed, as we have said, this brief formulary of their future preaching, each contributing his several sentence to one common summary: and they ordained that the rule thus framed should be given to those who believe.[56]

As the opening words 'our forefathers have handed down to us the tradition' indicate, Rufinus did not make up this story. To quote Kelly again 'it represented in his eyes an ancient and hallowed tradition.' [57] We do not know how far back this story goes, but what we do know is that it was accepted throughout the Middle Ages until it began to be questioned by scholars such as Lorenzo Valla and Reginald Pecock in the fifteenth century and came to be generally abandoned from the seventeenth century onwards.

---

[56] Rufinus, *A Commentary on the Apostles' Creed* in *The Nicene and Post-Nicene Fathers*, 2nd series, Vol. III (Edinburgh and Grand Rapids: T&T Clark/Eerdmans 1996), p.542.
[57] Kelly, p.2.

What has since come to be the accepted view of the origins of the Apostles' Creed is helpfully summarised by Charles Cranfield who writes that the Creed:

> ...can be traced back in almost precisely its present form to the eighth century of the church, and with only slight variations as far back as the sixth.
>
> The Old Roman Creed, an early statement of Christian beliefs used in connection with baptism, was quoted in Greek by Marcellus of Ancyra in A.D. 340 and in Latin by Rufinus about A.D. 400. It is found in Greek in question form Hippolytus's *Apostolic Tradition* early in the third century and Hippolytus's use of it probably implies that it existed in the latter part of the second century, when the Roman church still used Greek. This early creed is recognisably akin to our Apostles' Creed.
>
> Apparently, the Roman Creed was elaborated a little north of the Alps, and then, after the time of Charlemagne (who died in A.D. 814), this elaborated form of the creed - now in the form we know as the Apostles' Creed - was received back in Rome.
>
> So the Apostles' Creed has been used for well over 1000 years. It was accepted and used in the mediaeval Western Church and by the sixteenth-century Reformers and is used today by both Roman Catholics and Protestants.[58]

What Cranfield tells us is that the Apostles' Creed was the result of a six-hundred-year process of doctrinal development by means of which the Old Roman Creed of the late second century became the Apostles' Creed which is still in use today. The changes which this process of development involved can be seen if we compare the form of the Creed found in the *Apostolic Tradition* and the form used today.

---

[58] Charles Cranfield, *The Apostles' Creed – A faith to live by* (Edinburgh: T&T Clark, 1993).

The form found in the *Apostolic Tradition* runs as follows:

> Dost thou believe in God the Father almighty?
> Dost thou believe in Christ Jesus, the Son of God,
> Who was born by the Holy Spirit from the Virgin Mary,
> Who was crucified under Pontius Pilate, and died,
> and rose again on the third day living from the dead,
> and ascended into the heavens,
> and sat down at the right hand of the Father,
> and will come to judge the living and the dead?
> Dost thou believe in the Holy Spirit in the holy Church? [59]

By contrast the form used today, in the version found in the *Book of Common Prayer*, runs as follows:

> I believe in God the Father Almighty, **Maker of heaven and earth**:
>
> And in Jesus Christ his only Son **our Lord,** Who was **conceived by the Holy Ghost**, Born of the Virgin Mary, Suffered under Pontius Pilate, Was crucified, dead, **and buried: He descended into hell;** The third day he rose again from the dead; He ascended into heaven, And sitteth on the right hand of God the Father **Almighty**; From thence he shall come to judge the quick and the dead.
>
> I believe in the Holy Ghost; The holy **Catholick** Church; **The Communion of Saints; The Forgiveness of sins; The Resurrection of the body, And the Life everlasting**. Amen.

The change from an interrogatory to a declaratory format reflects the fact that first version is intended for use at baptism with the questions being asked of those seeking to be baptised whereas the second version is intended for general congregational use, and the additions marked in bold are intended to make the Creed a more comprehensive summary of the apostolic teaching found in the New Testament.

---

[59] Text from Kelly, p.114.

The Apostles' Creed is thus a clear example of doctrinal development. It started in one form and ended in another, but the result has been viewed positively across the Western Church because, to quote Cranfield again: 'it is a concise but comprehensive summary of New Testament teaching and as such an invaluable aid toward a reasonably clear understanding of the Christian faith.[60]

The Nicene Creed

The Nicene Creed is a fourth century creed, which was originally written in Greek. The reason it is called the Nicene Creed is because it embodies the belief in the divinity of God the Son upheld by the First Council of Nicaea in 325 AD. This creed seems to have been used at the First Council of Constantinople in 381 AD, which re-affirmed the theology agreed at Nicaea, and it was officially recognised as summarising the theology of the Council of Constantinople by the Council of Chalcedon in 451 AD.

Because of its association with both the Council of Nicaea and the Council of Constantinople it is sometimes referred to by scholars as the 'Niceno-Constantinopolitan Creed.'

The fact that the Nicene Creed was a development of doctrine can be seen if we compare the texts of the creed agreed at the Council of Nicaea (the 'Creed of Nicaea') and the Nicene Creed. The differences between the two are shown by the words in bold in the text of the latter.

The Creed of Nicaea

We believe in one God, the Father almighty, maker of all things visible and invisible;

And in one Lord, Jesus Christ, the Son of God, begotten from the Father, only-begotten, that is, from the substance of the Father, God from God, light from light, true God from true God, begotten not made, of one substance with the Father, through Whom all

---

[60] Cranfield, p.6.

things came into being, things in heaven and things on earth, Who because of us men and because of our salvation came down, and became incarnate and became man, and suffered, and rose again on the third day, and ascended to the heavens, and will come to judge the living and dead,

And in the Holy Spirit.

But as for those who say, There was when He was not, and, Before being born He was not, and that He came into existence out of nothing, or who assert that the Son of God is of a different hypostasis or substance, or created, or is subject to alteration or change - these the Catholic and apostolic Church anathematizes.[61]

The Nicene Creed

I believe in one God the Father Almighty, **Maker of heaven and earth**, And of all things visible and invisible:

And in one Lord Jesus Christ, **the only-begotten Son of God, Begotten of his Father before all worlds,** God of God, Light of Light, Very God of very God, Begotten, not made, Being of one substance with the Father, By whom all things were made: Who for us men and for our salvation came down from heaven, **And was incarnate by the Holy Ghost of the Virgin Mary,** And was made man, **And was crucified also for us under Pontius Pilate.** He suffered **and was buried**, And the third day he rose again **according to the Scriptures**, And ascended into heaven, **And sitteth on the right hand of the Father.** And he shall come again **with glory** to judge both the quick and the dead: **Whose kingdom shall have no end.**

And I believe in the Holy Ghost, **The Lord and giver of life, Who proceedeth from the Father and the Son, Who with the Father**

---

[61] 'The Creed of Nicaea' at *Early Church Texts*:
https://www.earlychurchtexts.com/public/creed_of_nicaea_325.htm.

and the Son together is worshipped and glorified, Who spake by the Prophets.

And I believe one Catholick and Apostolick Church. I acknowledge one Baptism for the remission of sins. And I look for the Resurrection of the dead, And the life of the world to come. Amen[62]

If we look at the differences between the two creeds, we find that the Nicene Creed does not reject anything that is present in the Creed of Nicaea. What it does is add to it.

In the first paragraph the biblical affirmation that God the Father is 'maker of heaven and earth' (Genesis 1:1, Psalm 121:1, Psalm 124:8) is added.

In the second paragraph what is said about the Sons eternal existence, his incarnate existence, his ascension, and his coming again are filled out from the New Testament and the words 'whose kingdom will have no end' are added to clarify that although the Son will deliver the kingdom to God the Father (1 Corinthians 15:24), he will nonetheless continue to reign with the Father for all eternity.

In the third paragraph the brief affirmation of belief in the Holy Spirit[63] contained in the Creed of Nicaea is expanded to affirm the divinity of the Holy Spirit in the face of a heresy known as Macedonianism, which held that the Holy Spirit was a spiritual entity created by the Father and the Son.[64] In this paragraph the Spirit's divinity is expressed by the description of him as 'Lord and giver of life' and by the declaration that he is 'worshipped and glorified' alongside the Father and the Son.

---

[62] Text of the Nicene Creed in the *Book of Common Prayer*.
[63] The word 'Ghost' used in the Prayer Book version of the Creed is simply an old English word for 'Spirit.'
[64] For the Macedonian heresy see John Kelly, *Early Christian Doctrines*, 5th ed (London: A&C Black, 1977), p.259-260.

In addition, the fourth paragraph was included to add further additional material concerning the Holy Spirit. To quote Justin Holcomb, this additional paragraph declares:

> To the Holy Spirit, and to his activity belong the holy catholic and apostolic church, its teaching, its confessions, its sacraments, and its ultimate new birth into the resurrection of everlasting life. Put simply, the Holy Spirit is the one who leads the church in its worship and its confession of the triune God. [65]

The Prayer Book version of the Nicene Creed cited above, like other Western versions of the Nicene Creed adds the words 'and the Son' to the Creed's original statement that the Spriit 'proceeds from the Father'. This addition is known as the filioque clause (from the Latin word *filioque*, 'and the Son'). Under the influence of Western theologians such Hilary of Poitiers and Augustine of Hippo the belief that the Holy Spirit proceeds from both the Father and the Son formed part of Western theology from the fourth century onwards and from the end of the sixth century onwards the use of the filioque clause spread from Spain across the Western Church and was eventually accepted by the Papacy in the eleventh century. [66]

In summary we can say that the Nicene Creed exhibits four forms of doctrinal development.

- It follows the development pioneered in the Creed of Nicaea by affirming that that the Son is of 'one substance' (*homoousios*) with the Father.

- It adds additional biblically based material to the clauses on the Father and the Son.

- It affirms the divinity of the Holy Spirit and a description of the activity of the Holy Spirit in the life of the Church

---

[65] Holcomb, pp.37-38.
[66] See Kelly, *Early Christian Creeds*, pp.358-367.

- It affirms that the Spirit proceeds from the Father (and its Western form that the Spirit also proceeds from the Son).

The Chalcedonian Confession

The Chalcedonian Confession, also known as the Chalcedonian Definition, is the statement concerning the person of Christ produced at the Council of Chalcedon in 451. It runs as follows:

> Following the holy Fathers we teach with one voice that the Son [of God] and our Lord Jesus Christ is to be confessed as one and the same [Person], that he is perfect in Godhead and perfect in manhood, very God and very man, of a reasonable soul and [human] body consisting, consubstantial with the Father, as touching his Godhead, and consubstantial with us as touching his manhood; made in all things like unto us, sin only excepted; consubstantial with the Father as touching his Godhead, and consubstantial with us as touching his manhood; made in all things like unto us, sin only excepted; begotten of his Father before the worlds according to his godhead; but in these last days for us men and for our salvation born [into the world] of the Virgin Mary, the mother of God according to his manhood. This one and the same Jesus Christ, the only-begotten Son [of God] must be confessed to be in two natures, unconfusedly, immutably, indivisibly, inseparably [united], and that without the distinction of natures being taken away by such union, but rather the peculiar property of each nature being preserved and being united in one Person and one subsistence, not separated or divided into two persons, but one and the same Son and only-begotten, God the Word, our Lord Jesus Christ, as the Prophets of old time have spoken concerning him, and as the Lord Jesus Christ hath taught us, and as the Creed of the Fathers hath delivered two us.[67]

---

[67] Text in *Nicene and Post Nicene Fathers* vol XIV Edinburgh & Grand Rapids: T&T Clark/Eerdmans 1997 pp.264-265.

The opening words of the Confession 'following the Holy Fathers' indicates that the bishops meeting at Chalcedon believed that they were re-affirming the faith taught by the bishops who had met together at the earlier Councils held at Nicaea, Constantinople and Ephesus in affirming in affirming the teaching of the Bible about Christ's true deity and true humanity.

However, what the bishops agreed at Chalcedon was in fact a new development in that it not only ruled out the Arian heresy by following the Councils of Nicaea and First Constantinople in affirming that the Son is 'consubstantial with the Father' but also ruled out a number of other heresies which troubled the Early Church by making two further affirmations.

- Over against the Docetic heresy which claimed that Christ only appeared to be human, the Apollinarian heresy which denied that he had a rational human soul, and the Eutychian heresy which claimed that his humanity was swallowed up by His deity, it affirmed that Christ is truly human and therefore possesses a human nature that is like the nature of all other human beings 'sin only excepted.'

- Over against the Nestorian heresy which claimed that Christ was a union of two separate persons, one human and one divine, it affirms that that there is one person, one self, God the Son, who possesses the two natures and operates through both.

As in the case of the Apostles and Nicene Creed, what is said in the Chalcedonian Confession upholds biblical teaching, but what is said in the Chalcedonian Confession is also a development of doctrine in that the revealed truths of Christ's full humanity and divinity had never been defined and taught in precisely this way before.

The Athanasian Creed

The Athanasian Creed is a Western creed which was originally written in Latin and was composed in the area of Lérins in Southern France at the end of the fifth or the beginning of the sixth century.

Although it was not written by Athanasius, who had died in 373 AD, calling it the creed of Athanasius, who had been persecuted for his loyalty to orthodox Trinitarian theology in the face of Arianism, was a way of saying to Christians whose rulers were Arian Visigoths: 'This is the faith to which Athanasius remained loyal and for which he was prepared to suffer. You should be prepared to follow his example by remaining equally loyal to it.'

This creed is also known as the *Quicunque vult* (English 'whoever wishes') which are its opening words in Latin. Although it was probably written as a teaching tool rather than for liturgical use, it came to be used in the liturgy across the Western Church (including the Church in England) from the eighth century onwards.

The Athanasian Creed is in three parts. It begins and ends with what are known as the 'damnatory clauses' so called because they declare that belief in the Catholic faith is necessary to avoid damnation. In the words of the opening two verses:

> Whosoever will be saved: before all things it is necessary that he hold the Catholick Faith. Which faith except every one do keep whole and undefiled: without doubt he shall perish everlastingly.

These damnatory clauses in the creed are a stumbling block to many who can accept the rest of its teaching. However, they make sense once one understands that according to the New Testament salvation involves faith in Christ (see Mark 16:16, John 3:16-18, Romans 3:28). Faith in Christ in turn means faith in the teaching of the apostles who are the ambassadors appointed by Christ to speak on his behalf (2 Corinthians 5:20) and by extension faith in later Church teaching ('the catholic faith') which embodies the teaching of the apostles.

Accordingly, to turn away from the catholic faith is, as the creed says, to exclude oneself from salvation by rejecting faith in Christ himself.

The rest of the creed is divided into two sections, the first concerned with the Trinity and the second concerned with person and work of Christ. In between them are two verses that serve as a hinge holding the two main sections together and further emphasising the importance of right belief for salvation.

On the subject of the Trinity the Athanasian Creed teaches that there is one God who exists as three Persons, the Father, the Son and the Holy Spirit. Because they are all God, all three persons possess the same divine attributes (thus they are all 'uncreated,' 'infinite' and 'eternal' and they possess the same divine names ('Almighty', 'God' and 'Lord').

What distinguishes the Persons is their relationships of origin, the Father being neither created nor begotten, the Son being not created but begotten from the Father, and the Spirit being neither created nor begotten, but proceeding from the Father and the Son.

On the person and work of Christ the Athanasian Creed teaches in line with the Chalcedonian Confession that Christ is 'perfect God and perfect Man,' one person with both a divine and human nature. It also teaches that as the God-Man he died, descended to the place of the dead, rose, ascended and will come to judge the living and the dead.

In terms of its theology the Athanasian Creed says nothing new. It draws on the writings of earlier theologians such as Ambrose of Milan, Augustine of Hippo and Caesarius of Arles and it reflects the theology proclaimed by the Councils of Nicaea, First Constantinople and Chalcedon. However, it does something novel by unflinchingly declaring the necessity for salvation of adherence to the orthodox faith and by setting out the content of that faith in a clearer, more comprehensive and more systematic fashion than anyone had achieved before. In this sense it is a development of Christian doctrine.

4. The confessions of faith of the Reformation period

In the sixteenth and seventeenth centuries the Protestant Reformation and the corresponding Roman Catholic Counter-Reformation resulted in the development of new statements of Christian doctrine by both Protestants and Roman Catholics alike.

This development was the result of two factors. The first factor was the need felt by both Protestants and Roman Catholics to affirm that they stood by the faith taught by the New Testament and by the orthodox theologians and Councils of the Early Church. The second factor was the need felt by both Protestants and Roman Catholics to define their faith in a way that ruled out the errors of belief and practice which they believed existed in other churches, whether Roman Catholic or Protestant.

In the remainder of this section, I shall illustrate the way that the Reformation and Counter-Reformation led to the development of new statements of Christian doctrine by looking at material from the Lutheran *Augsburg Confession* of 1530, the Reformed *Scots Confession* of 1560, the Anglican *Thirty-Nine Articles* of 1571 and the Roman Catholic *Creed of the Council of Trent* of 1564.

The Augsburg Confession

The *Augsburg Confession* was a statement of Lutheran faith, written by Philip Melancthon with assistance from other Lutheran theologians including Martin Luther himself, that was presented to the Emperor Charles V in 1530 by the princes and city authorities of those territories within the Holy Roman Empire that had accepted the Lutheran Reformation.

In the words of its Preface, in the *Augsburg Confession* these princes and city authorities:

> ...offer and present a confession of our pastors' and preachers' teaching and of our own faith, setting forth how and in what manner, on the basis of the holy Scriptures, these things are

preached, taught, communicated, and embraced in our lands, principalities, dominions, cities, and territories.[68]

As Mark Noll explains. the body of the Confession is in two parts. 'Its first twenty-one articles present convictions that the Lutherans hoped could be accepted by Catholics. The last eight offer lengthier explanations of matters in dispute.' [69]

An example of the sort of material found in the first twenty-one articles is Article 3 on the person of Christ. This declares:

> It is also taught among us that God the Son became man, born of the Virgin Mary, and that the two natures, divine and human, are so inseparable united in one person that there is one Christ, true God and true man, who was truly born, suffered, was crucified, died, and was buried in order to be a sacrifice not only for original sin but also for all other sins and to propitiate God's wrath. The same Christ also descended into hell, truly rose from the dead on the third day, ascended into heaven, and sits on the right hand of God, that he may eternally rule and have dominion over all creatures, but through the Holy Spirit he may sanctify, purify, strengthen and comfort all who believe in him, that he may be bestow on them life and every grace and blessing, and that he may protect and defend them against the devil and against sin. The same Lord Jesus Christ will return openly to judge the living the dead, as stated in the Apostles' Creed. [70]

This article builds on the teaching of the New Testament, the *Chalcedonian Confession and* the *Apostles' Creed*. However, in comparison with what is said in the latter two sources it emphasises that the purpose of Christ's suffering and death was to be a sacrifice for all sin and to propitiate the wrath of God and explains the benefits

---

[68] Text from Mark Noll (ed), *Confessions and Catechisms of the Reformation* (Vancouver: Regent College Publishing, 2004), p. 85.
[69] Noll, p.83.
[70] Noll, p.88

that Christ bestows through the Holy Spirit on all who believe in him. These new features make the article a form of doctrinal development.

An example of the sort of material found in the final eight articles is article 24 on the Mass. This article explains that in order to counter errors concerning the Mass that had crept in during the Middle Ages:

> ...instruction was given so that our people might know how the sacrament is to be used rightly. They were taught, first of all, that the Scriptures show in many places but there is no sacrifice for original sin, or for any other sin, except the one death of Christ. For it is written in the Epistle to the Hebrews that Christ offered himself once and by this offering made satisfaction for all sin. It is an unprecedented novelty in church doctrine that Christ's death should have been made satisfaction only for original sin and not for other sins as well. Accordingly it is to be hoped that everyone will understand that this error is not unjustly condemned.
>
> In the second place, Saint Paul taught that we obtain grace before God through faith and not through works. Manifestly contrary to this teaching is the misuse of the Mass by those who think that grace is obtained through the performance of this work, for it is well known that the Mass is used to remove sin and obtain grace and all sorts of benefits from God, not only for the priest himself but also for the whole world and for others, both living and dead.
>
> In the third place, the holy sacrament was not instituted to make provision for a sacrifice for sin - for that sacrifice has already taken place - but to awaken our faith and comfort our consciences when we perceive that through the sacrament grace and forgiveness of sin are promised to us by Christ. Accordingly, the sacrament requires faith, and without faith it is used in vain.[71]

This article represents a development of doctrine in that it represents fresh teaching, based on the teaching of the New Testament, that is

---

[71] Noll, 102-103.

designed to explain why the Lutheran understanding of the purpose of the Mass is to be preferred to the teaching on this subject previously given by the Medieval Church.

The Scots Confession

The *Scots Confession* of 1560 was one of the first fruits of the Scottish Reformation. In that year the Scottish Parliament commissioned ministers of the Scottish Church to produce a statement of the Protestant Christian Faith. John Knox and five other ministers undertook this task and resultant confession of faith was officially adopted on 17 August 1560 as 'wholesome and sound doctrine grounded upon the infallible truth of God's word.'

The fact that the *Scots Confession* is an example of the development of doctrine can be seen if we look at what is said in chapters 10 and 11 concerning Christ's resurrection and ascension.

Chapter X
The Resurrection

We undoubtedly believe, since it was impossible that the sorrows of death should retain in bondage the Author of Life, that our Lord Jesus crucified, dead, and buried, who descended into hell, did rise again for our justification, and the destruction of him who was the author of death, and brought life again to us who were subject to death and its bondage. We know that His resurrection was confirmed by the testimony of His enemies, and by the resurrection of the dead, whose sepulchres did open, and they did rise and appear to many within the city of Jerusalem. It was also confirmed by the testimony of His angels, and by the senses and judgement of His apostles, and of others, who had conversation, and did eat and drink with Him after His resurrection.

Chapter XI
The Ascension

We do not doubt but that the self-same body which was born of the virgin, was crucified, dead and buried, and which did rise again, did ascend into the heavens, for the accomplishment of all things, where in our name and for our comfort He has received all power in heaven and earth, where He sit at the right hand of the Father, having received His kingdom, the only advocate and mediator for us. Which glory, honour, and prerogative, He alone amongst the brethren shall possess till all His enemies are made His footstall, as we undoubtedly believe they shall be in the Last Judgment. We believe that the same Lord Jesus shall visibly return for this Last Judgment as He was seen to ascend. And then, we firmly believe, the time of refreshing and restitution of all things shall come, so that those who from the beginning have suffered violence, injury, and wrong for righteousness' sake, shall inherit that blessed immortality promised them from the beginning. But, on the other hand, the stubborn, disobedient, cruel persecutors, filthy persons, idolators, and all sorts of the unbelieving, shall be cast into the dungeon of utter darkness, where their worm shall not die, nor their fire be quenched. The remembrance of that day, and of the Judgment to be executed in it, is not only a bridle by which our carnal lusts are restrained but also such inestimable comfort that neither the threatening of worldly princes, nor the fear of present danger or of temporal death, may move us to renounce and forsake that blessed society which we, the members, have with our Head and only Mediator, Christ Jesus: whom we confess and avow to be the promised Messiah, the only Head of His Kirk, our just Lawgiver, our only High Priest, Advocate, and Mediator. To which honours and offices, if man or angel presume to intrude themselves, we utterly detest and abhor them, as blasphemous to our sovereign and supreme Governor, Christ Jesus.[72]

While belief in Christ's resurrection and ascension has been part of Christian doctrine since the time they occurred (as Peter's sermon on the day of Pentecost as recorded in Acts 2:22-36 makes clear), the way that this faith is affirmed in chapters X and XI of the Scots Confession is a new development in that no one affirmed this belief in

---

[72] G D Henderson and John Bulloch, *The Scots Confession of 1560* (Edinburgh: The St Andrew Press, 1960), pp. 59-60.

quite this way before. As far as we know, no one before Knox and his colleagues had linked together the reasons for the resurrection and the evidence for the resurrection in the way that is done in chapter X, and as far as we know no one had linked together the ascension, the nature of the last judgement, and the spiritual benefits of remembering the last judgement in the way that is done in chapter XI.

The Thirty-Nine Articles
Following the breach with Rome in the 1530s, the leaders of the Church of England felt it needed to draw up a statement of its faith and practice, 'for avoiding of diversities of opinion, and for the establishment of consent touching true religion.' By 'true religion' they meant the teaching and practice of Jesus and his Apostles as recorded in the New Testament, expounded by the orthodox Fathers and Councils of the Church during the first few centuries of its history, and summarised in the Creeds. *The Thirty-Nine Articles*, which reached their final form in 1571 were intended to help embody true religion in the life of the Church of England both by setting out a pattern for its faith and practice based on these sources, and by ruling out the errors of Medieval Catholicism on the one hand and of the radical Reformation on the other.

Although the Articles were based on the teaching of the Bible and the early Fathers and Councils of the Church, and although they were influenced by the theology produced by the continental Protestant reformers, what they say is nevertheless novel and distinctive and for this reason constitutes a fresh development of Christian doctrine. We can see this for example if we consider what is said in Articles XVII and XXXVII.

Article XVII, 'Of Predestination and Election,' runs as follows:

> Predestination to life is the everlasting purpose of God, whereby, before the foundations of the world were laid, He hath constantly decreed by His counsel secret to us, to deliver from curse and damnation those whom He hath chosen in Christ out of mankind, and to bring them by Christ to everlasting salvation as vessels

made to honour. Wherefore they which be endued with so excellent a benefit of God be called according to God's purpose by His Spirit working in due season; they through grace obey the calling; they be justified freely; they be made sons of God by adoption; they be made like the image of His only-begotten Son Jesus Christ; they walk religiously in good works; and at length by God's mercy they attain to everlasting felicity.

As the godly consideration of Predestination and our Election in Christ is full of sweet, pleasant, and unspeakable comfort to godly persons and such as feeling in themselves the working of the Spirit of Christ, mortifying the works of the flesh and their earthly members and drawing up their mind to high and heavenly things, as well because it doth greatly establish and confirm their faith of eternal salvation to be enjoyed through Christ, as because it doth fervently kindle their love towards God: so for curious and carnal persons, lacking the Spirit of Christ, to have continually before their eyes the sentence of God's Predestination is a most dangerous downfall, whereby the devil doth thrust them either into desperation or into wretchlessness of most unclean living no less perilous than desperation.

Furthermore, we must receive God's promises in such wise as they be generally set forth in Holy Scripture; and in our doings that will of God is to be followed which we have expressly declared unto us in the word of God.[73]

Predestination and election were not new topics in Christian theology and what Article XVII says about them is rooted in the teaching of Paul in Romans 8:28-30, Romans 9:23-24, Ephesians 1:4-5 and Ephesians 1:11-12 and was also probably influenced by the writings of Augustine of Hippo and Prosper of Aquitaine from the Patristic period and the writings of the Protestant reformers Peter Martyr Vermigli and Philip Melancthon. Nevertheless, what the Article itself

---

[73] Text in Noll, p. 219.

says is novel. No one before had produced the combination of biblical teaching about predestination, explanation of the benefits and dangers of thinking about predestination and election, and insistence on seeking the will of God in the promises and commandments given to all human beings in God's word that we find in this article. This combination makes what is said in this Article a new development.

Article XXXVII, 'Of the Civil Magistrate,' runs as follows:

> The Queen's Majesty hath the chief power in this realm of England and other her dominions, unto whom the chief government of all estates of this realm, whether they be ecclesiastical or civil, in all causes doth appertain, and is not nor ought to be subject to any foreign jurisdiction.
>
> Where we attribute to the Queen's Majesty the chief government, by which titles we understand the minds of some slanderous folks to be offended, we give not to our princes the ministering either of God's word or of sacraments, the which thing the Injunctions also lately set forth by Elizabeth our Queen doth most plainly testify: but that only prerogative which we see to have been given always to all godly princes in Holy Scriptures by God himself, that is, that they should rule all estates and degrees committed to their charge by God, whether they be ecclesiastical or temporal, and restrain with the civil sword the stubborn and evil-doers.
>
> The Bishop of Rome hath no jurisdiction in this realm of England.
>
> The Laws of the Realm may punish Christian men with death for heinous and grievous offences.
>
> It is lawful for Christian men at the commandment of the Magistrate to wear weapons and serve in the wars.[74]

---

[74] Text in Noll, p.226.

What is said in Article XXXVII draws on the teaching of Romans 13:1-7 and reflects debates about the relationship between the respective jurisdictions of secular rulers and the Papacy that had taken place in England and across Western Christendom throughout the Middle Ages. However, the specifics of what Article XXXVII says about this matter, and in particular its complete repudiation of Papal jurisdiction in England, is new, as is the combination of discussion of this matter with the rejection of the claim made by some Anabaptist groups that it was unlawful for Christians to ever kill people. As in the case of Article XVII what we have here is therefore a new development of doctrine.

The Creed of the Council of Trent

The Council of Trent was a council of the Roman Catholic Church that began on in December 1545 and ran with long interruptions until December 1563. It was a response to the Protestant Reformation that sought to define the faith of Catholic Church in response to the challenges to it posed by Protestant teaching and to bring about the Church's moral and spiritual renewal in the face of the abuses that had brought the Church into disrepute and thus contributed to the rise of Protestantism.

The *Creed of the Council of Trent*, which was promulgated by Pope Pius IV in 1564, was a summary of the doctrines agreed by the Council of Trent. It states:

> I, N, with firm faith believe and profess age and every article contained in the Symbol of faith which the holy Roman church uses; namely; [Constantinopolitan Creed with Western additions].
>
> I resolutely accept and embrace the apostolic and ecclesiastical traditions and the other practises and regulations of that same Church. In like manner I accept Sacred Scripture according to the meaning which has been held by holy Mother Church and which she now holds. It is her prerogative to pass judgement on the true meaning and interpretation of Sacred Scripture. And I will never

accept or interpret it in a manner different from the unanimous agreement of the Fathers.

I also acknowledge that there are truly and properly seven sacraments of the New Law, instituted by Jesus Christ our Lord, and that they are necessary for the salvation of the human race, although it is not necessary for each individual to receive them all. I acknowledge the seven sacraments are: baptism, confirmation, Eucharist, penance, extreme function, holy orders, and matrimony; and that they confer grace; and that of the seven, baptism, confirmation, and holy orders cannot be repeated without committing a sacrilege. I also accept and acknowledge it the customary and approved rites of the Catholic Church in the solemn administration of these sacraments. I embrace each and every article on original sin and justification declared and defined in the most holy Council of Trent.

I likewise professed that in the Mass a true, proper, and propitiatory sacrifice is offered to God on behalf of the living and the dead, and that the body and blood together with the soul and divinity of our Lord Jesus Christ is truly, really, and substantially present in the most holy sacrament of the Eucharist, and that there is a change of the whole substance of the bread into the body, and of the whole substance of the wine into blood; And this changed the Catholic Church calls transubstantiation. I also profess that the whole and entire Christ and a true sacrament is received under each separate species.

I firmly hold that there is a purgatory, and that the souls detained there are helped by the prayers of the faithful. I likewise hold that the Saints reigning together with Christ should be honoured and invoked, that they offer prayers to God on our behalf, and that their relics should be venerated. I firmly assert that images of Christ, of the Mother of God ever Virgin, and of the other saints should be owned and kept, and that due honour and veneration should be given to them. I affirm that the power of indulgences was left in the keeping of the Church by Christ, and that the use of indulgences is very beneficial to Christians.

I acknowledge, the holy, Catholic, and apostolic Roman Church as the mother and teacher of all churches; and I promise and swear true obedience to the Roman Pontiff, vicar of Christ and successor of Blessed Peter, Prince of the Apostles.

I unhesitatingly accept and profess all the doctrines (especially those concerning the primacy of the Roman Pontiff and his infallible teaching authority) handed down, defined, and explained by the sacred canons and ecumenical councils and especially those of this most holy Council of Trent (and by the ecumenical Vatican Council). And at the same time I condemn, reject, and anathematize everything that is contrary to those propositions, and all heresies without exception that have been condemned comment rejected, and anathematized by the Church. I, N., promise, vow, and swear that, with God's help, I shall most constantly hold and profess this true Catholic faith, outside which no one can be saved and which I now freely profess and truly hold. With the help of God I shall profess it whole and unblemished to my dying breath; and to the best of my ability, I shall see to it that my subjects or those entrusted to me by virtue of my office hold it, teach it, and preach it, so help me God and his holy Gospel.[75]

Although the purpose of the Creed was to summarise what was seen as the unchanging teaching of the Church over against Protestant innovations it can be seen to be an example of doctrinal development in a number of ways.

First, the version of the Nicene Creed it uses is the Western version of the Creed that has the filioque clause added to the original text.

Secondly, the decisions of the Council of Trent which it summarises were themselves a development of doctrine in that they defined the

---

[75] Text in Leith, pp. 440-442.

limits of Christian orthodoxy in a new way by 'excluding not only the Protestant position but other positions that had been permissible in Mediaeval Catholicism.'[76] In addition the summary of the teaching of Trent which it offers was in itself a new text that added to what Trent itself had said.

Thirdly, following the definition of Papal infallibility by the First Vatican Council in 1870 the words in brackets in the final paragraph were added to the original text by Pope Pius IX in 1877 in order to reflect the teaching of that Council. Thus the text of the Creed of the Council of Trent was itself developed.

5. **Doctrinal Statements from the twentieth and twenty first centuries**

The Barmen Declaration 1934
The *Barmen Declaration* was a theological declaration agreed by representatives of Lutheran, Reformed and United Protestant churches in Germany at a Synod held in the German city of Barmen on May 29-30, 1934. The declaration, which was largely the work of the Swiss theologian Karl Barth, was a rejection of the idea put forward by the Nazi supporting 'German Christians' that the German Protestant churches should become subject ideologically and politically to the Nazi regime which had come to power in Germany the previous year.

The declaration, which has subsequently become widely influential across the Christian Church as a whole, runs as follows:

> In view of the errors of the 'German Christians' of the present Reich church government which are devastating the church and also therefore breaking up the unity of the German Evangelical Church, **we confess the following evangelical truths:**

---

[76] Leith p.399.

1. "I am the way, and the truth, and the life; no one comes to the Father, but by me." (Jn 14.6) "Truly, truly, I say to you, he who does not enter the sheepfold by the door, but climbs in by another way, that man is a thief and a robber...I am the door; if anyone enters by me, he will be saved." (Jn 10.1, 9)

Jesus Christ, as he is attested for us in holy scripture, is the one Word of God which we have to hear and which we have to trust and obey in life and in death.

We reject the false doctrine, as though the church could and would have to acknowledge as a source of its proclamation, apart from and besides this one Word of God, still other events and powers, figures and truths, as God's revelation.

2. "Christ Jesus, whom God has made our wisdom, our righteousness and sanctification and redemption." (1 Cor 1.30)

As Jesus Christ is God's assurance of the forgiveness of all our sins, so, in the same way and with the same seriousness he is also God's mighty claim upon our whole life. Through him befalls us a joyful deliverance from the godless fetters of this world for a free, grateful service to his creatures.

We reject the false doctrine, as though there were areas of our life in which we would not belong to Jesus Christ, but to other lords - areas in which we would not need justification and sanctification through him.

3. "Rather, speaking the truth in love, we are to grow up in every way into him who is the head, into Christ, from whom the whole body [is] joined and knit together." (Eph 4.15,16)

The Christian church is the congregation of the brethren in which Jesus Christ acts presently as the Lord in word and sacrament through the Holy Spirit. As the church of pardoned sinners, it has to testify in the midst of a sinful world, with its faith as with its obedience, with its message as with its order, that it is solely his property, and that it lives and wants to live solely from his comfort and from his direction in the expectation of his appearance.

We reject the false doctrine, as though the church were permitted to abandon the form of its message and order to its own pleasure or to changes in prevailing ideological and political convictions.

4. "You know that the rulers of the gentiles lord it over them, and their great men exercise authority over them. It shall not be so among you; but whoever would be great among you must be your servant." (Mt 20.25,26)

The various offices in the church do not establish a dominion of some over the others; on the contrary, they are for the exercise of the ministry entrusted to and enjoined upon the whole congregation.

We reject the false doctrine, as though the church, apart from this ministry, could and were permitted to give itself, or allow to be given to it, special leaders vested with ruling powers.

5. "Fear God. Honour the emperor." (1 Pet 2.17)

Scripture tells us that, in the as yet unredeemed world in which the church also exists, the state has by divine appointment the task of providing for justice and peace. [It fulfils this task] by means of the threat and exercise of force, according to the measure of human judgment and human ability. The church acknowledges the benefit of this divine appointment in gratitude and reverence before him. It calls to mind the kingdom of God, God's commandment and righteousness, and thereby the responsibility both of rulers and of the ruled. It trusts and obeys the power of the Word by which God upholds all things.

We reject the false doctrine, as though the state, over and beyond its special commission, should and could become the single and totalitarian order of human life, thus fulfilling the church's vocation as well.

We reject the false doctrine, as though the church, over and beyond its special commission, should and could appropriate the characteristics, the tasks, and the dignity of the state, thus itself becoming an organ of the state.

6. "Lo, I am with you always, to the close of the age." (Mt 28.20) "The word of God is not fettered." (2 Tim 2.9)

The church's commission, upon which its freedom is founded, consists in delivering the message of the free grace of God to all people in Christ's stead, and therefore in the ministry of his own Word and work through sermon and sacrament.

We reject the false doctrine, as though the church in human arrogance could place the word and work of the Lord in the service of any arbitrarily chosen desires, purposes, and plans.

The Confessional Synod of the German Evangelical Church declares that it sees in the acknowledgement of these truths and in the rejection of these errors the indispensable theological basis of the German Evangelical Church as a federation of confessional churches. It invites all who are able to accept its declaration to be mindful of these theological principles in their decisions in church politics. It entreats all whom it concerns to return to the unity of faith, love, and hope.[77]

Although the *Barmen Declaration* builds upon the teaching of Scripture and previous statements about the relationship between the Church and the state by Patristic theologians and theologians of the Protestant Reformation, it nevertheless constitutes a development of doctrine in two ways.

---

[77] Evangelische Kirche in Deutschland, 'The Barmen Declaration' at: https://www.ekd.de/en/The-Barmen-Declaration-303.htm

First, because its first article rejects the idea which had developed from the eighteenth century onwards that the theological authority for the Church should be the ' historical Jesus' supposedly discovered by critical historical study (which for the German Christian meant an anti-Jewish Aryan Jesus).[78] What the first article insists instead is that is the Jesus, and only the Jesus, witnessed to in Holy Scripture who is the final and authoritative word through whom God speaks to his people.

Secondly, because the remaining articles of the declaration go on to reject the subjection of the Christian Church to the sort of totalitarian political ideology and political organisation that the Nazis attempted to impose on Germany and on the German protestant churches (and which, on a different ideological basis, various Communist regimes have also sought to impose), a subjection which would effectively make the Church simply a propaganda tool of a totalitarian government.

Neither of these points had previously been emphasised as clearly as they are in the *Barmen Declaration* because the particular historical circumstances that produced the Barmen Declaration had not previously arisen.

The New Delhi Statement on unity 1961

As well as seeing the rise of right- and left-wing totalitarian regimes, the twentieth century also saw the rise of the ecumenical movement as an attempt to heal the divisions within the visible Church caused by the emergence of a range of separate Christian churches during the course of Christian history. One of the key achievements of the ecumenical movement was the foundation in 1948 of the World Council of Churches as a body representing all the main Christian churches around the world with the exception of the Roman Catholic Church.

---

[78] For details see Susanna Heschel, *The Aryan Jesus: Christian Theologians and the Bible in Nazi* Germany (Princeton: Princeton University Press, 2008).

At its third assembly held in New Delhi in 1961 the Word Council of Churches produced *the New Delhi Statement* which sets out the basis for Christian unity and a vision of what a united Christian Church, healed of the divisions of the past should look like. The key paragraphs of the statement declare:

1. The love of the Father and the Son in the unity of the Holy Spirit is the source and goal of the unity which the Triune God wills for all men and creation. We believe that we share in this unity in the Church of Jesus Christ, who is before all things and in whom all things hold together. In him alone, given by the Father to be Head of the Body, the Church has its true unity. The reality of this unity was manifest at Pentecost in the gift of the Holy Spirit, through whom we know in this present age the first fruits of that perfect union of the Son with his Father, which will be known in its fullness only when all things are consummated by Christ in his glory. The Lord who is bringing all things into full unity at the last is he who constrains us to seek the unity which he wills for his Church on earth here and now.
2. We believe that the unity which is both God's will and his gift to his Church is being made visible as all in each place who are baptized into Jesus Christ and confess him as Lord and Saviour are brought by the Holy Spirit into one fully committed fellowship, holding the one apostolic faith, preaching the one Gospel, breaking the one bread, joining in common prayer, and having a corporate life reaching out in witness and service to all and who at the same time are united with the whole Christian fellowship in all places and all ages in such wise that ministry and members are accepted by all, and that all can act and speak together as occasion requires for the tasks to which God calls his people.[79]

---

[79] World Council of Churches, 'New Dehli Statement on Unity' at: https://www.oikoumene.org/resources/documents/new-delhi-statement-on-unity.

These two paragraphs are a development of Christian doctrine because they are the first statement agreed by churches from around the world which describe what a future united church should look like. No such agreed ecumenical statement about the end goal of the work for visible unity had ever been produced before. As such the *New Delhi Statement* was a new development in the history of Christian theology.

The Jerusalem Declaration
At the beginning of the twenty first century the movement towards unity produced by the ecumenical movement began to go backwards. This was because a new source of division between and within churches opened up over the issue of whether churches should accept and bless same-sexual relationships, ordain those in such relationships and celebrate same-sex marriages.

In the Anglican Communion this issue came to the fore due to the decision of the diocese of New Westminster in the Anglican Church of Canada to permit the blessing of same-sex relationships and the appointment of Gene Robinsion, a man in a gay relationship, as Bishop of New Hampshire in The Episcopal Church in the United States. In response to these developments a movement called GAFCON[80] was founded in 2008 at a meeting in Jerusalem to: 'to guard and proclaim biblical truth globally and provide fellowship for orthodox Anglicans.' [81]

At this meeting a statement called *The Jerusalem Declaration* was agreed as the theological basis for the new movement. The declaration runs as follows:

> In the name of God the Father, God the Son and God the Holy Spirit:

---

[80] GAFCON is the acronym for Global Anglican Future Conference, which was the name of the meeting at which it was founded.
[81] GAFCON Global Anglicans, 'The history of GAFCON at a glance' at: https://www.gafcon.org/about/.

We, the participants in the Global Anglican Future Conference, have met in the land of Jesus' birth. We express our loyalty as disciples to the King of kings, the Lord Jesus. We joyfully embrace his command to proclaim the reality of his kingdom which he first announced in this land. The gospel of the kingdom is the good news of salvation, liberation and transformation for all. In light of the above, we agree to chart a way forward together that promotes and protects the biblical gospel and mission to the world, solemnly declaring the following tenets of orthodoxy which underpin our Anglican identity.

1. We rejoice in the gospel of God through which we have been saved by grace through faith in Jesus Christ by the power of the Holy Spirit. Because God first loved us, we love him and as believers bring forth fruits of love, ongoing repentance, lively hope and thanksgiving to God in all things.

2. We believe the Holy Scriptures of the Old and New Testaments to be the Word of God written and to contain all things necessary for salvation. The Bible is to be translated, read, preached, taught and obeyed in its plain and canonical sense, respectful of the church's historic and consensual reading.

3. We uphold the four Ecumenical Councils and the three historic Creeds as expressing the rule of faith of the one holy catholic and apostolic Church.

4. We uphold the Thirty-nine Articles as containing the true doctrine of the Church agreeing with God's Word and as authoritative for Anglicans today.

5. We gladly proclaim and submit to the unique and universal Lordship of Jesus Christ, the Son of God, humanity's only Saviour from sin, judgement and hell, who lived the life we could not live and died the death that we deserve. By his

atoning death and glorious resurrection, he secured the redemption of all who come to him in repentance and faith.

6. We rejoice in our Anglican sacramental and liturgical heritage as an expression of the gospel, and we uphold the 1662 Book of Common Prayer as a true and authoritative standard of worship and prayer, to be translated and locally adapted for each culture.

7. We recognise that God has called and gifted bishops, priests and deacons in historic succession to equip all the people of God for their ministry in the world. We uphold the classic Anglican Ordinal as an authoritative standard of clerical orders.

8. We acknowledge God's creation of humankind as male and female and the unchangeable standard of Christian marriage between one man and one woman as the proper place for sexual intimacy and the basis of the family. We repent of our failures to maintain this standard and call for a renewed commitment to lifelong fidelity in marriage and abstinence for those who are not married.

9. We gladly accept the Great Commission of the risen Lord to make disciples of all nations, to seek those who do not know Christ and to baptise, teach and bring new believers to maturity.

10. We are mindful of our responsibility to be good stewards of God's creation, to uphold and advocate justice in society, and to seek relief and empowerment of the poor and needy.

11. We are committed to the unity of all those who know and love Christ and to building authentic ecumenical relationships. We recognise the orders and jurisdiction of those Anglicans who uphold orthodox faith and practice, and we encourage them to join us in this declaration.

12. We celebrate the God-given diversity among us which enriches our global fellowship, and we acknowledge freedom in secondary matters. We pledge to work together to seek the mind of Christ on issues that divide us.

13. We reject the authority of those churches and leaders who have denied the orthodox faith in word or deed. We pray for them and call on them to repent and return to the Lord.

14. We rejoice at the prospect of Jesus' coming again in glory, and while we await this final event of history, we praise him for the way he builds up his church through his Spirit by miraculously changing lives.[82]

The Jerusalem Declaration is, and was intended to be, a conservative re-statement of Anglican doctrine. However, it can also be seen as an example of doctrinal development in three ways. First, there is no previous statement of Anglican identity that includes an equivalent of article 8. For the first time the traditional Christian view of sexual ethics has been included in a list of the marks of orthodox Anglican identity. Secondly, in article 11 'those Anglicans who uphold orthodox faith and practice,' and whose orders and jurisdictions are recognised, now means, among other things, those Anglicans (and only those Anglicans) who continue to uphold the traditional Christian view of sexual ethics. Thirdly, in article 13 there is a denial of 'the authority of those churches and leaders' who have rejected the traditional view of sexual ethics, since this is what the article means when it refers to those who have 'denied the orthodox faith in word or deed.' Previously, it had been generally assumed that a traditional view of Christian sexual ethics was part of being an orthodox Anglican, however the developments that had taken place in Canada and the United States meant that for the first time this belief was stated explicitly, as were its ecclesiological consequences.

---

[82] GAFCON,' Jerusalem Declaration – June 2008' at: https://civicrm.gafcon.org/about/jerusalem-Declaration.

6. Why we need to distinguish between legitimate and illegitimate development

In sections 2-5 of this chapter, we have seen that doctrinal development has been a feature of the life of the Church since New Testament times. The New Testament writings, the creeds and conciliar statements of the Patristic period, the confessions of faith produced by Protestants and Roman Catholics at the time of the Reformation, and theological statements produced by various bodies during the twentieth and twenty-first centuries are all examples of doctrinal development.

This being the case it is very difficult to maintain with Bossuet that every new development in theology is necessarily false. This is because to maintain this principle consistently we would have to say that everything said by every Christian theologian that differs in any way from what was said by Peter on the Day of Pentecost, the day the Church was founded (Acts 2:14-36), is by necessarily wrong simply because it is something that has not been said before.

As far as I am aware, no Christian, including Bossuet himself, has ever taken this extreme position. Bossuet himself believed in the theological authority of the New Testament, he believed in the Creeds and conciliar statements of the Patristic period, and he believed in the correctness of the theological statements produced by the Roman Catholic Church at the Council of Trent. He thus accepted that some development at least could be legitimate, even if he was not willing to admit this fact.

As Owen Chadwick explains, Bossuet held that when the Church used new language such as 'consubstantial' or 'transubstantiation' when describing the Trinity or the nature of Christ's presence at the Mass 'it was the words, not the ideas, which had changed.'[83] However, even the most conservative Roman Catholic theologians would now say that the evidence of Church history rules out this argument. Down the

---

[83] Chadwick, p.20.

centuries theologians have had new ideas, even if these new ideas have simply been about how to use new words to define and teach the revealed truth of God in new situations and in face of new theological challenges, and some of these new ideas have subsequently come to be regarded as having made a permanent contribution to orthodox Christian theology.

A classic example of this is Martin Luther's 1520 treatise *The Freedom of a Christian*. This treatise was the result of Luther having had a new idea about how to express the teaching about justification by faith taught in the letters of Paul in the face of what Luther saw as the misleading teaching of the late medieval Church. What resulted has been generally recognised by Protestant Christians (and now also by many Roman Catholics) as having made a permanent contribution to Christian thinking about justification and the nature of Christian freedom.[84]

However, although some new ideas that have emerged in the course of the history of the Church have thus been regarded as making a permanent contribution to orthodox Christian thought others have come to be regarded as heretical in the sense that they are 'thought by the Church to be wrong rather than right teaching or 'doctrine.'' [85]

Examples of such heretical ideas are:

- Marcionism: The rejection of the God of the Old Testament.
- Docetism: The rejection of the reality of the humanity of Christ.

---

[84] The text of *The Freedom of a Christian* can be found in Martin Luther, *Three Treatises* (Philadelphia, Fortress Press, 1978), pp. 262-316. For a study of its significance for Christian theology see Eberhard Jungel *The Freedom of a Christian: Luther's Significance for Contemporary Theology* (Minneapolis: Augsburg Press, 1988).
[85] Ben Quash, 'Prologue' in Quash and Ward, p.1.

- Gnosticism: The belief that people can be saved through acquiring secret knowledge.

- Arianism: The belief that God the Son is a created spiritual being

- Eutychianism: The belief that Christ's human nature was subsumed by his divine nature.

- Nestorianism: The belief that Christ was two distinct persons, one human and one divine.

- Pelgianism: The teaching that people can be saved through their own efforts. [86]

The fact that some new ideas have generally been seen as making a permanent contribution to Christian doctrine while others have been rejected as heretical raises the issue of the basis for making such a judgement. How is it possible to distinguish between positive developments of doctrine and those which are heretical? To put it another way, what is the mark of a legitimate development of Christian doctrine?

In the next three chapters of this book, we shall consider the answer to this last question by exploring the works of three writers on the development of doctrine, Vincent of Lerins, John Newman and Maurice Wiles.

Additional Note: Eastern Orthodox theology and doctrinal development

As Daniel Lattier notes,[87] objections to the idea of doctrinal development have been raised by modern Orthodox authors such as Georges Florovsky, Vladimir Lossky, Olivier Clément, Thomas Hopko, John Behr, and Andrew Louth. In the words of Louth, they argue that:

---

[86] For a useful introduction to these heresies see Quash and Ward.

[87] Daniel Lattier, 'The Orthodox Rejection of Doctrinal Development,' *The Holy Catholic Religion*, 7 May 2016 at: https://holycatholicreligion.blogspot.com/2016/05/the-orthodox-rejection-of-doctrinal.html2016.

'the idea of development itself is not an acceptable category in Orthodox theology.'[88] If we ask why these authors object to the ideas that doctrine develops, the answer seems to be that is because they see the idea of the development of doctrine as involving the claim that the Church increases in its knowledge about God and his ways, whereas from an Orthodox perspective such an increase in knowledge is impossible because the full truth about God has already been fully revealed in the Scriptures as understood in the light of the apostolic witness to Jesus Christ. To quote Louth again, 'There is no development beyond seeking, again and again, to deepen our understanding of the Scriptures in the light of the mystery of Christ.'[89]

There are two major problems with the rejection of doctrinal development by Orthodox writers such as those listed above.

First, history shows us that Orthodox doctrine has in fact developed over the centuries in that Orthodox theologians have expressed their faith in new ways.[90]

Secondly, as the Romanian Orthodox theologian Dumitru Staniloae explains, the concept of doctrinal development does in fact make sense on the basis of Orthodox theology, As he puts it:

> The fullness of the mystery of redemption, that is to say the divinity in its nearness and most perfect redemptive activity in the course of our earthly life, lived continuously in the Church, is a reality which cannot be fully expressed by words, metaphors or

---

[88] Andrew Louth, 'Is Development of Doctrine a Valid Category for Orthodox Theology?' in Valerie Hotchkiss and Patrick Henry (eds), *Orthodoxy and Western Culture: A Collection of Essays Honoring Jaroslav Pelikan on His Eightieth Birthday* (Crestwood: SVS Press, 2005), p.61.

[89] Louth, p.61.

[90] For the evidence for this point see Jaroslav Pelikan, *The Christian Tradition: A History of the Development of Doctrine, Volume 2: The Spirit of Eastern Christendom (600-1700)* (Chicago: Chicago University Press, 1977), and Kallistos Ware, 'Christian Theology in the East' in Hubert Cunliffe Jones and Benjamin Drewery (eds), *A History of Christian Doctrine* (Edinburgh: T&T Clark 1980).

formulas. For this reason new expressions are justified. But it is not only on account of the mysterious character of this action, but also because Christ, in guiding the world towards the general resurrection and the Kingdom of perfect love, by his Spirit which is found in the church and by his activity in history, draws closer to us, not only by reducing the number of years which separate us from these events, but also by making men more ready to receive them. Thus he aids men to go always further in the way of spirituality, of the likeness of Christ, of the ability to grasp and express the work which the Spirit of Christ carries out in them and in history, of understanding what the incarnation of the Son of God, his sacrifice for men, his resurrection and our resurrection truly mean.

In this way, Tradition signifies not only a continual experience of the mystery of redemption at the same level of spiritual apprehension, but also a progress in this experience and understanding, without this implying however transcending of the mystery of redemption and its fulfilment in Christ. Thus, Tradition not only means 'a living memory' constantly relived by the church, but also a tension and a constant self-transcendence towards the eschatological goal, a progress in the knowledge of the divine activity, lived without break by the Church in herself and grasped in history.

This is inevitably reflected in an enrichment of language, which constantly becomes diversified and more delicate, and thus capable of expressing always more subtly the mystery of the redemptive and spiritualizing activity of the Spirit of Christ in human nature and in his activity in history. Hence comes the justification and the necessity for employing new words, metaphors and formulas in order to express the mystery.[91]

---

[91] Dumitru Staniloae, 'The Orthodox Conception of Tradition and The Development of Doctrine,' *Sobornost* 5 (1969), pp.658-659.

Chapter 3
Noviter non nova - The Commonitory of Vincent of Lerins

1. Vincent of Lerins and the date of *The Commonitory*

The Commonitory of Vincent of Lerins is generally regarded as the major Patristic contribution to the discussion of the development of doctrine. Although it is not mentioned by medieval writers, it was rediscovered in the sixteenth century, when it was republished numerous times and appealed to by both Protestants and Roman Catholics as an authority supporting their theological position. Since then, it has been continuously in print and has been viewed as an important theological resource by theologians from a whole variety of different Christian churches.

The work itself is anonymous, with the author describing himself simply as 'peregrinus ('pilgrim') who am the least of all the servants of God.'[92]

All that we know of the authorship of the book comes from the chapter on Vincent in the work *Lives of Illustrious Men* by the fifth century monk and historian Gennadius of Marseilles. In chapter 65 of this work Gennadius writes:

> Vincentius, the Gaul, presbyter in the Monastery on the Island of Lérins,[93] a man learned in the Holy Scriptures and very well informed in matters of ecclesiastical doctrine, composed a powerful disputation, written in tolerably finished and clear language, which, suppressing his name, he entitled Peregrinus

---

[92] Vincent of Lerins, *The Commonitory*, Ch.I, in *The Nicene and Post-Nicene Fathers*, 2nd series, Vol.XI, (Edinburgh and Grand Rapids: T&T Clark: Eerdmans 1998), p.131.
[93] The Lérin islands are a group of four Islands in the Mediterranean off the French coast near Cannes. The monastery was on what is now the Ile Saint-Honorat.

against heretics. The greater part of the second book of this work having been stolen, he composed a brief reproduction of the substance of the original work, and published in one [book]. He died in the reign of Theodosius and Valentianus.[94]

We know that the Emperor Theodosius II died in July 450 so Vincent's death must have occurred before that date. When he was born and the details of his life are unknown, although his statement in chapter I: 'whereas I was at one time involved in the manifold and deplorable tempests of secular warfare, I have now at length, under Christ's auspices, cast anchor in the harbour of religion' [95] suggests that he was a soldier prior to becoming a monk.

The date of the writing of *The Commonitory* is fixed by a reference in chapter XXIX to 'the example of the holy council which some three years ago was held at Ephesus in Asia.'[96] The Council of Ephesus was held in 431 so this reference dates the writing of *The Commonitory* to 434. We have no direct evidence of when precisely it was published, but if we accept the evidence of Gennadius that Vincent himself published it, it must have been published sometime between 434 and 450.

The Commonitory as we now have it is not all that Vincent originally wrote. He refers at the start of chapter XXIX to a 'second Commonitory,'[97] the one which Gennadius reports as having been stolen. *The Commonitory* as we now have it seems to be made up of the first Commonitory, consisting of chapters I-XXVIII, and a summary of both the first and second Commonitories in chapters XXIX-XXXIII.

Reginald Moxon argues in his 1915 edition of *The Commonitory* that Gennadius' claim that the second Commonitory was stolen was

---

[94] Gennadius, *Lives of Illustrious Men*, in *The Nicene and Post-Nicene Fathers*, 2nd series (Edinburgh and Grand Rapids: T&T Clark: Eerdmans 1996), p.396.
[95] Vincent of Lerins, Ch.I, p.131.
[96] Vincent of Lerins, Ch.XXIX, p.154.
[97] Vincent of Lerins Ch.XXIX, p.153.

'nothing but a guess' and that the bulk of the material in it was left out of what was finally published because Vincent judged the detail about the Council of Ephesus which it contained to be too dull for publication.[98] However, we have no actual evidence that Vincent took this view of the material in his second book, and Gennadius' account that Vincent produced a short summary of what was in it because most of the original material had been stolen is equally plausible and has the advantage of being the testimony of someone who was writing shortly after the events which he is describing. There is therefore no good reason to doubt that what Gennadius wrote was true.

2. The purpose of The Commonitory

The word commonitory (*commonitorium* in Vincent's original Latin) means an 'aid to memory' and, as Vincent explains at the start of his work, its original purpose was to refresh his memory about how best to address the issue which his work covers.

He makes this point twice in chapter I. At the beginning of the chapter, he writes:

> I, Peregrinus, who am the least of all the servants of God, remembering the admonition of Scripture, 'Ask your fathers and they will tell you, your elders and they will declare unto you,' [Deuteronomy 32:7] and again, 'Bow down your ear to the words of the wise,' [Proverbs 22:17] and once more, 'My son, forget not these instructions, but let your heart keep my words:' [Proverbs 3:1] remembering these admonitions, I say, I, Peregrinus, am persuaded, that, the Lord helping me, it will be of no little use and certainly as regards my own feeble powers, it is most necessary, that I should put down in writing the things which I have truthfully received from the holy Fathers, since I shall then have ready at

---

[98] Reginald Moxon, *The Commonitorium of Vincent of Lerins* (Cambridge: CUP, 1915), pp. XVII-XXI.

hand wherewith by constant reading to make amends for the weakness of my memory.[99]

At the end of the chapter, he adds:

> Let those cultivate elegance and exactness who are confident of their ability or are moved by a sense of duty. For me it will be enough to have provided a Commonitory (or Remembrancer) for myself, such as may aid my memory, or rather, provide against my forgetfulness: which same Commonitory however, I shall endeavor, the Lord helping me, to amend and make more complete little by little, day by day, by recalling to mind what I have learned.[100]

If we ask what Vincent wanted to remember, the answer is that he wanted to remember the correct method for distinguishing between truth and heresy.

3. The contents of the *Commonitory*
The search for a rule to distinguish the Catholic faith from heresy (Ch II)

In line with this purpose Vincent begins his argument in the *Commonitory* in chapter II with the statement:

> I have often then inquired earnestly and attentively of very many men eminent for sanctity and learning, how and by what sure and so to speak universal rule I may be able to distinguish the truth of Catholic faith from the falsehood of heretical pravity; and I have always, and in almost every instance, received an answer to this effect: That whether I or any one else should wish to detect the frauds and avoid the snares of heretics as they rise, and to continue sound and complete in the Catholic faith, we must, the Lord helping, fortify our own belief in two ways; first, by the

---

[99] Vincent of Lerins, Ch.I, p.131.
[100] Vincent of Lerins, Ch.I, p.132.

> authority of the Divine Law [i.e. the teaching of the Bible], and then, by the Tradition of the Catholic Church.[101]

Vincent then notes that at this point someone may object: 'Since the canon of Scripture is complete, and sufficient of itself for everything, and more than sufficient, what need is there to join with it the authority of the Church's interpretation?'[102] Vincent's response to this objection is:

> For this reason — because, owing to the depth of Holy Scripture, all do not accept it in one and the same sense, but one understands its words in one way, another in another; so that it seems to be capable of as many interpretations as there are interpreters. For Novatian expounds it one way, Sabellius another, Donatus another, Arius, Eunomius, Macedonius, another, Photinus, Apollinaris, Priscillian, another, Jovinian, Pelagius, Celestius, another, lastly, Nestorius another. Therefore, it is very necessary, on account of so great intricacies of such various error, that the rule for the right understanding of the prophets and apostles should be framed in accordance with the standard of Ecclesiastical and Catholic interpretation.[103]

The Vincentian Canon (Ch II)

Vincent goes on to explain what sticking to the standard of Ecclesiastical and Catholic interpretation involves. In a paragraph which sets out what has come to be known as the 'Vincentian canon,' or rule, he writes:

> ...all possible care must be taken, that we hold that faith which has been believed everywhere, always, by all. For that is truly and in the strictest sense 'Catholic,' which, as the name itself and the reason of the thing declare, comprehends all universally. This rule we shall observe if we follow universality, antiquity, consent. We

---

[101] Vincent of Lerins, Ch.II, p.132.
[102] Vincent of Lerins, Ch.II, p.132.
[103] Vincent of Lerins, Ch.II, p.132.

shall follow universality if we confess that one faith to be true, which the whole Church throughout the world confesses; antiquity, if we in no wise depart from those interpretations which it is manifest were notoriously held by our holy ancestors and fathers; consent, in like manner, if in antiquity itself we adhere to the consentient definitions and determinations of all, or at the least of almost all priests and doctors.[104]

The need to give attention to General Councils and acknowledged authorities (Ch III)

In chapter III Vincent addresses the objection that it is all very well saying we need to cleave to what has been held in the past, but what happens 'if in antiquity itself there be found error on the part of two or three men, or at any rate of a city or even of a province?' The answer he gives is that in this case attention should be given to the decrees of General Councils and failing that to the agreement of acknowledged authorities.

> Then it will be his care by all means, to prefer the decrees, if such there be, of an ancient General Council to the rashness and ignorance of a few. But what, if some error should spring up on which no such decree is found to bear? Then he must collate and consult and interrogate the opinions of the ancients, of those, namely, who, though living in various times and places, yet continuing in the communion and faith of the one Catholic Church, stand forth acknowledged and approved authorities: and whatsoever he shall ascertain to have been held, written, taught, not by one or two of these only, but by all, equally, with one consent, openly, frequently, persistently, that he must understand that he himself also is to believe without any doubt or hesitation.[105]

---

[104] Vincent of Lerins, Ch.II, p.132.
[105] Vincent of Lerins, Ch.III, p.133.

The evils resulting from novel doctrine and the witness of those who have rejected it (Chs IV-VI)

In chapters IV-VI Vincent illustrates with reference to the Donatist and Arian heresies the evils resulting from doctrinal novelty, notes the heroic example set by those who adhered to 'the faith of universality and antiquity' [106] in spite of facing persecution for so doing, and lauds the example of Pope Stephen in resisting the heretical idea that baptism ought to be repeated 'contrary to the divine canon, contrary to the rule of the universal Church, contrary to the customs and institutions of our ancestors'.[107]

Paul's warning against those who preach another Gospel (Chs VII-IX)

In chapter VII Vincent moves on to note how the 'crime of perverting the faith and adulterating religion' was censured by the apostle Paul.

> For every one knows how gravely, how severely, how vehemently, the blessed apostle Paul inveighs against certain, who, with marvellous levity, had 'been so soon removed from him who had called them to the grace of Christ to another Gospel, which was not another;' [Galatians 1:6] 'who had heaped to themselves teachers after their own lusts, turning away their ears from the truth, and being turned aside unto fables;' [2 Timothy 4:3-4] 'having damnation because they had cast off their first faith;' [1 Timothy 5:12] who had been deceived by those of whom the same apostle writes to the Roman Christians, 'Now, I beseech you, brethren, mark them which cause divisions and offenses, contrary to the doctrine which you have learned, and avoid them. For they that are such serve not the Lord Christ, but their own belly, and by good words and fair speeches deceive the hearts of the simple,' [Romans 16:17-18] 'who enter into houses, and lead captive silly women laden with sins, led away with diverse lusts, ever learning and never able to come to the knowledge of the truth;' [2 Timothy 3:6]

---

[106] Vincent of Lerins, Ch.V, p.134.
[107] Vincent of Lerins, Ch.VI, p.135. By 'the divine canon' he means Scripture.

'vain talkers and deceivers, who subvert whole houses, teaching things which they ought not, for filthy lucre's sake;' [Titus 1:10] 'men of corrupt minds, reprobate concerning the faith;' [2 Timothy 3:8] 'proud knowing nothing, but doting about questions and strifes of words, destitute of the truth, supposing that godliness is gain,' [1 Timothy 6:4] 'withal learning to be idle, wandering about from house to house, and not only idle, but tattlers also and busybodies, speaking things which they ought not,' [1 Timothy 5:13] 'who having put away a good conscience have made shipwreck concerning the faith;' [1 Timothy 1:19] 'whose profane and vain babblings increase unto more ungodliness, and their word does eat as does a cancer.' [2 Timothy 2:16-17] Well, also, is it written of them: 'But they shall proceed no further: for their folly shall be manifest unto all men, as theirs also was.' [2 Timothy 3:9]. [108]

Next, in chapters VIII-IX Vincent refers to Paul's warning in Galatians 1:8 'Though we, or an angel from heaven, preach any other Gospel unto you than that which we have preached unto you, let him be accursed.' He argues that this warning and those previously mentioned in chapter VII 'are intended for all ages' and show that:

> To preach any doctrine therefore to Catholic Christians other than what they have received never was lawful, never is lawful, never will be lawful: and to anathematize those who preach anything other than what has once been received, always was a duty, always is a duty, always will be a duty. Which being the case, is there any one either so audacious as to preach any other doctrine than that which the Church preaches, or so inconstant as to receive any other doctrine than that which he has received from the Church? [109]

---

[108] Vincent of Lerins, Ch.VII, p.136.
[109] Vincent of Lerins, Ch.IX, p.137.

Why God allows heresy (Ch X)

In Chapter X Vincent moves on to address the question 'How is it then, that certain excellent persons, and of position in the Church are often permitted by God to preach novel doctrines to Catholics?' [110] As he sees it, the answer to this question is given by the words of Moses in Deuteronomy 13:1-3:

> 'If a prophet arises among you, or a dreamer of dreams, and gives you a sign or a wonder, and the sign or wonder which he tells you comes to pass, and if he says, 'Let us go after other gods,' which you have not known, 'and let us serve them,' you shall not listen to the words of that prophet or to that dreamer of dreams; for the Lord your God is testing you, to know whether you love the Lord your God with all your heart and with all your soul.'

According to Vincent, these words apply to the Church, with the heretics being the modern false prophets and the 'other gods' being their false teachings, 'forasmuch as heretics pay the same sort of reverence to their notions as the Gentiles do to their gods.'[111]

Examples of false prophets in the history or the Church (Chs XI-XX)

In chapters XI-XVI Vincent identifies as examples of the sort of false prophets referred to in Deuteronomy the fourth and fifth century heretics Photinus, Apollinarius and Nestorius. He explains the nature of their heretical teachings about the Trinity and the person of Christ and contrasts these with the position of the Catholic Church which:

> ...holding the right faith both concerning God and concerning our Saviour, is guilty of blasphemy neither in the mystery of the Trinity, nor in that of the Incarnation of Christ. For she worships both one Godhead in the plenitude of the Trinity, and the equality of the Trinity in one and the same majesty, and she confesses one Christ Jesus, not two; the same both God and man, the one as truly

---

[110] Vincent of Lerins. Ch.X, p.137.
[111] Vincent of Lerins, Ch.X, p.138

as the other. One Person indeed she believes in Him, but two substances; two substances but one Person: Two substances, because the Word of God is not mutable, so as to be convertible into flesh; one Person, lest by acknowledging two sons she should seem to worship not a Trinity, but a Quaternity.[112]

In chapters XVII and XVIII he cites Origen and Tertullian as two further examples 'of persons who having had at the one time the reputation of being sound in the faith, eventually fell away to some sect already in existence, or else founded a heresy of their own.,'[113] and in chapter XIX-XX he summarises his argument in this section of his work by declaring:

It behoves us, then, to give heed to these instances from Church History, so many and so great, and others of the same description, and to understand distinctly, in accordance with the rule laid down in Deuteronomy, that if at any time a Doctor in the Church have erred from the faith, Divine Providence permits it in order to make trial of us, whether or not we love God with all our heart and with all our mind.

This being the case, he is the true and genuine Catholic who loves the truth of God, who loves the Church, who loves the Body of Christ, who esteems divine religion and the Catholic Faith above everything, above the authority, above the regard, above the genius, above the eloquence, above the philosophy, of every man whatsoever; who sets light by all of these, and continuing steadfast and established in the faith, resolves that he will believe that, and that only, which he is sure the Catholic Church has held universally and from ancient time; but that whatsoever new and unheard-of doctrine he shall find to have been furtively introduced by some one or another, besides that of all, or contrary to that of all the saints, this, he will understand, does not pertain to religion, but is

---

[112] Vincent of Lerins, Ch.XIII, p.140.
[113] Vincent of Lerins, Ch.XVII, p.143.

permitted as a trial, being instructed especially by the words of the blessed Apostle Paul, who writes thus in his first Epistle to the Corinthians, 'There must needs be heresies, that they who are approved may be made manifest among you:' [1 Corinthians 2:9] as though he should say, This is the reason why the authors of Heresies are not immediately rooted up by God, namely, that they who are approved may be made manifest; that is, that it may be apparent of each individual, how tenacious and faithful and steadfast he is in his love of the Catholic faith.[114]

Further warnings against doctrinal novelty from the Bible and the Apocrypha (Chs XXI-XXII)

In chapters XXI and XXII Vincent next quotes a series of passages from the Old Testament, the Apocrypha and the New Testament which underline the importance of the rule 'let what has once for all been revealed suffice':

'Remove not the landmarks, which your fathers have set,' [Proverbs 22:28] and 'Go not to law with a Judge,' [Sirach 8:14] and 'Whoever breaks through a fence a serpent shall bite him,' [Ecclesiastes 10:8] and that saying of the Apostle wherewith, as with a spiritual sword, all the wicked novelties of all heresies often have been, and will always have to be, decapitated, 'O Timothy, keep the deposit, shunning profane novelties of words and oppositions of the knowledge falsely so called, which some professing have erred concerning the faith.' [1 Timothy 6:20]. [115]

On 1 Timothy 6:20 Vincent comments that Paul:

...mourned in anticipation over the errors which he foresaw. Who is the Timothy of today, but either generally the Universal Church, or in particular, the whole body of The Prelacy, whom it behoves either themselves to possess or to communicate to others a complete knowledge of religion? What is 'Keep the deposit'? 'Keep

---

[114] Vincent of Lerins, Chs.XIX-XX, pp.145-146.
[115] Vincent of Lerins, Ch.XXI, pp.146-147.

it,' because of thieves, because of adversaries, lest, while men sleep, they sow tares over that good wheat which the Son of Man had sown in his field. 'Keep the deposit.' What is 'The deposit'? That which has been entrusted to you, not that which you have yourself devised: a matter not of wit, but of learning; not of private adoption, but of public tradition; a matter brought to you, not put forth by you, wherein you are bound to be not an author but a keeper, not a teacher but a disciple, not a leader but a follower. 'Keep the deposit.' Preserve the talent of Catholic Faith inviolate, unadulterate. That which has been entrusted to you, let it continue in your possession, let it be handed on by you. You have received gold; give gold in turn. Do not substitute one thing for another. Do not for gold impudently substitute lead or brass. Give real gold, not counterfeit.[116]

The nature of doctrinal progress (Ch XXIII)

In Chapter XXIII Vincent answers the objection 'Shall, there, then, be no progress in Christ's Church?' His answer is that there is 'all possible progress.' However, it has to be:

> ...real progress, not alteration of the faith. For progress requires that the subject be enlarged in itself, alteration, that it be transformed into something else. The intelligence, then, the knowledge, the wisdom, as well of individuals as of all, as well of one man as of the whole Church, ought, in the course of ages and centuries, to increase and make much and vigorous progress; but yet only in its own kind; that is to say, in the same doctrine, in the same sense, and in the same meaning.[117]

In his view, the growth of religion, both in the individual and in the Church needs to be:

> ...analogous to the growth of the body, which, though in process of years it is developed and attains its full size, yet remains still the

---

[116] Vincent of Lerins, Ch.XXII, pp.147.
[117] Vincent of Lerins, Ch.XXIII, pp.147-148.

same. There is a wide difference between the flower of youth and the maturity of age; yet they who were once young are still the same now that they have become old, insomuch that though the stature and outward form of the individual are changed, yet his nature is one and the same, his person is one and the same. An infant's limbs are small, a young man's large, yet the infant and the young man are the same. Men when full grown have the same number of joints that they had when children; and if there be any to which maturer age has given birth these were already present in embryo, so that nothing new is produced in them when old which was not already latent in them when children. This, then, is undoubtedly the true and legitimate rule of progress, this the established and most beautiful order of growth, that mature age ever develops in the man those parts and forms which the wisdom of the Creator had already framed beforehand in the infant. Whereas, if the human form were changed into some shape belonging to another kind, or at any rate, if the number of its limbs were increased or diminished, the result would be that the whole body would become either a wreck or a monster, or, at the least, would be impaired and enfeebled.

In like manner, it behoves Christian doctrine to follow the same laws of progress, so as to be consolidated by years, enlarged by time, refined by age, and yet, withal, to continue uncorrupt and unadulterate, complete and perfect in all the measurement of its parts, and, so to speak, in all its proper members and senses, admitting no change, no waste of its distinctive property, no variation in its limits.[118]

Changing his analogy from the growth of the human body to the cultivation of plants, Vincent further declares:

Our forefathers in the old time sowed wheat in the Church's field. It would be most un-meet and iniquitous if we, their descendants,

---

[118] Vincent of Lerins, Ch.XXIII, p.148.

instead of the genuine truth of grain, should reap the counterfeit error of tares. This rather should be the result — there should be no discrepancy between the first and the last. From doctrine which was sown as wheat, we should reap, in the increase, doctrine of the same kind — wheat also; so that when in process of time any of the original seed is developed, and now flourishes under cultivation, no change may ensue in the character of the plant. There may supervene shape, form, variation in outward appearance, but the nature of each kind must remain the same. God forbid that those rose-beds of Catholic interpretation should be converted into thorns and thistles. God forbid that in that spiritual paradise from plants of cinnamon and balsam, darnel and wolfsbane should of a sudden shoot forth.

Therefore, whatever has been sown by the fidelity of the Fathers in this husbandry of God's Church, the same ought to be cultivated and taken care of by the industry of their children, the same ought to flourish and ripen, the same ought to advance and go forward to perfection. For it is right that those ancient doctrines of heavenly philosophy should, as time goes on, be cared for, smoothed, polished; but not that they should be changed, not that they should be maimed, not that they should be mutilated. They may receive proof, illustration, definiteness; but they must retain withal their completeness, their integrity, their characteristic properties.[119]

Paul's warning against profane novelties (Ch XXIV)

In chapter XXIV Vincent returns to the words of Paul to Timothy in 1 Timothy 6:20 'shun profane novelties' and argues that the production of profane novelties is what distinguishes heretics from Catholics. Heresy is marked by someone separating themselves 'from the consentient agreement of the universality and antiquity of the Catholic Church'[120] Referring to the heresies of Pelagius, Arius, Sabellius, Novatian and Simon Magus as examples of this truth, he

---

[119] Vincent of Lerins, Ch.XXIII, p.148.
[120] Vincent of Lerins, Ch.XXIV, p.149.

argues that these examples, and numerous others which could be cited, show that:

> ...it is an established law, in the case of almost all heresies, that they evermore delight in profane novelties, scorn the decisions of antiquity, and, through oppositions of science falsely so called, make shipwreck of the faith. On the other hand, it is the sure characteristic of Catholics to keep that which has been committed to their trust by the holy Fathers, to condemn profane novelties, and, in the apostle's words, once and again repeated, to anathematize every one who preaches any other doctrine than that which has been received [Galatians 2:9].

The heretics appeal to Scripture (Ch XXV-XXVI)

In chapters XXV-XXVI Vincent notes that it is a characteristic of heretics to appeal to Scripture to support their heresies:

> Whether among their own people, or among strangers, in private or in public, in speaking or in writing, at convivial meetings, or in the streets, hardly ever do they bring forward anything of their own which they do not endeavour to shelter under words of Scripture. Read the works of Paul of Samosata, of Priscillian, of Eunomius, of Jovinian, and the rest of those pests, and you will see an infinite heap of instances, hardly a single page, which does not bristle with plausible quotations from the New Testament or the Old.[121]

However, in doing this they are acting as the 'false prophets' and 'false apostles' whom Christ and Paul warned against' (Matthew 7:13, 2 Corinthians 11:12) and are following the example of the Devil who quoted Scripture when tempting Christ in the wilderness (Matthew 4:1-11).

---

[121] Vincent of Lerins, Ch.XXV, p.150.

The need to follow universality, antiquity and consent (Chs XXVII-XXVII)

In chapters XXVII-XXVIII Vincent explains that the way for 'Catholics and the Sons of Mother Church' to avoid being misled by the heretics' appeal to Scripture is to follow the approach laid down at the start of the *Commonitory*:

> ...they must interpret the sacred Canon according to the traditions of the Universal Church and in keeping with the rules of Catholic doctrine, in which Catholic and Universal Church, moreover, they must follow universality, antiquity, consent. And if at any time a part opposes itself to the whole, novelty to antiquity, the dissent of one or a few who are in error to the consent of all or at all events of the great majority of Catholics, then they must prefer the soundness of the whole to the corruption of a part; in which same whole they must prefer the religion of antiquity to the profaneness of novelty; and in antiquity itself in like manner, to the temerity of one or of a very few they must prefer, first of all, the general decrees, if such there be, of a Universal Council, or if there be no such, then, what is next best, they must follow the consentient belief of many and great masters. Which rule having been faithfully, soberly, and scrupulously observed, we shall with little difficulty detect the noxious errors of heretics as they arise.[122]

Summary of the first and second *Commonitories* (Chs XXIX-XXXIII)

As previously explained, In the final section of his book, chapters XXIX-XXXIII Vincent summarises the contents of his first *Commonitory* and the stolen second *Commonitory*.

Summarising the contents of the first he declares:

> ...in the Church itself regard must be had to the consentient voice of universality equally with that of antiquity, lest we either be torn from the integrity of unity and carried away to schism, or be

---

[122] Vincent of Lerins, Ch.XVVII, p.152.

precipitated from the religion of antiquity into heretical novelties. We said, further, that in this same ecclesiastical antiquity two points are very carefully and earnestly to be held in view by those who would keep clear of heresy: first, they should ascertain whether any decision has been given in ancient times as to the matter in question by the whole priesthood of the Catholic Church, with the authority of a General Council: and, secondly, if some new question should arise on which no such decision has been given, they should then have recourse to the opinions of the holy Fathers, of those at least, who, each in his own time and place, remaining in the unity of communion and of the faith, were accepted as approved masters; and whatsoever these may be found to have held, with one mind and with one consent, this ought to be accounted the true and Catholic doctrine of the Church, without any doubt or scruple.[123]

Summarising the contents of the second, he explains that in that work he appealed to the Council of Ephesus as an example of the right approach to dealing with heresy, in that at this council the heresy of Nestorius regarding the person of Christ was condemned on the basis of the teaching of a series of 'holy Fathers' who were known to have faithfully adhered to the Catholic faith. As Vincent puts it, those bishops who took part in the Council:

> ...whom the very circumstance of their being assembled for the purpose, might seem to embolden to make some determination on their own authority, yet they innovated nothing, presumed nothing, arrogated to themselves absolutely nothing, but used all possible care to hand down nothing to posterity but what they had themselves received from their Fathers. And not only did they dispose satisfactorily of the matter presently in hand, but they also set an example to those who should come after them, how they

---

[123] Vincent of Lerins, Ch.XXIX, pp.153-154.

also should adhere to the determinations of sacred antiquity, and condemn the devices of profane novelty.[124]

4. Four objections to what Vincent teaches in the *Commonitory*

There are four main objections that have been made to what Vincent teaches in the *Commonitory*.

Objection 1 - Vincent's view of doctrine is too static

The first objection is that Vincent's work is excessively conservative. In the words of Thomas Guarino in his book *Vincent of Lerins and the Development of Christian Doctrine*:

> '…The theologian of Lérins is sometimes dismissed as a mere antiquarian, exceedingly concerned with preserving the faith in its original purity, but without any significant interest in its development over time. Even as astute a theologian as the young Joseph Ratzinger somewhat breezily dismissed Vincent's holding a notion of historical change and development that is untenable in the contemporary age. A similarly insightful commentator, who has written an oft-cited monument to the Lerinian's work, comes close to accusing him of mummifying doctrine, so great is his concern zealously to protect 'the faith once delivered to the saints' (Jude 1:3). The prosecutorial charge is that Vincent is so profoundly concerned to protect old time religion that he fails to allow the Christian faith to meet new challenges and develop new insights.'[125]

This objection to Vincent's work is misleading for two reasons.

First, the evidence shows that Vincent did allow the Christian faith to meet new challenges. As noted above, Vincent lauds the then recent

---

[124] Vincent of Lerins, Ch.XXXI, p.155.
[125] Thomas Guarino, *Vincent of Lerins and the Development of Christian Doctrine* (Grand Rapids: Baker Academic, 2013), p.xii. The second writer Guarino refers to is Jose Madoz.

Council of Ephesus as an example of the proper way to deal with heresy. That council was the result of the Church facing a new challenge, namely the heretical Christological teaching of Nestorius, and in the light of this challenge it adopted a series of twelve anathemas drawn up by Cyril of Alexandria that made new statements about the orthodox understanding of the person of Christ.[126] This fact does not seem to have worried Vincent at all, which would not have been the case if he held that the way that the orthodox faith is expressed has to remain static regardless of whatever new theological challenges the Church faces. For Vincent it seems adhering 'to the determinations of sacred antiquity' and condemning 'the devices of profane novelty' did not involve refusing to say anything new.

Secondly, as Guarino explains, Vincent's willingness to accept new things being said at the Council of Ephesus makes sense once one understands that:

> There is a dynamism inherent in Vincent's notion of tradition. The gospel is an active living presence in the world. Its intrinsic power allows Christian teaching to develop organically over time…

> Temporality, then, is never seen by Vincent in a purely dyslogic way as if the only task on Christians is preservative, battling against the effects of history. It is true that Vincent is aware of time's dangerously ravenous appetite, but he also thinks that the church may learn from the inexorable advance of history. The Lerinian does not regard time as an enemy against whom one must retain a hermetically sealed purity with the truth of Christianity entirely resistant to change. At the outset of his work, he says, 'Since time ravages all human things, we should in turn, seize from it's something that will profit us regarding eternal life' [Ch I]. And we may seize something profitable because time, properly used,

---

[126] These twelve anathemas can be found in *The Nicene and Post-Nicene Fathers,* 2nd series (Edinburgh and Grand Rapids, T&T Clark/Eerdmans, 1997), pp.21

participates in the work of the Holy Spirit; it allows for a true *profectus*, an advance in the understanding of Christian truth. That is why Vincent uses the phrase *dilatetur tempore*: the church's teaching is enlarged by time [Ch XXIII]; and again, *in semetipsa... res amplificetur* the matter grows within itself [Ch XXIII]. If time is used well, the church advances and develops its understanding of the gospel. This is the great advantage of ecumenical councils, which have served to elucidate and clarify the faith: 'By your explanations let that which was believed obscurely now be understood clearly. What antiquity venerated without comprehension let posterity now understand' [Ch XXII].

Vincent is fully aware, then, that change is intrinsic to human life. Because of this time can be doctrine's closest ally. For time allows the precious jewels of Christian teaching to be polished and burnished, freed from any impure alloys. Time - imbued with Judeo-Christian teleology - allows the gems of divine doctrine to be arranged with skill and wisdom, 'with splendour grace and beauty' [*splendorem, gratiam, venustatem*] [Ch XXII]. With time, then, the church develops and refines the unchangeable truth given in ancient Israel and in Jesus of Nazareth. The time, the church carefully distinguishes a true *profectus* which enriches and adorns the church for a permanent italic here fidelity which deprives it. Time properly used, is the locus of God's saving plan.[127]

As Guarino goes on to say, Vincent's positive view of doctrinal advance over time explains why:

...Vincent ardently insists that those who oppose development are 'hostile towards God' [*exosus Dei*] [Ch XXIII] and 'envious of others' [*invidus hominibus*]. Why this strong language? Because by trying to prohibit developments some fail to recognise that it is God himself who endorses progress. Why are opponents of development 'envious of others'? To answer this we need to

---

[127] Guarino, pp.84-85.

remember Vincent's comment that, thanks to councils, 'what antiquity venerated without comprehension, posterity now understands' [Ch XXII]. The Lerinian is alluding to the fact that a later generation may possess more clarity and depth than an earlier one. The Christian faith, in other words, becomes more lucid and precise over time. There has been a growth in 'understanding knowledge and wisdom' [*intelligentia, scientia, sapientia*] [Ch XXIII]. Some may be jealous that later ages have a clear understanding than earlier ones with the mystery of revelation in Christ now more transparently unfolded. Precisely this jealousy has inspired some to try to overthrow the landmarks of Nicaea (325) and Ephesus [431] councils that have clarified and advanced the faith with their teachings

For Vincent if the church is attentive to the channels of tradition that God has provided - always under the Divine Word - it will see that through history itself God's Word gradually comes to fruition. [128]

For Vincent the way in which God's word gradually comes to fruition is by the Church restating the truth it has received in a new way. Thus, as he puts it at the end of Chapter XXIII, one of the things accomplished by ecumenical Councils such as Nicaea or Ephesus is, as Guarino translates it, to 'designate by new and appropriate words some article of faith, which is, of itself. traditional' [*non novum fidei sensum, novae appellationis proprietate signando*]. [129] To quote Guarino again, the approach taken by Vincent is '*noviter, non nova*' – 'newly but not new.' Christians cannot rightly say new things (*nova*) when formulating doctrine (because the content of the faith is unchanging) but they can and should say the old things in new ways (*noviter*) when it is helpful to do so.

---

[128] Guarino, p.85.
[129] Guarino, p.86.

The objection that Vincent holds a static view of doctrine is thus mistaken. He is clear that doctrine can and should develop, but he has a particular idea of what development should involve.

Objection 2- Vincent's teaching leads the way to the Council of Trent

The second objection to Vicent's approach is that he gives too great a weight to the present teaching authority of the Church in a way that fails to do justice to the unique authority of Scripture. This objection was forcefully made by Karl Barth in volume 1.2 of his *Church Dogmatics*.

Barth notes that according to Vincent the Catholic faith is that which has been held *ubique, semper et ab omnibus* ('everywhere, always, and by all'). As Barth sees it, this formulation raises the question 'Who does *in concreto* decide the presence of what is universal in time and space?' [130] Vincent, declares Barth, 'gives the theoretical answer to this question' in that in the *Commonitory*:

> Beyond the constitutive *ubique* and *semper* there is a regulative *ab omnibus*. That is, the interpretation of tradition and – because tradition on its part is the authentic interpretation of Holy Scripture – the interpretation of Holy Scripture is the concern of the existing teaching office in its *consensio*.[131]

As Barth sees it, according to Vincent:

> ...the conserving and producing use of tradition is in one hand and under one guidance and responsibility, and this hand and guidance and responsibility is that of the Timothy addressed by Vincent, i.e., those who at any time bear the teaching office of the Church in their mutual *consensio*...Vincent drew the cords tighter than those who preceded him. He derived the one *corpus* of the *depositum*

---

[130] Karl Barth, *Church Dogmatics* 1.2 (London and New York; T&T Clark International, 2004) p.550.
[131] Barth, p.550.

from the unexplained combination of Scripture on the one hand with its need of exposition and development, and tradition on the other, which does expound and develop Scripture. He understood this *corpus* as a whole as a living thing, which even as it remains the same, can and must also grow. Above all, he put both the maintenance and development into the hands of the teaching office of the Church, thus making the latter the visible subject of tradition. In all this he shows plainly which way things were moving and had to move once the first steps had been taken. When we remember Vincent, we cannot say of the counter Reformation decision of the Tridentinum that it was hurried and exaggerated. Rather, the fathers of Trent, with perhaps too much sobriety and moderation, raised to the dignity of a confession a perception which had had a long life in the Popish Church and which it might have confessed much earlier, if it had not been restrained by what is (in the light of more recent developments) a puzzling timidity.[132]

To understand the point that Barth is making in these quotations it is necessary to understand that the 'Decree Concerning the Canonical Scriptures' issued by Council of Trent in 1546 [the 'Tridentinum'] laid down that the Council of Trent keeps 'constantly in view' the conviction that:

> This [Gospel], of old promised through the Prophets in the Holy Scriptures, our Lord Jesus Christ, the Son of God, promulgated first with His own mouth, then commanded it to be preached by His Apostles to every creature as the source at once of all saving truth and rules of conduct. It also clearly perceives that these truth and rules are contained in the written books and in the unwritten traditions, which, received by the Apostles from the mouth of Christ himself, of from the Apostles themselves, the Holy Ghost

---

[132] Barth, p.551.

dictating, have come down to us, transmitted as it were from hand to hand.[133]

In addition, as we saw in chapter 2, the second article of the Creed of the Council of Trent declares:

> I resolutely accept and embrace the apostolic and ecclesiastical traditions and the other practises and regulations of that same Church. In like manner I accept Sacred Scripture according to the meaning which has been held by holy Mother Church and which she now holds. It is her prerogative to pass judgement on the true meaning and interpretation of Sacred Scripture. And I will never accept or interpret it in a manner different from the unanimous agreement of the Fathers.

Taken together these two statements from the Council of Trent declare that the Gospel is made known to us through two sources,[134] partly through Holy Scripture, but also through unwritten traditions, and that it is the magisterium of the Roman Catholic Church that has authority to declare the true 'meaning and interpretation' of Scripture.

The Protestant Reformers, whose views Barth echoes on this point, rejected both the idea that there are two sources by which we know the Gospel, and the idea that it is the current magisterium of the Roman Catholic Church that should determine what Scripture teaches. Barth objects to what Vincent writes in the *Commonitory* because he thinks it leads inevitably to the acceptance of these mistaken ideas.

---

[133] Text in Leith pp.401-402.

[134] As Roman Catholic scholars have correctly pointed out, the Council of Trent does not teach that there are two sources of special revelation. There is one source of special revelation, the Gospel promised by the prophets and promulgated by Jesus Christ, but according to Trent there *are* two sources through which the Gospel is made known and the teaching of these two sources *is* authoritatively interpreted by the magisterium of the Roman Catholic church.

However, Barth's objection to Vincent is based on a misreading of Vincent's work. Unlike the Council of Trent, Vincent does not hold that the truth about what we should believe and how we should behave is revealed through the Scriptures *and* through unwritten traditions. As we have seen, he holds that 'the canon of Scripture is complete, and sufficient of itself for everything, and more than sufficient.' To quote Guarino again: 'in Vincent's work...an epistemic primacy is always accorded to Scripture. The Bible is the rule and rock on which all church practices and teachings are based.'[135]

For Vincent where tradition comes into picture is as a guide to reading to Scripture properly and as a warning against improper interpretations of Scripture. For him tradition is only ever a helpful commentary pointing to what Scripture in itself already means. Furthermore, if we ask where Vincent thinks this commentary is to be found it is not, as Barth suggests, in 'the teaching office of the church,' particularly if by this is meant the teaching office of the Roman Catholic Church.

Writing in the fifth century, before the split between the Eastern and Western churches and before the divisions of the Reformation and post-Reformation periods, Vincent has no conception of the Roman church having a unique authority with regard to the interpretation of Scripture. As Guarino puts it:

> For the Lerinian, a variety of 'courts' are necessary to guard the deposit faithfully, to interpret Scripture correctly. He places great emphasis on the body of bishops/overseers, particularly when gathered in council, as had already occurred at the great synods of Nicaea (325) and Ephesus (431). And he observes that the faithful at large are also bearers of the truth, as they, under the Spirit, preserve the deposit by their natural *instinctus* for Christian truth. This is why Vincent states flatly the deposit is secured 'by the universal church generally or, specifically, the entire body of

---

[135] Guarino, p.93.

overseers/bishops' [*vel generaliter universa ecclesia vel specialiter totum corpus praepositorum*] (Ch XXII).

In all cases Vincent emphasises the importance of consensus within the interpretive tradition. There must be a *consensus* of bishops in council; a *consensus* of holy, learned, and confessing doctors; and a *consensus* of the faithful generally. The bishop of Rome is dealt with as an individual, but even here, he speaks *with* the other bishops, as Stephen did in the controversy over rebaptism. Popes Celestine and Sixtus speak as individuals, but *individuals bound by the prior tradition*. Idiosyncrasy in interpretation is a sure mark of error. As Vincent insists, 'Even a holy and learned man, even a bishop, even a confess and martyr' is holding only a personal opinion if he advances some position that is 'other than all or even against all' [praeter omnes aut etiam contra omnes] [Ch XXVIII]. Even the shedding of one's blood for Christ constitutes no conclusive proof on the orthodoxy of one's interpretation.[136]

What all this means is that Barth is mistaken when he sees what Vincent writes in the *Commonitory* as a precursor of what was later taught by the Council of Trent. For Vincent, authority in matters of interpretation is not necessarily found in the current teaching of the Roman church. It is found in the consensus of the Church as a whole, a consensus which finds expression in a variety of different ways.

---

[136] Guarino, pp.94-95. It should be noted, that as a Roman Catholic scholar Guarino claims that Vincent 'supports a primatial ministry for the Roman bishop' (p.115), but the evidence that he himself cites from Vincent (pp.39-41) does not seem to justify this claim. Three bishops of Rome, Stephen, Callistus and Sixtus are seen as having played a significant role in counteracting heresy, but he does not suggest that they exercised a primatial ministry greater than that of all other bishops.

Objection 3 – The meaning of the Vincentian Canon is unclear

The third objection is that it is unclear what Vincent means when he says that what should be believed is that that which has been held 'everywhere, always and by all.' Thus, the Orthodox theologian George Florovsky writes:

> The well-known formula of the Lerinian is very inexact, when he describes the catholic nature of church life in the words *Quod ubique, quod semper, quod ab omnibus creditum est*...First of all, it is not clear whether this is an empirical criterion or not. If this be so, then the 'Vincentian Canon' proves to be inapplicable and quite false. For about what *omnes* is he speaking? Is it a demand for a general universal questioning of all the faithful, and even those who only deem themselves such?[137]

At first sight Florovsky's objection seems plausible. Who exactly does Vincent think should be consulted over the correct understanding of Scripture given that it is impossible to simply poll everyone who claims to be a Christian? However, Florovsky has not paid sufficient attention to what Vincent himself says about the matter. As the summary of the contents of the *Commonitory* given above shows, what Vincent argues is that the faith of the Catholic Church as a whole across space and time can be discovered by taking note of what has been laid down by the bishops of the Church meeting together in a General Council and by the witness of generally recognised theological authorities, what later Christian terminology would call the 'Doctors of the Church.' As we shall see shortly, this is something that it is quite possible to do.

Objection 4 – There is no consensus about what counts as orthodoxy and what counts as heresy

The final objection to what Vincent argues in the *Commonitory* is that the history of the Church shows that there has been no agreement

---

[137] Georges Florovsky, *Bible, Church, Tradition: An Eastern Orthodox View* (Belmont: Nordland, 1972), p.52.

about what constitutes orthodoxy and what constitutes heresy. This point is made, for example, by the Anglican reformer John Jewel who responds to the appeal made to the Vincentian Canon by the Roman Catholic writer Thomas Harding by declaring 'there was never any doctrine so catholic, no, not the confessed doctrine of Christ himself, that hath been received 'evermore' and 'everywhere' and 'of all men' without any exception.'[138]

Those who put forward this objection contend that if the study of the history of the Church shows that there never has been any doctrine that has been accepted by everyone, then labelling some forms of doctrine as orthodox and others as heretical is simply a matter of one group of Christians seeking to impose its views on everyone else.

Since the mid-twentieth century this position has become prominent in the world of theological scholarship as a result of the work of scholars such as Walter Bauer and Bart Ehrman. As Andreas Kostenberger and Michael Kruger explain in their book *The heresy of orthodoxy*:

> The new orthodoxy - the gospel of diversity - challenges head on the claim that Jesus and the early Christians taught a unified message that they thought was absolutely true and its denials absolutely false. Instead, advocates of religious diversity such as Walter Bauer and Bart Ehrman argue not only that contemporary diversity is good and historic Christianity unduly narrow, but that the very notion of orthodoxy is a later fabrication not true to the convictions of Jesus and the first Christians themselves.
>
> In the first century, claim Bauer, Ehrman and other adherents to the diversity doctrine, there was no such thing as 'Christianity' (in the singular), but only *Christianities* in the plural, different versions of belief, all of which claimed to be 'Christian' with equal

---

[138] John Jewel, 'The Defence of the Apology of the Church of England' in John Ayre (ed), *The Works of John Jewel, The Third Portion* (Cambridge: Parker Society/CUP, 1848), pp. 267-268.

legitimacy. The traditional version of Christianity that later came to be known as orthodoxy is but the form of Christianity espoused by the church in Rome, which emerged as the ecclesiastical victor in the power struggle waged during the second through the fourth centuries. What this means for us today is that we must try to get back to the more pristine a notion of diversity that prevailed in the first century before ecclesiastical and political power squashed and brutally extinguished the fragile notion that diversity - previously known as heresy - is the only orthodoxy there is. [139]

The problem with this argument is that the history to which it appeals simply does not support it. Early Church Fathers such as Irenaeus and Tertullian were right, a pattern of orthodox Christian belief rooted in the teaching of the apostles appointed by Jesus came first, and heresies were a deviation from it.[140] To quote Kostenberger and Kruger again, what historical study of the development of doctrine in the early Church shows us is that:

> ...heresy arose after orthodoxy and did not command the degree of influence in the later first and early second century that Ehrman and others claim. Moreover, the orthodoxy established by the third-and fourth century creeds stands in direct continuity with the teaching of the orthodox writers of the previous two centuries. In essence, when orthodoxy and heresy are compared in terms of their genesis and chronology, it is evident that orthodoxy did not emerge from a heretical morass; instead, heresy grew parasitically out of an already established orthodoxy. And while the Church

---

[139] Andreas Kostenberger and Michael Kruger, *The Heresy of Orthodoxy* (Nottingham: Apollos, 2010), p.16. The key works by Bauer and Ehrman are Walter Bauer, *Orthodoxy and Heresy in Earliest Christianity* (Philadelphia: Fortress Press, 1971) and Bart Ehrman, *Lost Christianities: The Battles for Scripture and the Faiths we never knew* (Oxford: OUP, 2003).

[140] Irenaeus, *Against Heresies* in *The Ante-Nice Fathers*, Vol I (Edinburgh and Grand Rapids: T&T Clark/Eerdmans 1996) and Tertullian, *The Prescription against Heretics in The Ante-Nice Fathers*, Vol III (Edinburgh and Grand Rapids: T&T Clark/Eerdmans 1997).

continued to set forth its doctrinal beliefs in a variety of creedal formulations, the DNA of orthodoxy remained essentially unchanged.[141]

In similar fashion, Gerald Bray writes concerning the Gnostic groups of the early centuries to whom scholars such as Bauer and Ehrman accord the same, or greater, historical importance as they accord to what has come to be known as orthodox Christianity:

> Modern discoveries have given us a more objective picture of what these groups were like, but they have not overturned the traditional picture of an essentially orthodox Church that was called to combat new and alien heresies in its midst. We can therefore state with complete confidence that the writings of the classical church fathers remained primary witnesses for what the early church believed and taught and that the underpinning they provide for the first article of the Nicene creed represents the authentic traditional Christian teaching, not a late and somewhat totalitarian deviation from it. Bauer's thesis and its variants will doubtless continue to circulate, but students of early Christian doctrine do not have to worry that the magisterial church fathers are unrepresentative of the beliefs of the mainstream Christian communities in ancient times.[142]

Furthermore, not only can it be shown that there is a direct line of theological succession between the teaching of the earliest days of the Church and the teaching of the orthodox Fathers and Councils of the third and fourth centuries, but it can also be shown that this line of theological succession has continued in the Christian Church over the succeeding centuries despite the divisions that have opened up

---

[141] Kostengerger and Kruger, pp.66-67.
[142] Gerald Bray, *Ancient Christian Doctrine 1, We Believe in One God* (Downers Grove: Inter-Varsity Press, 2009), p.XXXIX. For a detailed study and rebuttal of the Bauer thesis see H E W Turner, *The Pattern of Christian Truth* (London: Mowbray 1954).

between Roman Catholicism, Eastern Orthodoxy and the various forms of Protestantism.

This point is demonstrated in great detail, for example, by the American Methodist theologian Thomas Oden in his magisterial study *Classic Christianity*. In this work, which is a deliberate 'attempt to carry out the ecumenical method proposed by Vincent of Lerins,'[143] Oden sets out a systematic theology that draws upon the consensus of Christian thought from the New Testament onwards and which provides 'clear evidences of the unity of classic Christian teaching by presenting discrete, convincing and authoritative examples of it.'[144]

Among the key sources on which Oden draws are the seven 'ecumenical councils,' First Nicaea, (325), First Constantinople (381), Ephesus (431), Chalcedon (451), Second Constantinople (553), Third Constantinople (680-681) and Second Nicaea (787), the four great doctors of the Eastern Church, Athanasius, Basil, Gregory Nazianzus and John Chrysostom, the four great doctors of the Western Church, Ambrose, Augustine, Jerome and Gregory the Great and 'others who have been perennially valued for accurately stating points of ecumenical consensus' including Hilary of Poitiers, Cyril of Alexandria, Leo I, John of Damascus, Thomas Aquinas, Martin Luther and John Calvin. He also draws on female exegetes and saints such as Macrina, Perpetua, Caecilia of Rome, Agatha of Sicily, Margaret of Antioch, Paula, Eustochium and Anna Theodora.[145] He notes that most of these sources 'insofar as they were consensually received, thought of themselves as unoriginal in desiring especially *not to add anything to an already sufficient apostolic faith*, but only to receive and re-appropriate that faith accurately and honestly in their particular social and historical setting.'[146]

---

[143] Thomas Oden, *Classic Christianity* (London: Harper Collins, 2009), Kindle edition, Preface.
[144] Oden, Preface.
[145] Oden, Preface.
[146] Oden, Preface, italics in the original.

Oden concludes his study with an Epilogue in which he offers three overall conclusions.

His first conclusion is that:

> *The texts documenting the classic consensus are accessible, well known and exhaustively vetted for orthodoxy.* Classic Christian teaching prefers to reference only those texts most obviously consensual and least subject to quibbling as to their orthodoxy, and most pertinent to the subject being discussed. This implies a respectful resistance to texts that do not meet the criteria of consensuality and orthodoxy. This especially requires listening carefully to the councils, ecumenical and regional, then to the great doctors of the church, and then finally to the key teachers that have survived many centuries of the vetting process. This is what we have done.[147]

His second conclusion is that:

> *...consensual authority is grounded in general lay consent to apostolic teaching.* The apostles themselves had a fully formed and sufficient vision of the Lord's teaching. They were not in continuing competitive disagreement on the core of Christian teaching. Their shared encounter with Jesus drew them toward unity of witness from the outset. From this was derived the primitive rule of faith that was aptly summarised by the baptismal confession. The authority of the ecumenical councils is grounded in general lay consent under the guidance of the Spirit based on the written word. The tradition of general lay consent established in the patristic period continued and was largely received in the confessional and liturgical practises of the Reformation. The check against the abuse of councils is the whole laity over the whole of time. They remain in effect the jury for the councils, even if their decisions may have taken decades or even centuries to become

---

[147] Oden, p.846, italics in the original.

ecumenically confirmed. This is the democratic and populist aspect of the formation of classic Christian teaching.[148]

His third conclusion is that:

> *Though neglected, consensus clarification is entirely feasible, but more easily recognized only within long time frames.* Consensus is not intrinsically unreachable because it has a long history of being reached. The records of that history are found in the texts of the councils and consensual teachers. These achievements are known because they have a conspicuous textual history of authority in the worshipping community. This community has learned that heterodoxy may serve the truth by having the unexpected effect on further refining rough and incomplete orthodox consensual exegesis. Less well known, but increasingly recognized is the fact that the most durable consensus is far more indebted to minority and neglected voices, such as classic African and Asian texts of the first Millennium, than to later European ideas.[149]

The basic point that Oden is making, and which the historical sources he cites supports, is that we can distinguish between orthodoxy and heresy by using the method proposed by Vincent in the *Commonitory*. As C S Lewis argues, 'reading old books' shows us that there is such a thing as 'mere Christianity,' a pattern of Christian belief that has received general consent among God's people *ubique, semper et ab omnibus* and that can be appealed to correct the errors prevalent in particular periods of the history of the Church (including our own).

---

[148] Oden, p.851, italics in the original. By 'laity' he means the *laos*, the people of God as a whole.

[149] Oden, pp.856-857, italics in the original. Like the attention he has earlier drawn to female consensual exegetes, the final point here is intended to correct the idea that is sometimes suggested today that 'orthodoxy' simply means the opinions of dead white males and is therefore an expression of sexism and racism. To put the matter in terms of the Vincentian Canon, orthodoxy does meet the criteria of being believed everywhere and by all.

The reason why this consensus is to be preferred to the various forms of heresy that have also emerged over the history of the Church is because the consensus position, 'orthodoxy' to use the traditional term, can be traced back to the teaching of the apostles as recorded in the New Testament and through them to Jesus Christ himself, while the same is not true of heresy. All heresies have developed as a deviation from the consensus position and thus constitute in effect, if not in intention, a rejection of the message proclaimed by Christ and his apostles.

5. In summary

In summary, what we have seen in this chapter is as follows:

- Vincent of Lerins sees Christian doctrine as being based on the teaching of Scripture.

- Vincent notes that this means we have to decide how to interpret Scripture properly in order to fulfil the Pauline command to 'guard the deposit' (1 Timothy 6:20).

- Vincent proposes that the way to decide between proper and improper readings of Scripture is by taking note of how Scripture has been understood *ubique, semper et ad omnibus*. Such consensual reading is to be found in the decisions made by the bishops in the ecumenical councils of the Church and in the teachings of the Church's recognised theological teachers, decisions and teaching which reflect the faith of the Church as a whole.

- Vincent strongly believes that doctrine can and should develop, but he holds that genuine development has to represent the growth of existing orthodox teaching rather than a departure from it. Developments of Christian teaching should say old truths in a new way (*noviter*), but they should not presume to offer new truths that the Church has not held before (*nova*).

- The objections to Vincent's teaching that we have considered in this chapter are unpersuasive, and the study of the history of the Church shows that his appeal to consensual teaching as a guide to orthodoxy, and hence a guide for further doctrinal development, is one that should be accepted.

Additional note: Anglicanism and the Vincentian Canon

A study of Anglican history shows that Anglicanism has traditionally taken a Vincentian approach to the identification of orthodox doctrine.

For example, in the history of the Church of England we find that the Canons agreed by the bishops of the Church of England in 1571 as an accompaniment to the *Thirty-Nine Articles* declare that preachers shall:

> ...teach nothing in their preaching, which they would have the people religiously to observe, and believe, but that which is agreeable to the doctrine of the Old Testament and the New and that which the Catholic Fathers and Ancient Bishops have gathered out of that doctrine. [150]

Likewise, Archbishop Richard Bancroft laid down in 1609 that:

> ...this is and has been the open profession of the Church of England, to maintain no other Church, Faith and Religion, than that which is truly Catholic and Apostolic, and for such warranted not only by the written word of God, but also by the testimony and consent of the ancient and godly Fathers. [151]

It should also be noted that the purpose of the *Thirty-Nine Articles* themselves was to maintain the faith taught in Scripture and testified to by the orthodox bishops and theologians of the early centuries against what were seen as deviations from this faith by some aspects

---

[150] *The Canons of 1571 in English and Latin* (London: SPCK, 1899), p.77.
[151] Cited in *The Canons of 1571*, p.78.

of Medieval Catholicism on the one hand, and by the novel ideas of certain radical Protestant groups on the other.

Canon A5 of the Church of England's current Canon Law follows the same approach. It states:

> The doctrine of the Church of England is grounded in the Holy Scriptures and in such teachings of the ancient Fathers and councils of the Church as are agreeable to the said Scriptures.
>
> In particular such doctrine is to be found in the Thirty-nine Articles of Religion, the Book of Common Prayer and the Ordinal.[152]

To put this in Vincentian terms, what this means is that the Church of England's doctrine is based on the teaching contained in the Scriptures and in the legitimate development of that teaching, first by the orthodox Fathers and Councils of the Early Church and then by the three historic formularies of the Reformation period. It is for this reason that it is *noviter* but not *nova*.

In similar fashion the agreed statement *The Principles of Canon Law Common to the Churches of the Anglican Communion* published by the Anglican Communion Office in 2008 lays down as 'Principle 49: The sources of doctrine' that: 'The faith of our Lord Jesus Christ is taught in the Holy Scriptures, summed up by the Creeds, and affirmed by the ancient Fathers and undisputed General Councils' and that 'The Thirty-Nine Articles of Religion, the Book of Common Prayer and the Ordinal 1662 are grounded in the Holy Scriptures, and in such teachings of the ancient Fathers and Councils of the Church as are agreeable to the Holy Scriptures.' [153]

---

[152] *Canons of the Church of England*, Canon A5 at:
https://www.churchofengland.org/about/leadership-and-governance/legal-services/canons-church-england/section.
[153] *The Principles of Canon Law Common to the Churches of the Anglican Communion* (London: Anglican Communion Office, 2008), pp. 57-58.

Chapter 4
To be perfect is to have changed often - John Henry Newman on the development of doctrine

1. Newman's initial use of Vincent of Lerins against Rome

John Henry Newman (1801-1890) began his theological career as an Evangelical Anglican. Subsequently, he became one of the leaders of the High Church 'Tractarian' movement in the Church of England. Having become disillusioned with the Church of England, he was received into the Roman Catholic Church, and despite tensions with the Roman Catholic hierarchy and his misgivings over the definition of Papal infallibility at the First Vatican Council in 1870, he was made a Cardinal in 1879. He was canonised as a Catholic saint in 2019 and declared by the Roman Catholic Church to be a 'Doctor of the Universal Church' in 2025.

During his Tractarian period, Newman followed a traditional Anglican apologetic approach by arguing that what was said by Vincent of Lerins' in his *Commonitory* highlighted the subsequent errors of the Church of Rome. Vincent had explained that Christian orthodoxy is that which has been believed by Christians *ubique, semper et ab omnibus* and the study of Church history showed that Rome had departed from the faith and practice of the Early Church and thus fallen foul of this rule.

For example, Newman published a series of articles on Church history which he entitled *Records of the Church*. Article number XXIV, 'Vincentius of Lerins on the Tests of Heresy and Error,' which was published in 1834, was a partial translation of the *Commonitory* with additional comments from Newman.

In this article Newman quotes the words of Vincent

> What if some novel contagion attempt with its plague-spots, not only a portion, but even the whole Church? Then he will be careful

to keep close to antiquity, which is secure from the possibility of being corrupted by new errors.[154]

He then notes

> This case had been instanced even before Vincentius's time, in the history of the Arians. In our own day it is fulfilled in the case of the Church of Rome, which indeed has not erred vitally as the Arians did, nor has infected with its errors the whole Church, yet has to answer for very serious corruptions, which it has not merely attempted, but managed to establish in a great part of the Churches of Christendom. Here then apply Vincentius's test. Antiquity; — and the Church of Rome is convicted of unsoundness, as fully as those other sects among us which have already been submitted to the trial.[155]

Later in the article he quotes Vincent's words:

> I say, whoever he be, how holy and learned soever, whether Bishop, whether Confessor and Martyr, if he teaches aught beyond or contrary to the doctrine of all the Fathers, let it be set apart from the common, public, and general doctrine, which has authority, and numbered among his peculiar, hidden, and private surmises, lest, at the extreme risk of eternal ruin, we fall into the ways of heretics and schismatics, giving up the universally received truth, and following the novel error of an individual.[156]

As before, Newman applies Vincent's comments to the Church of Rome:

> As to cases of actual error, such as that of the false prophet introduced by Vincentius, there has been since his time a most

---

[154] John Newman *Records of the Church*, XXIV, p. 3. in *Tracts for the Times* (London: J H Rivington, 1840).
[155] Newman, Records of the Church, p.3. 'Those other sects' are various Protestant groups which Newman has already criticised.
[156] Newman, Records of the Church, p.7.

deplorable and astounding instance of this in the corruptions of the Latin Church, whether they be called heresy or not. Considering the high gifts and the strong claims of the Church of Rome and its dependencies on our admiration, reverence, love, and gratitude, how could we withstand it as we do; how could we refrain from being melted into tenderness and rushing into communion with it, but fur the words of Truth itself, which bid us prefer It to the whole world ? 'He that loveth father or mother more than Me, is not worthy of Me.' How could we learn to be severe, and execute judgment, but for the warning of Moses against even a divinely gifted teacher, who should preach new gods; and the anathema of St. Paul even against Angels and Apostles, who should bring in a new doctrine?[157]

For another example, in 1837 Newman published a work entitled *Lectures on the Prophetical Office of the Church*. In this work, he declares:

> The Rule or Canon which I have been explaining, is best known as expressed in the words or Vincentius of Lerins, in his celebrated treatise on the tests of Heresy and Error; viz, that is received as Apostolic which has been taught always everywhere and by all. Catholicity Antiquity, and consent of Fathers is the proper evidence of the fidelity or Apostolicity of a professed tradition.

By contrast, the Church of Rome:

> ...exalts the will and pleasure of the existing Church above all authority, whether of Scripture or Antiquity, interpreting the one and disposing of the other by its absolute and arbitrary decree.

What this shows, argues Newman, is that Vincent cannot be appealed to in support of Roman Catholicism:

---

[157] Newman *Records of the Church,* p.7.

If Vincentius had the sentiments and feelings of a modern Roman Catholic, it is incomprehensible that, in a treatise written to guide the private Christian in matters of Faith, he should have said not a word about the Pope's supreme authority, nay, not even about the infallibility of the Church Catholic. He refers the Inquirer to a triple rule, difficult, surely, and troublesome to use, compared with that which is ready furnished by Rome now. Applying his own rule to his work itself, we may unhesitatingly conclude the Pope's supreme authority in matters of faith, is no Catholic or Apostolic truth, because Vincent was ignorant of it.

In addition to papal authority, argued the Tractarian Newman, Rome has also added other blasphemous innovations to the faith and practice of the Early Church, including belief in transubstantiation, the sacrifice of the Mass, and purgatory as a place of torment, the traffic in indulgences and the veneration of relics and images. [158]

As Guarino puts it, for Newman at this stage in his career: 'Only the Anglican via media respects both antiquity and universality by refusing Rome's corruptions while simultaneously rejecting the Protestant jettisoning of the early church.' [159] In other words, only Anglicanism is truly Vincentian.

2. Newman's volte face in his *Essay on the Development of Christian Doctrine*

After Newman became disillusioned with the Church of England following the general rejection of his attempt to re-interpret the Thirty-nine Articles in a Catholic direction in Tract 90 of the *Tracts for The Times, Remarks on Certain Passages in the Thirty-Nine Articles*[160] he felt drawn to join the Roman Catholic Church. However, as a conscientious theologian this left him with a serious problem. How

---

[158] A list of corruptions which the Tractarian Newman identified in the Roman Catholic Church can be found in Avery Dulles, *John Henry Newman* (London: Continuum, 2002), p.73.
[159] Guarino, p51.
[160] Tract XC can be found at https://www.anglicanhistory.org/tracts/tract90/.

could he reconcile joining the Roman Catholic Church with his previous argument that the application of Vincent of Lerin's three tests for orthodoxy (*ubique, semper et ab omnibus*) showed that Rome was corrupt in its faith and practice?

Newman's *Essay on the Development of Christian Doctrine*, first published in 1845 and then revised in 1878, is his solution to this problem. The essay is in two parts. In the Introduction Newman explains why the study of Church History shows that Vincent's three tests of orthodoxy cannot consistently be used against the Roman Catholic Church, and in the body of the work, chapters 1-12, he then goes on to argue that a proper understanding of the nature of the development of Christian doctrine shows that the Roman Catholic Church is the sole authentic form of the Christian Church. [161]

The Introduction to the Essay

In the Introduction Newman notes that the study of the history of Christianity shows:

> ...that there are to be found, during the 1800 years through which it has lasted, certain apparent inconsistencies and alterations in its doctrine and its worship, such as irresistibly attract the attention of all who inquire into it. They are not sufficient to interfere with the general character and course of the religion, but they raise the question how they came about, and what they mean, and have in consequence supplied matter for several hypotheses. [162]

One of these hypotheses is that:

> ...Christianity has ever changed from the first and ever accommodates itself to the circumstances of times and seasons; but it is difficult to understand how such a view is compatible with

---

[161] In the summary that follows I am using the 1878 version since this is the version which reflects Newman's final thoughts on the matters which it covers.
[162] John Henry Newman, *An Essay on the Development of Christian Doctrine* (London: Longmans Green and co, 1909), p.7.

the special idea of revealed truth, and in fact its advocates more or less abandon, or tend to abandon, the supernatural claims of Christianity; so it need not detain us here.[163]

A second:

> ...and more plausible hypothesis is that of the Anglican divines, who reconcile and bring into shape the exuberant phenomena under consideration, by cutting and casting away as corruptions all usages, ways, opinions, and tenets, which have not the sanction of primitive times. They maintain that history first presents to us a pure Christianity in East and West, and then a corrupt; and then of course their duty is to draw the line between what is corrupt and what is pure, and to determine the dates at which the various changes from good to bad were introduced. Such a principle of demarcation, available for the purpose, they consider they have found in the dictum of Vincent of Lerins, that revealed and Apostolic doctrine is 'quod semper, quod ubique, quod ab omnibus,' a principle infallibly separating, on the whole field of history, authoritative doctrine from opinion, rejecting what is faulty, and combining and forming a theology. That 'Christianity is what has been held always, everywhere, and by all,' certainly promises a solution of the perplexities, an interpretation of the meaning, of history. What can be more natural than that divines and bodies of men should speak, sometimes from themselves, sometimes from tradition? what more natural than that individually they should say many things on impulse, or under excitement, or as conjectures, or in ignorance? what more certain than that they must all have been instructed and catechized in the Creed of the Apostles? what more evident than that what was their own would in its degree be peculiar, and differ from what was similarly private and personal in their brethren? what more conclusive than that the doctrine that was common to all at once was not really their own, but public property in which they had a

[163] Neman, *Essay*, p.7.

joint interest, and was proved by the concurrence of so many witnesses to have come from an Apostolical source? Here, then, we have a short and easy method for bringing the various informations of ecclesiastical history under that antecedent probability in its favour, which nothing but its actual variations would lead us to neglect. Here we have a precise and satisfactory reason why we should make much of the earlier centuries, yet pay no regard to the later, why we should admit some doctrines and not others, why we refuse the Creed of Pius IV. and accept the Thirty-nine Articles.[164]

This second way of understanding the matter, writes Newman,

…is the rule of historical interpretation which has been professed in the English school of divines; and it contains a majestic truth, and offers an intelligible principle, and wears a reasonable air. It is congenial, or, as it may be said, native to the Anglican mind, which takes up a middle position, neither discarding the Fathers nor acknowledging the Pope. It lays down a simple rule by which to measure the value of every historical fact, as it comes, and thereby it provides a bulwark against Rome, while it opens an assault upon Protestantism.

However, he claims, this way of understanding the matter does not in fact work for Anglicans, because if it rules out the Roman Catholic position, it rules out the traditional Anglican position as well.

The rule is more serviceable in determining what is not, than what is Christianity; it is irresistible against Protestantism, and in one sense indeed it is irresistible against Rome also, but in the same sense it is irresistible against England. It strikes at Rome through England. It admits of being interpreted in one of two ways: if it be narrowed for the purpose of disproving the catholicity of the Creed of Pope Pius, it becomes also an objection to the Athanasian; and if it be relaxed to admit the doctrines retained by the English Church,

[164] Newman, *Essay,* p.7.

it no longer excludes certain doctrines of Rome which that Church denies. It cannot at once condemn St. Thomas and St. Bernard, and defend St. Athanasius and St. Gregory Nazianzen.[165]

In order to justify this claim, Newman goes on in the introduction to give a series of historical examples to support it. He argues that there is as much, or as little, evidence in the ante-Nicene Fathers in support of the doctrine of the Trinity as set out in the Athanasian Creed, for the doctrine of original sin and for the real presence of Christ at Holy Communion (all of which Anglicans accept) as there is for purgatory, transubstantiation and Papal Supremacy (all of which Anglicans deny). This means that a consistent Vincentian appeal to history must mean either a rejection of the doctrines of the Trinity, original sin and the real presence, or the acceptance of purgatory, transubstantiation and Papal Supremacy as well.

What this shows, argues Newman, is that an approach based on an application of the Vincentian canon does not work as means by which to decide which forms of Christian doctrine are legitimate and which are not. In his words:

> It does not seem possible, then, to avoid the conclusion that, whatever be the proper key for harmonizing the records and documents of the early and later Church, and true as the dictum of Vincentius must be considered in the abstract, and possible as its application might be in his own age, when he might almost ask the primitive centuries for their testimony, it is hardly available now, or effective of any satisfactory result. The solution it offers is as difficult as the original problem.[166]

Faced with this problem, Newman then suggests an alternative approach, which is to adopt as one's criterion for distinguish truth from error the principle of the development of doctrine, a principle

---

[165] Newman, *Essay*, p.8.
[166] Newman, *Essay*, p.20.

which explains why what later came to be seen as orthodox doctrine only gradually became explicitly accepted in the history of the Church.

> The following Essay is directed towards a solution of the difficulty which has been stated, — the difficulty, as far as it exists, which lies in the way of our using in controversy the testimony of our most natural informant concerning the doctrine and worship of Christianity, viz. the history of eighteen hundred years. The view on which it is written has at all times, perhaps, been implicitly adopted by theologians, and, I believe, has recently been illustrated by several distinguished writers of the continent, such as De Maistre and Möhler: viz. that the increase and expansion of the Christian Creed and Ritual, and the variations which have attended the process in the case of individual writers and Churches, are the necessary attendants on any philosophy or polity which takes possession of the intellect and heart, and has had any wide or extended dominion; that, from the nature of the human mind, time is necessary for the full comprehension and perfection of great ideas; and that the highest and most wonderful truths, though communicated to the world once for all by inspired teachers, could not be comprehended all at once by the recipients, but, as being received and transmitted by minds not inspired and through media which were human, have required only the longer time and deeper thought for their full elucidation. This may be called the Theory of Development of Doctrine.[167]

The remainder of the Essay develops in detail the argument offered in this paragraph and also contends that acceptance of this argument leads inevitably to an acceptance of Roman Catholic teaching and practice.

---

[167] Newman, *Essay*, p.22.

3. Newman's detailed argument concerning the development of doctrine

Chapter 1 'The development of ideas'
In the first part of chapter 1 Newman puts forward his key proposal, which is that ideas in fields such as ethics, philosophy, politics, or religion will necessarily develop over the course of time in a way analogous to the germination and maturation of a plant. As he puts it:

> When an idea, whether real or not, is of a nature to arrest and possess the mind, it may be said to have life, that is, to live in the mind which is its recipient. Thus, mathematical ideas, real as they are, can hardly properly be called living, at least ordinarily. But, when some great enunciation, whether true or false, about human nature, or present good, or government, or duty, or religion, is carried forward into the public throng of men and draws attention, then it is not merely received passively in this or that form into many minds, but it becomes an active principle within them, leading them to an ever-new contemplation of itself, to an application of it in various directions, and a propagation of it on every side. Such is the doctrine of the divine right of kings, or of the rights of man, or of the anti-social bearings of a priesthood, or utilitarianism, or free trade, or the duty of benevolent enterprises, or the philosophy of Zeno or Epicurus, doctrines which are of a nature to attract and influence, and have so far a *primâ facie* reality, that they may be looked at on many sides and strike various minds very variously. Let one such idea get possession of the popular mind, or the mind of any portion of the community, and it is not difficult to understand what will be the result. At first men will not fully realise what it is that moves them, and will express and explain themselves inadequately. There will be a general agitation of thought, and an action of mind upon mind. There will be a time of confusion, when conceptions and misconceptions are in conflict, and it is uncertain whether anything is to come of the idea at all, or which view of it is to get the start of the others. New lights will be brought to bear upon the

original statements of the doctrine put forward; judgments and aspects will accumulate. After a while some definite teaching emerges; and, as time proceeds, one view will be modified or expanded by another, and then combined with a third; till the idea to which these various aspects belong, will be to each mind separately what at first it was only to all together. It will be surveyed too in its relation to other doctrines or facts, to other natural laws or established customs, to the varying circumstances of times and places, to other religions, polities, philosophies, as the case may be. How it stands affected towards other systems, how it affects them, how far it may be made to combine with them, how far it tolerates them, when it interferes with them, will be gradually wrought out. It will be interrogated and criticized by enemies, and defended by well-wishers. The multitude of opinions formed concerning it in these respects and many others will be collected, compared, sorted, sifted, selected, rejected, gradually attached to it, separated from it, in the minds of individuals and of the community. It will, in proportion to its native vigour and subtlety, introduce itself into the framework and details of social life, changing public opinion, and strengthening or undermining the foundations of established order. Thus in time it will have grown into an ethical code, or into a system of government, or into a theology, or into a ritual, according to its capabilities: and this body of thought, thus laboriously gained, will after all be little more than the proper representative of one idea, being in substance what that idea meant from the first, its complete image as seen in a combination of diversified aspects, with the suggestions and corrections of many minds, and the illustration of many experiences.

This process, whether it be longer or shorter in point of time, by which the aspects of an idea are brought into consistency and form, I call its development, being the germination and maturation of some truth or apparent truth on a large mental field. (pp.36-38)

In an oft quoted passage Newman then uses the image of the course of a river to argue that the development of an idea is something that needs to be viewed in a positive light:

> It is indeed sometimes said that the stream is clearest near the spring. Whatever use may fairly be made of this image, it does not apply to the history of a philosophy or belief, which on the contrary is more equable, and purer, and stronger, when its bed has become deep, and broad, and full. It necessarily rises out of an existing state of things, and for a time savours of the soil. Its vital element needs disengaging from what is foreign and temporary, and is employed in efforts after freedom which become more vigorous and hopeful as its years increase. Its beginnings are no measure of its capabilities, nor of its scope. At first no one knows what it is, or what it is worth. It remains perhaps for a time quiescent; it tries, as it were, its limbs, and proves the ground under it, and feels its way. From time to time it makes essays which fail, and are in consequence abandoned. It seems in suspense which way to go; it wavers, and at length strikes out in one definite direction. In time it enters upon strange territory; points of controversy alter their bearing; parties rise and fall around it; dangers and hopes appear in new relations; and old principles reappear under new forms. It changes with them in order to remain the same. In a higher world it is otherwise, but here below to live is to change, and to be perfect is to have changed often.[168]

Chapter 2 'On the antecedent argument in behalf of developments in Christian doctrine.'

In chapter 2 Newman goes on to argue that Christianity is an idea that impresses itself on our minds and that, this being the case, it is to be expected that it will develop in a variety of different ways and find clearer expression over time, because, as he has previously argued, it is in the nature of a living idea to do so.

[168] Newman, *Essay*, p.40.

If Christianity is a fact, and impresses an idea of itself on our minds and is a subject-matter of exercises of the reason, that idea will in course of time expand into a multitude of ideas, and aspects of ideas, connected and harmonious with one another, and in themselves determinate and immutable, as is the objective fact itself which is thus represented. It is a characteristic of our minds, that they cannot take an object in, which is submitted to them simply and integrally. We conceive by means of definition or description; whole objects do not create in the intellect whole ideas, but are, to use a mathematical phrase, thrown into series, into a number of statements, strengthening, interpreting, correcting each other, and with more or less exactness approximating, as they accumulate, to a perfect image. There is no other way of learning or of teaching. We cannot teach except by aspects or views, which are not identical with the thing itself which we are teaching. Two persons may each convey the same truth to a third, yet by methods and through representations altogether different. The same person will treat the same argument differently in an essay or speech, according to the accident of the day of writing, or of the audience, yet it will be substantially the same.

And the more claim an idea has to be considered living, the more various will be its aspects; and the more social and political is its nature, the more complicated and subtle will be its issues, and the longer and more eventful will be its course. And in the number of these special ideas, which from their very depth and richness cannot be fully understood at once, but are more and more clearly expressed and taught the longer they last, — having aspects many and bearings many, mutually connected and growing one out of another, and all parts of a whole, with a sympathy and correspondence keeping pace with the ever-changing necessities of the world, multiform, prolific, and ever resourceful, — among these great doctrines surely we Christians shall not refuse a foremost place to Christianity. Such previously to the determination of the fact, must be our anticipation concerning it from a contemplation of its initial achievements.[169]

Newman then goes on to contend that Christianity comes to us as a revelation that is guaranteed to be infallibly true. What follows from this is that developments which are the results of this revelation must likewise be true, and it is reasonable to expect that God will have made provision for them to be accredited as true.

> If the Christian doctrine, as originally taught, admits of true and important developments, as was argued in the foregoing section, this is a strong antecedent argument in favour of a provision in the dispensation for putting a seal of authority upon those developments. The probability of their being known to be true varies with that of their truth. The two ideas indeed are quite distinct, I grant, of revealing and of guaranteeing a truth, and they are often distinct in fact. There are various revelations all over the earth which do not carry with them the evidence of their divinity. Such are the inward suggestions and secret illuminations granted to so many individuals; such are the traditionary doctrines which are found among the heathen, that ' vague and unconnected family of religious truths, originally from God, but sojourning, without the sanction of miracle or a definite home, as pilgrims up and down the world, and discernible and separable from the corrupt legends with which they are mixed, by the spiritual mind alone.' There is nothing impossible in the notion of a revelation occurring without evidences that it is a revelation; just as human sciences are a divine gift, yet are reached by our ordinary powers and have no claim on our faith. But Christianity is not of this nature: it is a revelation which comes to us as a revelation, as a whole, objectively, and with a profession of infallibility; and the only question to be determined relates to the matter of the revelation. If then there are certain great truths, or duties, or observances, naturally and legitimately resulting from the doctrines originally professed, it is but

---

[169] Newman, *Essay*, pp.55-56.

> reasonable to include these true results in the idea of the revelation itself, to consider them parts of it, and if the revelation be not only true, but guaranteed as true, to anticipate that they too will come under the privilege of that guarantee. Christianity, unlike other revelations of God's will, except the Jewish, of which it is a continuation, is an objective religion, or a revelation with credentials; it is natural, I say, to view it wholly as such, and not partly *sui generis*, partly like others. Such as it begins, such let it be considered to continue; granting that certain large developments of it are true, they must surely be accredited as true. [170]

Newman next argues that true developments of the Christian idea possess the two marks of prominence and permanence. That is to say, they need to have been positive developments of Christian doctrine which been accepted across Christendom as a whole throughout the history of the Church. As he sees it, the only developments which meet these criteria are those beliefs which are held by the Roman Catholic Church and summarised in the teaching of the Council of Trent. The heresies that occurred in the Early Church were short lived, in the medieval period the Eastern Orthodox churches offered nothing positive, but simply objected to aspects of Western (Latin) Christianity, and following the Reformation the teaching of the various Protestant churches has failed to offer a positive and coherent alternative to the doctrine set forth at the Council of Trent. In Newman's own words:

> Next, we have to consider that from first to last other developments there are none, except those which have possession of Christendom; none, that is, of prominence and permanence sufficient to deserve the name. In early times the heretical doctrines were confessedly barren and short-lived, and could not stand their ground against Catholicism. As to the medieval period I am not aware that the Greeks present more than a negative opposition to the Latins. And now in like manner the Tridentine

---

[170] Newman, *Essay*, pp.79-80.

> Creed is met by no rival developments; there is no antagonist system. Criticisms, objections, protests, there are in plenty, but little of positive teaching anywhere; seldom an attempt on the part of any opposing school to master its own doctrines, to investigate their sense and bearing, to determine their relation to the decrees of Trent and their distance from them. And when at any time this attempt is by chance in any measure made, then an incurable contrariety does but come to view between portions of the theology thus developed, and a war of principles; an impossibility moreover of reconciling that theology with the general drift of the formularies in which its elements occur, and a consequent appearance of unfairness and sophistry in adventurous persons who aim at forcing them into consistency;' and, further, a prevalent understanding of the truth of this representation, authorities keeping silence, eschewing a hopeless enterprise and discouraging it in others, and the people plainly intimating that they think both doctrine and usage, antiquity and development, of very little matter at all; and, lastly, the evident despair of even the better sort of men, who, in consequence, when they set great schemes on foot, as for the conversion of the heathen world, are afraid to agitate the question of the doctrines to which it is to be converted, lest through the opened door they should lose what they have, instead of gaining what they have not. [171]

In addition, declares Newman, the developments which have taken place in the Roman Catholic Church are claimed to be infallibly true, in line with the antecedent probability that God would provide infallible developments of the original Christian revelation.

> To the weight of recommendation which this contrast throws upon the developments commonly called Catholic, must be added the argument which arises from the coincidence of their consistency and permanence, with their claim of an infallible sanction, — a claim, the existence of which, in some quarter or other of the

[171] Newman, *Essay*, pp.94-95.

Divine Dispensation, is, as we have already seen, antecedently probable. All these things being considered, I think few persons will deny the very strong presumption which exists, that, if there must be and are in fact developments in Christianity, the doctrines propounded by successive Popes and Councils, through so many ages, are they. [172]

Chapter 3 'On the historical argument in behalf of the existing developments.'

Newman begins chapter 3 of his Essay by arguing that there are certain developments (the doctrines accepted by the Roman Catholic Church) which claim to be apostolic, whose historical lineage can be traced back to early times, which together form a coherent system of belief and practice and reflect the ethos of the Early Church, the Apostles and the Prophets, and whose claim to authority fits in with the antecedent probability that God would provide a continuing authoritative development of the Christian revelation.

> It seems, then, that we have to deal with a case something like the following: Certain doctrines come to us, professing to be Apostolic, and possessed of such high antiquity that, though we are only able to assign the date of their formal establishment to the fourth, or the fifth, or the eighth, or the thirteenth century, as it may happen, yet their substance may, for what appears, be coeval with the Apostles., and be expressed or implied in texts of Scripture. Further, these existing doctrines are universally considered, without any question, in each age to be the echo of the doctrines of the times immediately preceding them, and thus arc continually thrown back to a date indefinitely early, even though their ultimate junction with the Apostolic Creed be out of sight and unascertainable. Moreover, they are confessed to form one body one with another, so that to reject one is to disparage the rest; and they include within the range of their system even those primary articles of faith, as the Incarnation, which many an impugner of the

---

[172] Newman, *Essay*, pp.95-96.

said doctrinal system, as a system, professes to accept and which, do what he will, he cannot intelligibly separate, whether in point of evidence or of internal character, from others which he disavows. Further, these doctrines occupy the whole field of theology, and leave nothing to be supplied, except in detail, by any other system; while, in matter of fact, no rival system is forthcoming, so that we have to choose between this theology and none at all. Moreover, this theology alone makes provision for that guidance of opinion and conduct, which seems externally to be the special aim of Revelation; and fulfils the promises of Scripture, by adapting itself to the various problems of thought and practice which meet us in life. And, further, it is the nearest approach, to say the least, to the religious sentiment, and what is called ethos, of the early Church, nay, to that of the Apostles and Prophets; for all will agree so far as this, that Elijah, Jeremiah, the Baptist, and St. Paul are in their history and mode of life (I do not speak of measures of grace, no, nor of doctrine and conduct, for these are the points in dispute, but) in what is external and meets the eye (and this is no slight resemblance when things are viewed as a whole and from a distance), — these saintly and heroic men, I say, are more like a Dominican preacher, or a Jesuit missionary, or a Carmelite friar, more like St. Toribio, or St. Vincent Ferrer, or St. Francis Xavier, or St. Alphonso Liguori, than to any individuals, or to any classes of men, that can be found in other communions. And then, in addition, there is the high antecedent probability that Providence would watch over His own work, and would direct and ratify those developments of doctrine which were inevitable.[173]

Given these arguments in their favour declares Newman, it follows that we should treat these developments 'not with suspicion and criticism, but with a frank confidence' and be 'patient with difficulties in their application, with apparent objections to them drawn from

---

[173] Newman, *Essay*, pp.99-100.

other matters of fact, deficiency in their comprehensiveness, or want of neatness in their working.' [174]

Newman then goes on to argue that this general attitude of confidence towards these doctrines should govern our attitude to the gaps in the historical record concerning precisely how they developed, what Newman calls 'omissions.' Such omissions exist, but their existence is not fatal to the theory of development he is proposing. This is for two reasons.

First, Scripture itself contains omissions:

> Scripture has its unexplained omissions. No religious school finds its own tenets and usages on the surface of it. The remark applies also to the very context of Scripture, as in the obscurity which hangs over Nathanael or the Magdalen. It is a remarkable circumstance that there is no direct intimation all through Scripture that the Serpent mentioned in the temptation of Eve was the evil spirit, till we come to the vision of the Woman and Child, and their adversary, the Dragon, in the twelfth chapter of the Apocalypse.[175]

Secondly, there are frequently good reason why there are gaps in the historical record:

> Omissions, thus absolute and singular, when they occur in the evidence of facts or doctrines, are of course difficulties; on the other hand, not unfrequently they admit of explanation. Silence may arise from the very notoriety of the facts in question, as in the case of the seasons, the weather, or other natural phenomena; or from their sacredness, as the Athenians would not mention the mythological Furies; or from external constraint, as the omission of the statues of Brutus and Cassius in the procession. Or it may proceed from fear or disgust, as on the arrival of unwelcome news;

[174] Newman, *Essay*, p.101.
[175] Newman, *Essay*, p.116.

or from indignation, or hatred, or contempt, or perplexity, as Josephus is silent about Christianity, and Eusebius passes over the death of Crispus in his life of Constantino; or from other strong feeling, as implied in the poet's sentiment, 'Give sorrow words;' or from policy or other prudential motive, or propriety, as Queen's Speeches do not mention individuals, however influential in the political world, and newspapers after a time were silent about the cholera. Or, again, from the natural and gradual course which the fact took, as in the instance of inventions and discoveries, the history of which is on this account often obscure; or from loss of documents or other direct testimonies, as we should not look for theological information in a treatise on geology.[176]

At the end of chapter 3 Newman notes a further argument against his view of development, which is that Christian theologians have disagreed about what constitutes a valid development of Christian doctrine. Newman acknowledges that this is true, but argues (a) that such disagreements are an inevitable part of doctrinal development and (b) that the Church as whole, acting through Popes and Councils, has maintained a consistent doctrinal position:

> And, if it be said in reply that the difficulty of admitting these developments of doctrine lies, not merely in the absence of early testimony for them, but in the actual existence of distinct testimony against them, — or, as Chillingworth says, in 'Popes against Popes, Councils against Councils,' — I answer, of course this will be said; but let the fact of this objection be carefully examined, and its value reduced to its true measure, before it is used in argument. I grant that there are 'Bishops against Bishops in Church history, Fathers against Fathers, Fathers against themselves,' for such differences in individual writers are consistent with, or rather are involved in the very idea of doctrinal development, and consequently are no real objection to it; the one essential question is whether the recognized organ of teaching, the

[176] Newman, *Essay*, pp.116-117.

Church herself, acting through Pope or Council as the oracle of heaven, has ever contradicted her own enunciations. If so, the hypothesis which I am advocating is at once shattered; but, till I have positive and distinct evidence of the fact, I am slow to give credence to the existence of so great an improbability. [177]

Chapter 4 'Instances in Illustration'

In his fourth chapter Newman goes on to illustrate the process of development by giving a series of examples of the way in which large parts of Christian doctrine came to receive general recognition by the Church as a whole in spite of the fact that the early evidence for them is relatively sparse, and that it was only over the course of time that their importance became recognised as the Church's thinking progressed. In Newman's words:

> It follows now to inquire how much evidence is actually producible for those large portions of the present Creed of Christendom, which have not a recognised place in the primordial idea and the historical outline of the Religion, yet which come to us with certain antecedent considerations strong enough in reason to raise the effectiveness of that evidence to a point disproportionate, as I have allowed, to its intrinsic value. In urging these considerations here, of course I exclude for the time the force of the Church's claim of infallibility in her acts, for which so much can be said, but I do not exclude the logical cogency of those acts, considered as testimonies to the faith of the times before them.

> My argument then is this:—that, from the first age of Christianity, its teaching looked towards those ecclesiastical dogmas, afterwards recognized and defined, with (as time went on) more or less determinate advance in the direction of them; till at length that advance became so pronounced, as to justify their definition and to bring it about, and to place them in the position of rightful

---

[177] Newman, *Essay*, pp.120-121.

interpretations and keys of the remains and the records in history of the teaching which had so terminated.[178]

Newman provides seven examples to support this argument. They are:

- The Canon of the New Testament
- Original sin
- The propriety of infant baptism
- The propriety of receiving communion in one kind
- The use of the term *homoousios* to describe the relationship between God the Father and God the Son
- The doctrine of the person of Christ and linked to this recognition of the dignity of Mary as the 'Mother of God.'
- Papal supremacy.

Neman's arguments with regard to the first two items on this list illustrate his overall approach.

On the Canon of the New Testament, Newman argues the extent of the New Testament Canon was established by a judgement of the Church in the fourth and fifth centuries based the testimony of the preceding centuries, the issue not having been able to be decided before that time:

> On what ground, then, do we receive the Canon as it comes to us, but on the authority of the Church of the fourth and fifth centuries? The Church at that era decided, — not merely bore testimony, but passed a judgment on former testimony, — decided, that certain books were of authority. And on what ground did she so decide? on the ground that hitherto a decision had been impossible, in an age of persecution, from want of opportunities for research,

---

[178] Newman, *Essay*, p.122.

discussion, and testimony, from the private or the local character of some of the books, and from misapprehension of the doctrine contained in others. Now, however, facilities were at length given for deciding once for all on what had been in suspense and doubt for three centuries.[179]

On the doctrine of original sin, Newman declares:

> ...the recognition of Original Sin, considered as the consequence of Adam's fall, was, both as regards general acceptance and accurate understanding, a gradual process, not completed till the time of Augustine and Pelagius. St. Chrysostom lived close up to that date, but there are passages in his works, often quoted, which we should not expect to find worded as they stand, if they had been written fifty years later. It is commonly, and reasonably, said in explanation, that the fatalism, so prevalent in various shapes pagan and heretical, in the first centuries, was an obstacle to an accurate apprehension of the consequences of the fall, as the presence of the existing idolatry was to the use of images. If this be so, we have here an instance of a doctrine held back for a time by circumstances, yet in the event forcing its way into its normal shape, and at length authoritatively fixed in it, that is, of a doctrine held implicitly, then asserting itself, and at length fully developed.[180]

Chapter 5 'Genuine developments contrasted with corruptions'

In chapter 5 Newman argues that he has shown that the form of religion that is found in the Roman Catholic Church is the historical continuation of that found in the Church of the early centuries. 'the heir of the religion of Cyprian, Basil, Ambrose and Augustine.' [181] However, with Protestant critics of Catholicism in mind, he then concedes that someone might object that:

---

[179] Newman, *Essay,* p. 125.
[180] Newman, *Essay*, pp.126-127.
[181] Newman, *Essay*, p. 169.

...it is not enough that a certain large system of doctrine, such as that which goes by the name of Catholic, should admit of being referred to beliefs, opinions, and usages which prevailed among the first Christians, in order to my having a logical right to include a reception of the later teaching in the reception of the earlier; that an intellectual development may be in one sense natural, and yet untrue to its original, as diseases come of nature, yet are the destruction, or rather the negation of health; that the causes which stimulate the growth of ideas may also disturb and deform them; and that Christianity might indeed have been intended by its Divine Author for a wide expansion of the ideas proper to it, and yet this great benefit hindered by the evil birth of cognate errors which acted as its counterfeit; in a word, that what I have called developments in the Roman Church are nothing more or less than what used to be called her corruptions; and that new names de not destroy old grievances.[182]

In order to meet this objection, he says, it is necessary 'to discriminate healthy developments of an idea from its state of corruption and decay.'[183] In the rest of the chapter he therefore offers seven tests by means of which the existence of a healthy development of an idea may be discerned. These seven tests are helpfully summarised by Peter Toon as follows:

1. *The preservation of the idea or type* The essence of a philosophical or political system must be preserved as it meets changing circumstances or it can be said that corruption has occurred. For example, if the members of a monastic institution abandoned their vows then the institution has not preserved the type.

2. *The continuity of principles* The basic principles of a country or movement must be preserved as it meets changing circumstances or it can be said that corruption has occurred. For example, when 'we talk of the spirit of the people being

---

[182] Newman, *Essay*, p.170.
[183] Newman, *Essay*, p.171.

lost, we do not mean that this or that act has been committed, or measure carried, but that certain lines of thought or conduct by which it is grown great are abandoned.'

3. *The power of assimilation* In the physical world to grow is to live and it means taking in air and food. This assimilation is not always natural, for it may take effort. Yet, when a plant or animal ceases to assimilate into its body that which makes it live it dies. Likewise, any system of thought shows itself alive and grows as it assimilates into itself new material.

4. *Early anticipation* Though vague and isolated, anticipations of later larger developments occur in histories in nations and movements. For example, in the very early history of monasticism which had as an essential feature manual labour, there are indications that monks will in the future spend their times in literary pursuits. And, fulfilling this anticipation, much academic scholarship has come from monastic communities in modern times - such as the Benedictines of Paris who edited the works of the Fathers.

5. *Logical sequence* Newman did not mean a conscious reasoning from premises to a conclusion but that the faithful unfolding of an idea will produce developments which upon examination are logically related to the initial idea.

6. *Preservative additions*

    'A true development may be described as one which is conservative of the course of development which went before it, which is that development and something besides: it is an addition which illustrates not obscures, corroborates not corrects, the body of thought from which it proceeds and this is its characteristic as contrasted with a corruption.'

7. *Chronic (of long duration) continuance* Corruption is distinguished from decay by its energetic action and it is distinguished from a development by its transitory character.

Heresies for example, are vibrant but do not last long whereas true developments continued through all difficulties. [184]

Chapter 6 'Preservation of type'

In chapters 6-12 Newman explains why he thinks Roman Catholicism meets these seven tests for healthy development.

In chapter 6 Newman argues that the same type or form of Christianity is found in both the Church of the early centuries and in the Church of the fifth and sixth centuries. Furthermore, he declares:

> If then there is now a form of Christianity such, that it extends throughout the world, though with varying measures of prominence or prosperity in separate places; — that it lies under the power of sovereigns and magistrates, in various ways alien to its faith; — that flourishing nations and great empires, professing or tolerating the Christian name, lie over against it as antagonists;—that schools of philosophy and learning are supporting theories, and following out conclusions, hostile to it, and establishing an exegetical system subversive of its Scriptures; — that it has lost whole Churches by schism, and is now opposed by powerful communions once part of itself; — that it has been altogether or almost driven from some countries; — that in others its line of teachers is overlaid, its flocks oppressed, its Churches occupied, its property held by what may be called a duplicate succession; — that in others its members are degenerate and corrupt, and are surpassed in conscientiousness and in virtue, as in gifts of intellect, by the very heretics whom it condemns; — that heresies are rife and bishops negligent within its own pale; — and that amid its disorders and its fears there is but one Voice for whose decisions the peoples wait with trust, one Name and one See to which they look with hope, and that name Peter, and that

---

[184] Peter Toon *The Development of Doctrine in the Church* (Grand Rapids: Eerdmans 1979) pp.11- 12.

see Rome; — such a religion is not unlike the Christianity of the fifth and sixth Centuries.[185]

This form of Christianity, which is like the form of Christianity found in the fifth and sixth centuries, and, as such, like the form of Christianity found in the first century, is, according to Newman, that found in the Roman Catholic Church.

Chapter 7 'Continuity of principles'

In chapter seven Newman notes that the doctrine of the Incarnation is the central truth of the Christian faith. This doctrine is referred to in passages such as John 1:14, 1 John 1:1-2, 2 Corinthians 8:9 and Galatians 2:20, and, in his view, nine principles can be deduced from these passages:

> 1. The principle of dogma, that is, supernatural truths irrevocably committed to human language, imperfect because it is human, but definitive and necessary because given from above.
>
> 2. The principal of faith, which is the correlative of dogma, being the absolute acceptance of the divine Word with an internal assent, in opposition to the informations, if such, of sight and reason.
>
> 3. Faith, being an act of the intellect, opens a way for inquiry, comparison and inference, that is, for science in religion, in subservience to itself; this is the principle of theology.
>
> 4. The doctrine of the Incarnation is the announcement of a divine gift conveyed in a material and visible medium, it being thus that heaven and earth are in the Incarnation united. That is, it establishes in the very idea of Christianity the sacramental principle as its characteristic.
>
> 5. Another principle involved in the doctrine of the Incarnation, viewed as taught or as dogmatic, is the necessary use of language,

---

[185] Newman, *Essay*, pp.331-332.

e. g. of the text of Scripture, in a second or mystical sense. Words must be made to express new ideas, and are invested with a sacramental office.

6. It is our Lord's intention in His Incarnation to make us what He is Himself; this is the principle of grace, which is not only holy but sanctifying.

7. It cannot elevate and change us without mortifying our lower nature: — here is the principle of asceticism

8. And, involved in this death of the natural man, is necessarily a revelation of the malignity of sin, in corroboration of the forebodings of conscience.

9. Also, by the fact of an Incarnation we are taught that matter is an essential part of us, and, as well as mind, is capable of sanctification.[186]

According to Newman the Roman Catholic Church alone has maintained these nine principles:

...while the development of doctrine in the Church has been in accordance with, or in consequence of these immemorial principles, the various heresies, which have from time to time arisen, have in one respect or other, as might be expected, violated those principles with which she rose into existence, and which she still retains. Thus, Arian and Nestorian schools denied the allegorical rule of Scripture interpretation; the Gnostics and Eunomians for Faith professed to substitute knowledge; and the Manichees also, as St. Augustine so touchingly declares in the beginning of his work *De Utilitate Credendi*. The dogmatic Rule, at least so far as regards its traditional character, was thrown aside by all those sects which, as Tertullian tells us, claimed to judge for themselves from Scripture; and the Sacramental principle was

---

[186] Newman *Essay*, pp.335-336.

violated, ipso facto, by all who separated from the Church,—was denied also by Faustus the Manichee when he argued against the Catholic ceremonial, by Vigilantius in his opposition to relics, and by the Iconoclasts. In like manner the contempt of mystery, of reverence, of devoutness, of sanctity, are other notes of the heretical spirit. As to Protestantism it is plain in how many ways it has reversed the principles of Catholic theology.[187]

Chapter 8 'Assimilative power'

In Chapter 8 Newman contends that in the early days of the Church, the Church's unwavering belief in the existence of one true God meant that the:

> ...cardinal distinction between Christianity and the religions and philosophies by which it was surrounded, nay even the Judaism of the day, [was] that it referred all truth and revelation to one source, and that the Supreme and Only God. Pagan rites which honoured one or other out of ten thousand deities; philosophies which scarcely taught any source of revelation at all; Gnostic heresies which were based on Dualism, adored angels, or ascribed the two Testaments to distinct authors, could not regard truth as one, unalterable, consistent, imperative, and saving. But Christianity started with the principle that there was but "one God and one Mediator," and that He, "who at sundry times and in divers manners spake in time past unto the fathers by the Prophets, had in these last days spoken unto us by His Son." He had never left Himself without witness, and now He had come, not to undo the past, but to fulfil and perfect it. His Apostles, and they alone, possessed, venerated, and protected a Divine Message, as both sacred and sanctifying; and, in the collision and conflict of opinions, 'in ancient times or modern, it was that Message, ' and not any vague or antagonist teaching, that was to succeed in purifying, assimilating, transmuting, and taking into itself the many-coloured beliefs, forms of worship, codes of duty, schools of

---

[187] Newman, *Essay*, p.354.

thought, through which it was ever moving. It was Grace, and it was Truth.[188]

The earliest form of Christianity therefore demonstrated 'assimilative power.' Today, says Newman, rejection or acceptance of the principle of assimilation is what divides Protestants from Catholics. Protestant theologians:

> ...imply that Revelation was a single, entire, solitary act, or nearly so, introducing a certain message; whereas we, who maintain the other, consider that Divine teaching has been in fact, what the analogy of nature would lead us to expect, 'at sundry times and in divers manners,' various, complex, progressive, and supplemental of itself. We consider the Christian doctrine, when analyzed, to appear, like the human frame, 'fearfully and wonderfully made;' but they think it some one tenet or certain principles given out at one time in their fulness, without gradual enlargement before Christ's coming or elucidation afterwards. They cast off all that they also find in Pharisee or heathen; we conceive that the Church, like Aaron's rod, devours the serpents of the magicians. They are ever hunting for a fabulous primitive simplicity; we repose in Catholic fulness. They seek what never has been found; we accept and use what even they acknowledge to be a substance. They are driven to maintain, on their part, that the Church's doctrine was never pure; we say that it can never be corrupt. We consider that a divine promise keeps the Church Catholic from doctrinal corruption; but on what promise, or on what encouragement, they are seeking for their visionary purity does not appear.[189]

Chapter 9 'Logical sequence'
In this chapter Newman explains that logical sequence means one doctrine leading to another, and he argues that such logical sequence

---

[188] Newman, *Essay*, pp.356-357.
[189] Newman, *Essay*, p.382.

can be shown in the various doctrines that have emerged from the doctrine of baptism.

Newman argues that in the 'primitive church' it was held that the distinctive gift given at baptism: 'was the plenary forgiveness of sins past. It was also held that the Sacrament could not be repeated.'[190] The question that followed from these convictions was

> ...how, since there was but 'one Baptism for the remission of sins,' the guilt of such sin was to be removed as was incurred after its administration. There must be some provision in the revealed system for so obvious a need. What could be done for those who had received the one remission of sins, and had sinned since?[191]

The Catholic doctrines of penance, purgatory, and meritorious works and the development of monasticism emerged as ways of answering this question, all setting out ways of dealing with post baptismal sin.

Chapter 10 'Anticipation of the future'

In chapter 10 Newman argues that the history of Roman Catholic doctrine meets the test of 'anticipation of the future' in that the later doctrines concerning saints, relics and the special spiritual privileges of Mary as the Mother of God are all anticipated in the basic teaching of the early Church about the goodness of created matter. As Newman puts it:

> Christianity began by considering Matter as a creature of God, and in itself "very good." It taught that Matter, as well as Spirit, had become corrupt, in the instance of Adam; and it contemplated its recovery. It taught that the Highest had taken a portion of that corrupt mass upon Himself, in order to the sanctification of the whole; that, as a first fruits of His purpose, He had purified from all sin that very portion of it which He took into His Eternal Person, and thereunto had taken it from a Virgin Womb, He had filled with

---

[190] Newman, *Essay*, p.384.
[191] Newman, *Essay*, p.384.

the abundance of His Spirit. Moreover, it taught that during His earthly sojourn He had been subject to the natural infirmities of man, and had suffered from those ills to which flesh is heir. It taught that the Highest had in that flesh died on the Cross, and that His blood had an expiatory power; moreover, that He had risen again in that flesh, and had carried that flesh with Him into heaven, and that from that flesh, glorified and deified in Him, He never would be divided. As a first consequence of these awful doctrines comes that of the resurrection of the bodies of His Saints, and of their future glorification with Him; next, that of the sanctity of their relics; further, that of the merit of Virginity; and, lastly, that of the prerogatives of Mary, Mother of God. All these doctrines are more or less developed in the Ante-Nicene period, though in very various degrees, from the nature of the case.[192]

Chapter 11 'Conservative action on its past'

In this chapter Newman notes that a true development is conservative, but also allows for the addition of something more. In his view:

> This character of addition, — that is, of a change which is in one sense real and perceptible, yet without loss or reversal of what was before, but, on the contrary, protective and confirmative of it, — in many respects and in a special way belongs to Christianity.[193]

Such additions, he says, can be found in the Catholic Church from earliest times.

In Catholicism:

- The virtue of Love was added to fear,
- The Church conquered the Empire but maintained the virtues of meekness and poverty,

---

[192] Newman, Essay, pp.401-402.
[193] Newman, Essay, p.420

- It was taught that Christ remained God while becoming fully Man,

- The oneness of God was maintained alongside his threeness,

- Idolatry remained forbidden while images were allowed,

- Unique devotion to God was maintained while forms of devotion to Mary were also allowed.

Chapter twelve 'Chronic vigour'

In this final chapter Newman highlights the constant renewal of the Roman Catholic Church as evidence that it passes the final test of possessing 'chronic vigour.' In the words of the penultimate paragraph of the *Essay*:

> It is true, there have been seasons when, from the operation of external or internal causes, the Church has been thrown into what was almost a state of *deliquium*; but her wonderful revivals, while the world was triumphing over her, is a farther evidence of the absence of corruption in the system of doctrine and worship into which she has developed. If corruption be an incipient disorganization, surely an abrupt and absolute recurrence to the former state of vigour, after an interval, is even less conceivable than a corruption that is permanent. Now this is the case with the revivals I speak of. After violent exertion men are exhausted and fall asleep; they awake the same as before, refreshed by the temporary cessation of their activity; and such has been the slumber and such the restoration of the Church. She pauses in her course, and almost suspends her functions; she rises again, and she is herself once more; all things are in their place and ready for action. Doctrine is where it was, and usage, and precedence, and principle, and policy; there may be changes, but they are consolidations or adaptations; all is unequivocal and determinate, with an identity which there is no disputing. Indeed it is one of the most popular charges against the Catholic Church at this very time, that she is "incorrigible;'—change she cannot, if we listen to St

Athanasius or St. Leo; change she never will, if we believe the controversialist or alarmist of the present day.[194]

4. Summarizing Newman's argument

Newman's argument in his *Essay on the Development of Christian Doctrine* can be summarised as follows:

The traditional Anglican appeal to the Vincentian canon as ruling out the legitimacy of aspects of Roman Catholic teaching and practice does not work because the same arguments from history which Anglicans use to rule out Catholic teaching and practices also rule out accepted Anglican beliefs and practices as well. An alternative approach to distinguishing truth from error in the development of Christian doctrine is therefore required.

This alternative approach starts from the recognition that ideas develop over time and it good that they do ('to live is to change, and to be perfect is to have changed often'). Christianity is an idea given to us in a divine revelation. We should therefore expect it to develop and for its correct development to be divinely accredited.

The teaching and practice of the Roman Catholic Church is the only form of Christianity that can plausibly claim to be a divinely accredited development of the Christian idea. Only the Roman Catholic Church can trace the lineage of its beliefs and practices back to Apostolic times (gaps in the historical evidence notwithstanding), it alone provides a coherent body of positive teaching, it alone reflects the ethos of the Early Church and it alone meets the antecedent expectation of the divine accreditation of doctrinal development by means of the authoritative decisions made by its Councils and by the Popes.

Furthermore, the study of a range of historical examples shows that the developments of the Christian idea found in Roman Catholicism meet the seven tests for healthy development, the preservation of the

---

[194] Neman, *Essay*, p.444, 'Deliquium' means 'melting away.'

idea or type, continuity of principles, power of assimilation, early anticipation, logical sequence, preservative additions and chronic continuance.

5. Assessing Newman's argument

There can be no doubt about the historic significance of Newman's *Essay on the Development of Doctrine*. As J M Cameron puts it in his introduction to the Penguin edition of the *Essay*:

> There are certain works in the history of theology of which we can say that after their appearance nothing was ever again quite the same. We can say this of Augustine's *De Civitate Dei* of the *Summa Theologiae* of Aquinas of Calvin's *Institutes*. The *Essay on Development* is a work of this order and the first work by an Englishman - at least since the day of William of Ockham- to shake the theological schools of Europe…the man whose genius had been given to the leadership of a counter revolution in a national church…is now become a power in Europe and in the world.[195]

Although Newman's *Essay* was deeply controversial when it was originally published, not only among Protestants, but also among many in the Roman Catholic Church, in the course of the twentieth century it became generally accepted as a landmark work in the history of Christian thinking about the development of doctrine and its approach became highly influential within the Roman Catholic Church (a fact reflected in the recent decision to recognise Newman as a Doctor of the Universal Church).

As Guarino notes:

> …it is Newman who is often credited (along with the nineteenth-century theologians from Tubingen) with having restored to Roman Catholic theology a notion of tradition that is active and dynamic as well as properly preservative. Many of these elements

---

[195] J M Cameron (ed), John Henry Newman, *An Essay on the Development of Doctrine* (Harmondsworth: Penguin, 1974), Introduction, p.7.

found voice at Vatican II (1962-1965), so much so that Paul VI in 1975 declared Vatican II to be 'Newman's hour.' [196]

In the words of Tony Lane, such has been Newman's influence within the Roman Catholic Church: 'It has even been claimed, with tongue in cheek, that in the long run it was the Roman Catholic Church that was converted to Newman, not vice versa.'[197]

However, the fact that Newman's *Essay* has thus been highly influential does not mean that his argument is correct, and there are in fact four very serious problems with Newman's argument.

The first problem is that Newman's starting point, that the arguments from history that Anglicans have used to rule out developments in Roman Catholic teaching and practice also rule out accepted Anglican beliefs and practices, is incorrect. This is because it can be perfectly consistently argued that the beliefs defended in the early Ecumenical Councils and summarised in the Nicene, Athanasian and Apostles Creeds (which are the beliefs which the Anglican tradition has accepted) can be traced back through the early centuries of the Church's existence to the teaching of the apostles as witnessed to by the New Testament, whereas the same is not true of the distinctive

---

[196] Guarino, p.80. The full quotation from Pope Paul VI runs:
'He who was convinced of being faithful throughout his life, with all his heart devoted to the light of truth, today becomes an ever-brighter beacon for all who are seeking an informed orientation and sure guidance amid the uncertainties of the modern world-a world which he himself prophetically foresaw...Not only this Council but also the present time can be considered in a special way as Newman's hour, in which, with confidence in divine providence, he placed his great hopes and expectations: 'Perhaps my name is to be turned to account as a sanction and outset by which others who agree with me in opinion should write and publish instead of me, and thus begin the transmission of views in religious and intellectual matters congenial with my own, to the generation after me' (cf. W. Ward, *The Life of Cardinal Newman*, London, 1912, vol. 2, p. 202.).'
L'Osservatore Romano (English edition), 17 April 1975.
[197] Tony Lane, *The Lion Handbook of Christian Thought* (Oxford: Lion, 1984), p.230.

beliefs which distinguish the Roman Catholic Church from other Christian traditions.

Two examples will serve to illustrate this point.

The first example is the teaching of the Nicene Creed about the divinity of Christ. In the words of Jacob Mozley in his response to Newman:

The Nicene Creed only asserted and guarded a doctrine which had been held from the first, viz., that of Christ's true and proper Divinity. The original Christian Revelation declared that Christ was God. If Christ was God, He was true God; He had true and proper Godhead. The Nicene Creed asserted this of Him, and no more; it expressed this truth, and no more, by the word *Homoousion*. The word *Homoousion* declared that Christ was very God with God the Father. His oneness of substance with the Father was the term by which the Nicene Fathers declared His true Godhead with the Father. And this true Godhead was attributed to Christ by the original Christian Revelation, which declared Him to be God, and commanded Him to be worshipped as God.[198]

The second is the doctrine of purgatory as this developed in Roman Catholic teaching, which holds that the souls of Christian believers have to undergo an extended period of penal suffering after death to make satisfaction for the sins which they have committed after baptism, a period which can be shortened by the prayers of the faithful here on earth. What Newman does not show, and what cannot be shown, is that a belief in purgatory, understood in this sense can be found in the New Testament or in the teaching of Church in the early centuries of its existence. In the words of Gerald Bray:

> In modern times scholars, including Roman Catholics, have established beyond doubt that the doctrine of purgatory was a

---

[198] Jacob Mozley, *The theory of development* (Oxford: Rivingtons, 1848). p.163.

medieval invention. It did not exist before the twelfth century, and it is unknown in the Eastern churches.[199]

Given the difference between these two beliefs just noted it would be perfectly reasonable to do what Anglicanism has done since the Reformation, which is to accept the teaching of the Nicene Creed while rejecting the doctrine of purgatory. Ruling out the latter does not entail ruling out the former.

Newman's response to the Anglican argument that the Roman Catholic Church's teaching about purgatory was not present in the teaching of the New Testament and the Early Church would be to say that it nevertheless forms part of the Christian idea which was gradually apprehended by the Church as doctrine developed.

This brings us to the second problem with Newman's argument, which is his notion that Christianity is an idea. The key thing to grasp is that for Newman Christianity is an idea about God and his relationship to the world that is known partly explicitly and partly implicitly, with that which is known implicitly becoming known explicitly over the course of time.

As Ian Ker explains in his Foreword to his 1989 edition of the *Essay on the Development of Christian Doctrine*, Newman's belief that the Christian idea is known both explicitly and implicitly enables him to avoid having to say that the developments that have taken place in Roman Catholic belief and practice over the centuries are the result of a continuing revelation that supplements the revelation given by Christ to the apostles.

Newman was clear that 'the Church does not know more than the Apostles knew,'[200] and yet it would appear that there are things that the Church now knows, such as the existence or the immaculate

---

[199] Gerald Bray, *The faith we confess* (London: Latimer Trust, 2009), p.119.
[200] Private letter by Newman in Charles Dessain and Thomas Gornall (eds) *John Newman, Letters and Diaries*, vol 25 (Oxford: Clarendon Press, 1973), p.418.

conception of the Virgin Mary that the evidence we have indicates that the apostles did not know. The notion that the apostles possessed implicit as well as explicit knowledge of the Christian ideas enables Newman to get round this problem.

As Ker writes, according to Newman:

> ...the fact that the Apostolic Church was not conscious of later dogmas does not necessarily mean that she was not unconsciously cognizant of them, in the sense that she had an implicit though not explicit knowledge of them. As Newman put it in 'The Theory of Developments in Religious Doctrine,' it is no proof that persons are not possessed, because they are not conscious, of an idea. It is because he thought the Apostles had an implicit rather than explicit understanding of the whole of the revelation committed to them that Newman can say in the *Essay* that they 'would without words know all the truths concerning the high doctrines of theology which controversialists after them have...reduced to formulae and developed through argument.' What was implicitly believed becomes explicitly professed, as the mind of the Church develops the 'ideas, which it has hitherto held implicitly and without subjecting them through its reflection and reasoning powers.'[201]

Ker further notes that in an unpublished paper written in 1868 Newman:

> ...amplifies and throws light on the distinction between implicit or unconscious and explicit or conscious knowledge. In it Newman is very emphatic that:
>
>> ...the Apostles had the *fullness* of revealed knowledge, a fullness which they could as little realize to themselves, as the human

---

[201] Ian Ker, Foreword, in *John Henry Cardinal Newman, An Essay on the Development of Christian Doctrine* (Notre Dame: University of Notre Dame Prees, 1989). Kindle edition, p.xxiii.

> mind as such, can have all its thoughts present before it once. They are elicited according to the occasion. A man of genius cannot go about with his genius in his hand: in an Apostle's mind great part of his knowledge is from the nature of the case latent or implicit...

Indeed, the 'idea' which the Church has received is cognitive enough to be called a 'Divine Philosophy' -

> ...not a number of formulas...but a system of thought...in such sense that a mind that was possessed of it, that is, the Church's mind, could definitely and unequivocally say whether this part of it, as traditionally expressed, means this or that, and whether this or that was agreeable to or inconsistent with it whole or in part. I wish to hold that there is nothing which the Church has defined or shall define but what an Apostle, if asked, would have been fully able to answer and would have answered, as the Church has answered, the one answering by inspiration of the other from its gift of infallibility.... [202]

This means, for example, that:

> St. Paul could hardly have understood what was meant by the 'Immaculate Conception,' but if he had been asked whether or not our Lady had the grace of the Spirit anticipating all sin whatever, including Adam's imputed sin, I think he would have answered in the affirmative. The 'living idea' then, of Christianity, or what Newman as a Roman Catholic calls the 'deposit of faith:'

> > ...is in such sense committed to the Church or to the Pope, that when the Pope sits in St. Peters chair, or when a Council of Fathers and doctors is collected around him, it is capable of being presented to their minds with that fullness and exactness...with which it habitually, not occasionally, resided in the minds of the Apostles; - a vision of it, not logical, and

---

[202] Ker, pp.xxiii - xxiv.

therefore consistent with errors of reasoning and of fact in the enunciation after the manner of an intuition or an instinct.[203]

To put it simply, according to Newman the Church (by which he means the Roman Catholic Church) knows everything that that the Apostles knew, both explicitly and implicitly, and it is able to draw on this implicit knowledge to formulate new developments of doctrine. The person who has the ability to formulate such new developments is the Pope, acting either on his own as the occupant of the chair of St. Peter, or in the context of a Church Council (such as the Council of Trent). The gift of infallibility given to the Pope means that the new doctrinal formulation will be correct because intuited correctly, even if the arguments put forward to support it contain mistakes.

There are two difficulties with this argument.

The first difficulty is that the idea that the Apostles possessed implicit knowledge which the later Church also possesses, and which can form the basis for developments in doctrine is a new idea which is not found in the history of the Church prior to Newman. The traditional view going back to New Testament times was that there was a deposit of explicit teaching concerning Christian belief and conduct which had been passed on by the Apostles to the later Church with the New Testament being the most authoritative (because divinely inspired) form of this deposit. All legitimate doctrine had to be in accordance with this deposit. Newman's idea of implicit knowledge possessed by the Apostles and then by the Church is a new concept and he does not offer any evidence that it is true. If we ask how we know that the Church possesses implicit knowledge that the Apostles also possessed, Newman simply does not give us an answer.

The second difficulty is that for Newman the guarantee that the Church has correctly understood the implicit knowledge it possesses

---

[203] Ker, p.xxv quoting J Derek Holmes (ed), *The Theological Papers of John Henry Newman on Biblical Inspiration and on Infallibility (*Oxford: Clarendon Press, 1979), pp.156-159.

and is therefore able to correctly use this knowledge to formulate new doctrine is the gift of infallible teaching given to the Pope as the successor of St. Peter. However, as the nineteenth century Irish Anglican critic of Newman, William Butler, points out, the belief that the Pope has infallible teaching authority is itself a development of doctrine based on the antecedent probability that God will have provided such an authority, so what Newman is in fact doing is using one development of doctrine to then guarantee the truth of other developments of doctrine in an entirely circular argument.

> ...the probability of the hypothesis is solely to be found in the service it can render towards making the innovations tolerable, we find the whole argument revolve in as pretty a circle as any the schools can furnish. I believe certain doctrines, because of infallible authority. I believe infallible authority, because of its antecedent necessity. I believe it antecedently necessary, because of developments wanting to be directed. I believe developments to want direction, because they must exist in great variety. I believe they must exist, because certain doctrines exist which I cannot otherwise prove to be part of the Christian religion. I believe them to be part of the Christian religion, because of infallible authority. This again, as before, I conclude from its antecedent necessity. And so on, the theological cycloid is anew described, as the circle rotates *in omne volubilis oevum*.[204]

Furthermore, as Mozley argues in his critique of Newman, the idea that it is antecedently probable that God will provide an infallible authority to protect his Church is based on a questionable presumption by Newman about how God will act, namely that having provided an original revelation God will provide an infallible guide to ensure that this revelation continues to be understood and developed correctly in the life of the Church. Everything follows logically from this presumption. In Mozley's words:

---

[204] William Butler, *Lectures on Romanism* (London: Macmillan, 1854), p. 271

We have then, on the one hand, a great presumptive ground asserting that if a revelation is given it must go on; that human nature wants a present infallible guide; that 'Christianity must, humanly speaking, have an infallible expounder.' Upon this original notion of what is necessary arises immediately the assertion of what is, and with that assertion a whole corresponding view of the existing matter-of-fact Church, and its established body of ideas, however and wherever derived. A whole, to use the word, perfectionist view of the historical progress of thought and growth of truth in the Church earthly, and the Christian world is ultimately imposed by an original basis of presumption like the present. The hypothesis of a standing revelation cannot afford to make any large established ideas in the earthly Church erroneous, it would interfere with such a standing revelation to do so; a pledge for the absolute correctness of all that growth of opinion which the infallible guide sanctions is contained in the notion of that infallible guide. Thus, inevitably arises the great general view that whatever is is right. The fact of certain ideas getting established becomes itself the proof of their truth. We see this view immediately in the tone of the arguer. The arguer reposes in fact; he carries the sensation about with him of largeness, extent, numbers; a doctrine that spreads over a large surface, that is held de facto by a large mass, is its own evidence. His tone of reasoning is a perpetual memento of the de facto ground. It is almost a condescension for him to argue at all; he has the fact, that is his argument. That his use of the fact is an assumption is lost sight of in the largeness of the fact itself; the authority of fact becomes itself a fact, and is ever seen in the background as the supreme authority, beyond which no appeal lies. The arguer is thus less occupied in proving than in simply unfolding his assumption. He explains how it was that such opinions arose, the need that was felt for them, their convenience in filling up certain chasms in the original revelation. It was thus, he explains, that their truth became known. This desire became, in course of ages, stronger and stronger, till at last it formally expressed itself: the mass of Christendom resolved that these opinions were true, and accordingly they became known truths, and have continued so up to the present day. Such is the account of the rise of this doctrine, of this article of faith: the arguer simply traces the progress of their discovery and adjustment from the very first dawn of the want to the climax of the supply. The completeness and rotundity of the formed system are then urged; the coincidence of the fact that such doctrines exist, with the fact that they were wanted; the coincidence of the various results and ramifications of developed doctrine with each other; the coincidence of the permanency of their reception with the fact of that profession of infallibility which first sanctioned it. 'When we are convinced that large developments do exist in matter of fact professing to be true and legitimate, our first impression naturally must be that these developments are what they pretend to be. The very scale on which they have been made, their high antiquity, yet present promise, their gradual formation, yet precision, affect the imagination most forcibly.' We need hardly say that Mr. Newman, in accordance with the whole tone of his book, and his appeal to the living and real, as opposed to merely historical and formal, of course understands by these developments of doctrine not the simple statements on paper, but doctrine as generally understood and believed, — the practical and energising opinions of the Christian body. Here, then, is what may be called a perfectionist view of the progress of truth in the Christian world. The ideas which establish themselves time after time in the Church are ipso facto true. What exists is right; each successive stage of thought improves on the following one; truth advances with the certainty of a mathematical problem; an infallible centre produces a perfect, ever operating self- correction; and the present state of things, as regards our relations to truth, becomes all that, humanly speaking, we could wish it to be.[205]

---

[205] Mozley, pp. 117-199. The quotations are from the 1845 edition of Newman's Essay.

A better approach, argues Mozley, is to follow the argument from analogy put forward by the Anglican theologian Joseph Butler in his book *The Analogy of Religion, Natural and Revealed* (a book to which Newman himself appeals). Butler explains that our experience shows us that we have no reason to think that we can know in advance how God will choose to act. What this means is that contrary to Newman's argument, we cannot assume from the fact of a revelation having been given that the reception of that revelation in the Church will be protected from any possibility of error. In fact, human nature being what it is, what is likely is that error will occur. In Mozley's words:

> The argument of analogy, on the other hand, gives a basis upon which a more qualified system erects itself. Its maxim that we are not judges of what a revelation should be, and consequent confinement of us to the fact of what revelation there has been, tends immediately this way. That there has been a revelation rests upon evidence of fact; its continuance rests upon presumption. That revelation, then, as far as it went, and as much as it said; the whole of it, in whatever mode communicated; everything for the institution and communication of which, as a fact, there is evidence, the argument of analogy gives us; but for the rest, it tells, us that we have no revelation, and that we cannot, by any notion on our part that we ought to have one, make one. It leaves the revelation which God gave, among them to whom he gave it, exposed to the same chances of abuse, perversion, or neglect, in the carrying out, which attend on the truths of nature; in all respects, except those in which it is, as a matter of fact, divinely guaranteed. The Christian revelation is divinely guaranteed against total corruption; it has the direct promise that the 'gates of hell shall not prevail against it' and stands in a different position from natural religion, in consequence of this promise. With this safeguard, however, the argument of analogy sends it down exposed all the same to common degrees of corruption, and those changes which are consistent with the substance of the revelation continuing. It prepares us, in consequence, for such abuses, if they occur; it makes it most likely beforehand that they will, in a greater

or less degree, occur. To the divine truth, thrown into the imperfect human mass, a positive likelihood of distortion and discolourment of some kind attaches. Not to mention lower and rougher causes, the mere tendencies of the human mind to go off upon particular thoughts, refine upon the natural substance of the truth put before it, and idolise its own conceptions and points of view, are against the probability of a revelation which offered the materials and supplied the occasions for abuse, being carried out without it; and running through centuries of intricate and agitating contact with the collective Christian intellect, without any deflection whatever from original soundness. If the rise of such deflections, again, is probable, their permanency is no matter to be surprised at; for the same course of things which originally established them makes them also last: it was their adaptation to some large and prevalent tastes which caused them to spread at first; and the same keeps them going. [206]

As Mozley goes on to say:

On the whole then, we say — according to the argument from analogy — an original creed or revelation thrown into the world of human intelligence is exposed to all common chances of human discolourment in the carrying out; the substantial original creed remaining throughout notwithstanding, and secured, if there be evidence for this fact, against failure to the end. And however, in reasoning a priori, out of our own heads, respecting revelation, we might expect it to do more for us because it did much, and look forward to a progress of truth pure, divinely guaranteed against error: the argument of analogy on the other hand bids us expect no such thing, but take the facts as they stand. It tells us not to expect all must be truth because there is truth; or again, to think all must be error because there is error; but to expect both truth and error. It supplies a dogmatic basis on the one side, and it allows for uncertainty on the other; and bids us neither be unbelievers nor

[206] Mozley, pp.119-121.

perfectionists. It says — This is a mixed world, and expect mixtures in it. Do not think that the progress of things will be wholly one way, or wholly another; that it will entirely submerge truth, or unfold it unimpeachably. There is much of both good and evil in it. The earthly Church partakes of the mixed character of the world in which it is placed, and which it has more or less received into its own pale. And its best members too are not perfect, but have their own undue biases of intellect, temper, taste, sometimes more open and palpable, sometimes more refined and internal.[207]

Mozley is surely right. We must accept the facts that God has given us a divine revelation and has promised that the gates of hell will not ultimately prevail against his Church, but beyond these two facts we cannot go. We cannot presume that God will supernaturally preserve his Church from all error and probability and experience lead us to reject the idea that he has or will do so. This being the case, Newman's antecedent argument for an infallible papacy preserving the Church from error as it progressively unpacks the Christian idea on the basis of implicit knowledge has to be judged to be unconvincing.

The third problem with Newman's argument is that he fails to demonstrate the truth of his claim that the teaching and practice of the Roman Catholic Church is the only form of Christianity that can plausibly claim to be a divinely accredited development of the Christian idea.

It is simply not the case that only the Roman Catholic Church can trace the lineage of its beliefs and practices back to Apostolic times.

- Other Christian traditions can equally convincingly make this claim. The Orthodox churches of the East, for example, have as long an unbroken history as the Church of Rome and even the Protestant churches that emerged out of the Reformation can

---

[207] Mozley, pp.124-125.

trace the origins of their beliefs and practices back to New Testament times.

- Other Christian traditions besides the Roman Catholic Church also provide coherent bodies of positive theological teaching such as for example the Lutheran *Augsburg Confession*, the Anglican *Thirty Nine Articles* and the Reformed *Heidelberg Catechism*.

- Other Christian churches besides the Roman Catholic Church reflect the ethos of the Early Church in various ways in their teaching and practice. For example, if we take the account of the practice of the Early Church provided Justin Martyr in his *First Apology* [208] as evidence for what the Early Church was like we can see a fundamental similarity between what Justin describes and the practice of a variety of different Christian churches today, Protestant and Orthodox as well as Roman Catholic. There is nothing distinctively Roman Catholic in what Justin describes.

- Other Christian churches besides the Roman Catholic Church can be seen to meet the seven tests for healthy development, the preservation of the idea or type, continuity of principles, power of assimilation, early anticipation, logical sequence, preservative additions and chronic continuance.

The basic problem is that Newman fails to explore the reality of other Christian churches. He describes what he sees as the unique virtues of the Roman Catholic Church and then dismisses other churches without proper investigation.

The fourth and final problem is that Newman's famous declaration in his *Essay* 'here below to live is to change, and to be perfect is to have changed often' is only half true. It is true that in this would 'to live is to change' – that is undeniable. However, having changed often does

---

[208] Justin Martyr, *First Apology*, Chapters LXV-LXVII in *The Ante-Nicene Fathers*, Vol.1 (Edinburgh and Grand Rapids T&T Clark/Eerdmans), pp. 185-186.

not in itself make someone perfect. This depends on the nature of the change that has occurred. From a Christian perspective, someone who has undergone a course of change that has made them more and more sinful in their behaviour, and increasingly hardened against Christian truth, cannot for this reason be said to have become perfect. In a similar fashion simply observing that the Roman Catholic Church (or any other church) has changed its doctrine and its practices over the centuries is not a plausible argument for its perfection. Likewise, it cannot be argued that a church that has changed its doctrine and practice frequently is necessarily better than a church that has not done so.

What these problems mean is that, for all its historical and contemporary importance, Newman's essay simply does not provide a reliable account of the development of Christian doctrine. Newman is too concerned with justifying the correctness of his decision to convert to Rome to give a properly balanced account of the matter.

Chapter 5
Schleiermacher's ghost - Maurice Wiles on the Making and Remaking of Christian Doctrine

1. The context of Maurice Wiles's work

The Revd Professor Maurice Wiles (1923-2005) was an Anglican clergyman and theologian. A specialist in the theology of the Patristic period, he taught at the universities of Ibadan, Cambridge and London before finishing his career as the Regius Professor of Divinity at the University of Oxford.

The background to his two books on the development of Christian doctrine, *The Making of Christian Doctrine* and the *Remaking of Christian Doctrine* was what the Roman Catholic Church historian Adrian Hastings describes as 'the social, intellectual, religious crisis of the 1960s' [209] As Hastings goes on to explain, this was a crisis:

> ...of the relevance (or capability for sheer survival) of long-standing patterns of thought and institutions of all sorts in a time of intense, and rather self-conscious, modernization. If the first long phase of post Second World War society was a conservative one, an attempt to recreate a fairly traditional world, that phase had gone with a steady escalation of secondary and tertiary education - most of it unquestioned unquestioningly secular - major shifts in academic preoccupation and a massive rise in the standard of living. Suddenly the mood changed, neo- traditionalism crumbled in ridicule and the pendulum swung rather warmly to the other extreme, the glorification of the modern. [210]

---

[209] Adrian Hastings, *A History of English Christianity 1920-1985* (London: Fount, 1987), p.580.
[210] Hastings, pp.580-581.

In the face of this situation the Church of England Bishop and Theologian John Robinson, famously declared that what was called for was:

> ...far more than a restating of traditional orthodoxy in modern terms. Indeed, if our defence of the Faith is limited to this, we shall find in all likelihood that we have lost out to all but a tiny religious remnant. A much more radical recasting, I would judge, is demanded, in the process of which the most fundamental categories of our theology - of God, of the supernatural, and of religion itself must go into the melting.[211]

Other Church of England theologians, such as Geoffrey Lampe, Don Cupitt, Hugh Montefiore and Dennis Nineham, took a similar approach to that put forward by Robinson, and Wiles was one of them. His two books on the development of doctrine are an attempt at the sort of 'radical recasting' called for by Robinson.

2. The Making of Christian Doctrine
The Development of Doctrine: The Nature of the Problem

Wiles' book *The Making of Christian Doctrine* [212] was published in 1967 at the end of his time as Dean of Clare College Cambridge. As its subtitle notes, it is 'A study in the principles of early doctrinal development.' It considers how Christian doctrine developed in the early centuries of the Church's existence, why it developed in this way, and what lessons we can learn for the direction that doctrinal development should take in the contemporary world.

Wiles begins the first chapter of his book, 'The Development of Doctrine: The Nature of the Problem,' by observing that reading Owen Chadwick's book *From Bossuet to Newman* about the discussions about the possibility of the development of Christian doctrine that took place from the seventeenth to the nineteenth centuries (the

---

[211] *John Robinson, Honest to God* (London: SCM, 1963), p.7.
[212] Maurice Wiles, *The Making of Christian Doctrine* (Cambridge: CUP, 1967).

discussions of which Newman's *Essay on the Development of Christian Doctrine* was the major fruit):

> ...is like reading a debate about the movement of the planets before the invention of the telescope. The general problems with which they were concerned are real problems; but the particular problems to which they addressed themselves so vigorously are not ours; and, more emphatically still, the way in which they approached them is not and cannot be ours. And so it is only in the most general manner that the historical treatment points on to the theological. The study of doctrinal development is a study of importance; but the debates of the eighteenth and nineteenth centuries must not be expected to throw any great light on the road we have to tread in pursuit of it at the present time. [213]

According to Wiles, the primary difference between the approach that he thinks is now called for and the approach taken by people like Newman in the nineteenth century is:

> ...an unreadiness to accept in advance that doctrinal development, even within the narrowly prescribed limits of, for example, the early conciliar decisions most generally acceptable to Anglicans, can be assumed with confidence to have been wholly true in direction and in conclusion.[214]

As Wiles sees it, while an *a priori* case can be made in favour of the Bible being infallible, 'an empirical approach to Scripture,' that is to say, a critical study of the biblical material, 'rules out decisively any question of its infallibility' [215] In similar fashion, he declares, a critical study of the development of doctrine also rules out the argument for the infallibility of the Church put forward by Newman:

---

[213] Wiles, *Making*, pp.1-2.
[214] Wiles, *Making*, p.11
[215] Wiles, *Making*, p.12.

> When the method of historical inquiry is applied with the same kind of rigour as has been used in the case of the study of Scripture, the results would seem to be similar. Newman's infallible developing authority becomes as difficult to maintain as the infallibility of scripture. The historical process of doctrinal development seems as unlikely to lead to infallible decisions as the oral transmission of gospel material to lead to an infallible record of the life of Jesus. The element of human fallibility is present in the bishops and theologians of the early church as evidently as it is in the persons of the apostles and evangelists. We have as much reason in the one case as in the other to believe either that fallibility was totally suppressed or that it was incapable of reflecting enough of the inspiration of the divine Spirit to provide us with valuable guidance for the Church's life. [216]

In Wiles' view:

> In the case of the study of Scripture we have gone a long way towards accepting the implications of such critical and empirical study. It was often a painful process; but few of us would want to go back to the security of the old fundamentalism. We know well enough that we have to study the early history of doctrinal development in the same spirit. Up to a point that is what we do. But I do not think we have fully faced the implications of our approach for our attitude to the creeds and other early formulations of doctrinal belief. As far as they are concerned we are still in the painful process of reappraisal and readjustment.
>
> We ought not, therefore, to begin with any preconceived theory concerning the pattern of doctrinal development. We can only proceed by a patient study of historical evidence. We must trace out as carefully as we can the way in which doctrinal belief actually did develop.[217]

---

[216] Wiles, *Making,* p.13.
[217] Wiles, *Making*, p.15.

In chapters 2-5 of his book Wiles seeks to undertake this kind of careful study of the historical evidence concerning the development of doctrine in the Patristic period. He looks in turn at the motives for doctrinal development, the role of Scripture, worship and beliefs about salvation in shaping doctrinal development, the sort of arguments that were used to support doctrinal development, and how new ideas about doctrine came to be assimilated in the course of doctrinal development.

Motives for Development in the Patristic Age
In chapter 2, 'Motives for Development in the Patristic Age,' Wiles argues that there were 'three outstanding motives by which the Church was led on along the path of doctrinal development.' [218]

According to Wiles these three motives:

> ...can be defined epigrammatically as the Church's self-understanding in relation to those outside, in relation to those half outside and half inside her borders, and finally in relation to herself. First was the apologetic motive, the need to express Christian truth in a form that would meet the requirements and answer the objections of the surrounding world. Secondly, there was the problem of heresy, the problem of those who standing to a greater or lesser degree within the fold of the Church, yet defined the tenets of the faith in a manner which seemed to the majority wrong-headed and dangerously mis-leading. Thirdly (though never in isolation from the other two, since no thought is unrelated to its environment), there was the natural desire of some Christians to think out and to think through the implications of their faith as deeply and as fully as possible. [219]

Scripture as a Source of Doctrine
In chapter 3, 'Scripture as a Source of Doctrine,' Wiles considers two questions:

---
[218] Wiles, *Making*, p.19
[219] Wiles, *Making*, p.19.

> What was the effect on the development of doctrine of the fact that the content of the revelation came to be recorded in specific documents? and What was the effect of the particular way in which those documents were regarded and interpreted? [220]

According to Wiles, in the earliest days of the Church the two key sources of Christian doctrine were the Old Testament Scriptures and the oral transmission of the 'specifically Christian content of the faith, both the historical facts and the pattern of their interpretation.' [221] However, by the end of the second century a generally recognized set of New Testament documents came to take the place of oral tradition, and this was a change of great significance.

In Wiles' words:

> The source of the Christian revelation was God himself. Of that there had never been any doubt. The tradition which had been handed down in the life of the Church had been conceived as deriving from the apostles, who had received it from Christ, who in his turn had received it from God. But as long as it was a matter of oral tradition there was room for a measure of flexibility - room, indeed, as experience had shown, for a measure of flexibility too great to be tolerated. So it had proved necessary for that revelation to be recorded in authoritative writings. The author of the revelation was the same, none other than God himself. Christians therefore believe themselves to have within their hands a written record whose ultimate author was God. Once such a conviction was firmly established, Scripture was bound to be the primary conscious source or subsequent doctrine.[222]

Furthermore, two principles followed from the belief that Scripture's ultimate author was God:

---

[220] Wiles, *Making*, p.42.
[221] Wiles, *Making,* p.43.
[222] Wiles, *Making,* pp.45-46.

...the unity of the whole and the significance of detail since God can neither be inconsistent with himself nor do anything without purpose. These two principles of expecting consistency and of paying attention to detail are sensible and important principles for the guidance of any interpreter, but both are capable of being seriously overworked. In the third and fourth centuries both were seriously overworked. [223]

The problem with the application of the first principle was that it led to a view of the relationship between the Old and New Testaments in which there was seen to be 'a unity without diversity, in which the newness of the New Testament was obscured, if not denied altogether.' [224] In Wiles' view:

The primary outcome of this minimising of the difference between the two testaments was an illegitimate reading back into the Old Testament of Christian ideas drawn in reality from the New. Such allegorization of the Old Testament has important repercussions for the student of exegesis; it is relatively unimportant for the student of doctrine. But this kind of evening out the differences between the two Testaments did not always work in the same direction. It could result not only in the Christianizing of the Old Testament but also in the Judaizing of the New. [225]

Wiles gives two examples of such Judaizing:

The outstanding example of this kind is the way in which Paul's teaching about a radical freedom from the curse of the law was tamed in order to make it as wholly consistent as possible with the straightforward teaching of the Old Testament. Another example, less widely recognised but equally far reaching in its effects, is Cyprian's teaching about the Christian ministry. It is well known that in the discussions about the role and function of the ministry

---

[223] Wiles, *Making*, p.47.
[224] Wiles, *Making*, p.49,
[225] Wiles, *Making*, p.50.

which figure so largely in the short but troubled period of his episcopate Cyprian frequently quotes from Old Testament teaching about the Jewish priesthood. A careful study of his writing shows that these quotations are of much more than purely illustrative significance; they are the main ground upon which his ideas are based.[226]

With regard to the second principle, Wiles gives as examples of a misleading interpretation of the details of Scripture Athanasius' use of Proverbs 8:22 and Psalm 110:3 to show the uncreated nature of God the Son, Origen's appeal to John 8:40 and John 11:50 to show that it was the human Jesus rather that the divine Word who died, and Augustine's appeal to the Latin text of Romans 5:12 to show that all human beings sinned in Adam.

At the end of the chapter Wiles declares that: 'Much of the doctrinal work of the early centuries is grounded on the evidence of Scripture in a way to which no exception can be taken.' However, he adds, this

> …is not the whole truth about the way in which Scripture served as a source of doctrine in those early years. We do no service to the cause of truth by laying claim to a perfection in the development of doctrine which was never there. If we are to hold fast to the true, we must be able to distinguish the false. The emphasis on the unity of the whole Bible and the concern for detail could, as I have tried to show, be used in ways which we cannot but regard as wholly invalid. [227]

Lex Orandi

In chapter 4, 'Lex Orandi,' Wiles explores the relationship between doctrine and worship in the Early Church.

He begins his exploration by giving two examples of the influence of worship on the development of doctrine in the New Testament

---
[226] Wiles, *Making*, p.51.
[227] Wiles, *Making*, p.60.

period. The first example is 2 Timothy 2:11-12 'Faithful is the saying: For if we died with him, we shall also live with him; if we endure we shall also reign with him.' According to Wiles, these words are probably a quotation from a baptismal hymn and they 'convey very effectively the Pauline doctrine of baptism as death and resurrection with Christ.' This means that 'liturgical practice has here provided the effective medium for conserving and transmitting to the next generation an important doctrinal concept.'[228] The second example is the use of the divine title 'Lord' to refer to Jesus in 1 Corinthians 16:21 which shows how 'a title given to him in worship and continually used of him in that context helped to give expression to some of the highest Christological affirmations in the whole of the New Testament' [229]

Wiles then goes on to argue that:

> The continuing practice of invoking the name of Jesus in worship helped to ensure that when the time came for more precise doctrinal definition of his person that it would be in terms which did not fall short of his address in worship.[230]

Wiles develops this point by contending that while in the early Church the Church's formal liturgical practice involved 'prayers offered to God through Jesus Christ'[231] popular piety, influenced by Gnosticism, was characterised by the worshipping of Jesus. It was this popular piety that led to rejection of the idea known as 'dynamic monarchianism' which held that Jesus was a man endowed with spiritual power (*dunamis*) by God and led to the development of the idea known as 'modalist monarchianism' that held that the Son was simply a form of mode of the being of God the Father.

---

[228] Wiles, *Making*, p.63.
[229] Wiles, *Making*, p.64.
[230] Wiles, *Making*, p.65.
[231] Wiles, *Making*, p.65.

He then goes on to further declare that Origen held that liturgical prayer should be offered to the Father alone because 'The Father alone is God in the fullest sense of the word' while 'the Son has his deity and the proper attributes of deity in a lesser sense.' [232] However, once Arianism had been defeated, fuelled by the demands of popular piety which worshipped Jesus as God, the result was the development of liturgical prayers being addressed directly to Jesus.

In addition, he goes on to argue that the reason why the Church came to accept the fully divinity of the Holy Spirit, even though this is 'so difficult to establish on scriptural grounds' was 'the fact that baptism was regularly administered in the threefold name of Father, Son and Holy Spirit.'[233]

In summary, declares Wiles:

> Whatever the intellectual merits of Dynamic Monarchianism, Origenist subordinationism and philosophical Arianism, they failed very largely because they did not do justice to Christian apprehension of the Son as a fitting object of worship and adoration. The full divinity of the Holy Spirit could still be doubted more than three and a half centuries after Pentecost, but no one factor was of greater importance for the settlement of the issue than the long-hallowed institution of triple immersion into the threefold name at baptism. [234]

Wiles concludes the chapter by noting, however, that the example of popular Marian piety:

> ...forces us to recognise that popular devotion is no infallible guide. We must be ready to admit that the popular devotion of the ante-Nicene period may have been more powerful as a historical and psychological force leading to the triumph of orthodoxy then it is

---

[232] Wiles, *Making,* p.74.
[233] Wiles, *Making*, p.79.
[234] Wiles, *Making*, pp.87-88.

as a rational ground of appeal for the truth of that doctrine today. It may still serve as one link in the chain of evidence but there are limits to the weight that it can bear by itself. [235]

Furthermore, with regard to the threefold baptism formula in Matthew 28:19:

> If it is evidence that conjoining of the three names in a baptismal context belongs to the earliest stage of the New Testament tradition, it is also evidence that the conjunction was possible without implying identity of role or status to the three persons concerned.[236]

Soteriology

In Chapter 5, 'Soteriology,' Wiles surveys the inter-relationship between understandings of salvation and the development of doctrine in the case of the Arian, Gnostic and Monophysite controversies. He declares:

> From this brief survey it is clear that two great soteriological principles played an immensely important part in the doctrinal debates of the fourth and fifth centuries. On the one hand was the conviction that a saviour must be fully divine; on the other was the conviction that what is not assumed is not healed. Or, to put the matter in other words, the source of salvation must be God; the locus of salvation must be man. It is quite clear that these two principles often pulled in opposite directions. The council of Chalcedon was the Church's attempt to resolve, or perhaps rather to agree to live with that tension. Indeed, to accept both principles as strongly as did the early Church is already to accept the Chalcedonian faith.[237]

He then suggests that:

---

[235] Wiles, *Making*, p.90.
[236] Wiles, *Making*, p.91.
[237] Wiles, *Making*, p.106.

If then these two principles are of such paramount importance, we must not shirk a critical examination of them and of their outworking working in the early doctrinal debates. How, we must ask, can we be so sure of the truth of these two axioms - that only a fully divine saviour can save and what is not assumed is not healed? Are they necessary presuppositions for all theological reasoning? Certainly, they can be stated in a form which makes them appear to be self-evident propositions. That only God can be the author of ultimate salvation seems to follow from any adequate understanding of the word 'God.' Similarly, it seems to follow from the very meaning of the word 'salvation' that it must reach down to where man is. But when stated in this bare form the axioms are of little value for determining the true expression of Christian doctrine. We may still ask whether it would not be possible for God to be the ultimate author of salvation and man the recipient without the agent or mediator of that salvation being himself necessarily of a fully divine or fully human nature - let alone both.[238]

As Wiles sees it:

...If salvation be thought of in personal terms, then its effective outworking is through the experience of divine grace in the human soul. Whatever media may be involved, the locus of salvation is the sphere of ordinary personal existence in which God establishes fellowship with man. Is this experience of divine grace, then, a meeting of the fully divine and fully human of the kind which the soteriological principle defines as a necessary precondition for the realisation of man's salvation? Difficulties arise whatever answer we give to that question. In one sense the experience of divine grace is a meeting of the human and the divine. But if we return an affirmative answer to our question, the whole argument of the Fathers falls to the ground. For it was of the essence of Athanasius' case against the early Antiochenes that on soteriological grounds

---

[238] Wiles, *Making*, pp.106-107.

Christ must be unique and not just a supreme example of saint or prophet; the heart of the soteriological argument was that it required there to be in Christ a meeting of the fully divine and the fully human which is different in kind from that which characterises the experience of divine grace in ordinary human life. But if we therefore return a negative answer, a different problem arises. Why should the axioms of salvation which we have been considering be a requisite condition in the primary archetypal instance of the life of Christ but not be applicable to the outworking in contemporary human experience of the salvation which he brought? If salvation be understood to be that personal knowledge of God which is open to man through divine grace, can its achievement require as of logical necessity the prior existence of a divine human meeting of a radically different and superior kind?[239]

The Form of the Arguments

In chapter 6, 'The Form of the Arguments,' Wiles moves on to consider the form of argument that was employed in the development of doctrine in the Patristic period.

He begins by noting that the 'framework of thought in terms of which early doctrine was developed was provided by Greek philosophy' [240] In his view this framework led to:

> ...an approach to theology in which its affirmations are regarded as descriptive accounts (albeit very imperfect accounts) of ultimate realities existing in the spiritual world. The fact that patristic theology grew up against such a background gave it an ontological urge and an ontological confidence which are both its glory and its weakness. [241]

---

[239] Wiles, *Making,* pp.111-112.
[240] Wiles, *Making,* p.115.
[241] Wiles, *Making,* p.118.

As his first example of the problems resulting from this ontological urge and ontological confidence Wiles points to the issue of Eucharistic theology:

> At the last supper Jesus spoke of the bread which he gave to his disciples as his body. Paul in his epistles wrote of the Church as the body of Christ. Both concepts are rich in religious meaning and have entered deeply into the piety of Christians throughout the ages. In neither instance is it self-evident that the statement is a definition, whose meaning can be properly elucidated in terms of substance and accidents, yet that is in course of time how the former affirmation has come to be regarded. [242]

Also on the issue of Eucharistic theology, Wiles observes that the Eucharist came to be seen both as 'the body and blood of Christ which we receive for the nourishment of our spiritual lives' and the pure offering or sacrifice prophesied in Malachi 1:11.[243] According to Wiles:

> Each of these concepts has a clear and distinctive meaning of its own. They bring out different aspects of what is happening in the religious reality of eucharistic worship. But if each be treated as an ontological affirmation describing in some absolute sense the nature of the eucharistic elements end of the eucharistic action, then it becomes natural to coordinate them in a new way. If the elements *are* the body and blood of Christ and the offering *is* a sacrifice, then the eucharist as a whole must be a sacrificial offering of the body and blood of Christ. This concept we find explicitly affirmed in the teaching of Cyprian. But the composite idea thus created is in fact something very different from the ideas of the two component parts before they had been thus combined.

---

[242] Wiles, *Making*, pp.118-119.
[243] Wiles, *Making*, p.121.

It is my contention this kind of combination of concepts without reference to their contextual difference is a very dangerous form of theological construction. [244]

As his second example Wiles points to the development of Trinitarian theology. He argues that this developed in two contradictory stages:

In the first stage differences between the persons of the Trinity are recognised and on the strength of these differences the distinctness of the persons is established. In the second stage the full co-equality of the persons is established by denying all differences between them, necessarily including those differences which were the initial evidence for asserting the distinct existence of the three persons. This process therefore involves not merely the forgetting but the practical repudiation of the lines of argument used at the earliest stage. If we put together the basic reasoning of the ante-Nicene and the post-Nicene periods, the outcome reads something like this: to fail to distinguish the persons of the Father and the Son and thereby to involve the Father in the experiences of the incarnation is to commit the enormity of Patripassianism, involving the impossible Father in suffering. The incarnation and crucifixion must therefore be affirmed of the Son who is co-equally impassible with the Father.[245]

Furthermore, argues Wiles:

If the principle that the persons of the Trinity never act towards the world in separation from one another (*opera trinitatis ad extra sunt indivisa*) is accepted as a summary of orthodox conviction on the matter, then only one kind of argument is left open for the establishment of the anti - modalist case by which the distinctness of the persons is demonstrated. It cannot be derived from reflection upon our response to the divine activity at all; it can only

---

[244] Wiles, *Making*, p.122.
[245] Wiles, *Making*, p.127.

be known if it has been imparted to us as a verbal disclosure about the inner nature of the godhead in Scripture or the apostolic tradition…Patristic reasoning about the Trinity can only be saved from the charge of inconsistency by allowing that it is grounded on an appeal to scripture of a kind which is totally at variance with one that would find general acceptance in the modern world. [246]

Finally, Wiles claims that it is paradoxical to follow the Cappadocian fathers by 'affirming a co-equal Trinity whose members stand to one another in relation of cause to effect' [247] and goes on to observe that:

> Quite apart from the particular nature of the distinctions affirmed, there seems to be an arbitrariness about the claim that they leave the divine simplicity unimpaired. If the unity and simplicity of the divine *ousia* are compatible with its existence in three distinguishable *hupostaseis*, it is difficult to see why they should not be equally compatible with a modalist - or to use the word most commonly used in the Eastern Church, a Sabellian - interpretation also, according to which the one God expressed himself in different modes, now as Father, now as Son, now as Holy Spirit, as his purposes of self-revelation to the world may require. The Cappadocians could argue that since the three *hupostasesis* are eternal and permanent existences, their understanding preserves, as the Sabellian does not, the eternal changelessness of God. It is not easy to feel that they also preserved his full simplicity. [248]

According to Wiles, the lesson to be drawn from the development of Trinitarian theology is the need to think about God in a different way:

> If in attempting to give philosophical expression to conflicting aspects of our experience, we are led to an apparently irreconcilable antinomy in our thinking, we do best to go back to the apparent conflict in experience in the hope that in due course

---

[246] Wiles, *Making*, pp.128-129.
[247] Wiles, *Making*, p.137.
[248] Wiles, *Making*, p.137.

some other form of philosophical expression may throw new light upon our problem. [249]

The Assimilation of New Ideas
In chapter 7 'The Assimilation of New Ideas' Wiles argues that there are two methods by which new ideas can be incorporated into an existing pattern of thought. The first is 'the assimilation of new ideas by the addition of new refinements to the old' and the second is 'the assimilation of new ideas by modification of the old.' [250]

According to Wiles the Fathers preferred the former approach, but in reality, what they achieved was often a compromise between the two approaches. In his words:

> ...the general aim of the Fathers was always to accommodate any new ideas in the way which involved the least possible alteration to the officially formulated notions of the past. In practise the two methods were not always as clearly distinct as I have described them. The facts usually constitute something of a compromise between the two. There was usually some modification of the old pattern but not enough to incorporate the new ideas altogether satisfactorily into a new synthesis. The far-reaching effect of a difference of method at this point can be illustrated by the comparison of two closely related doctrines whose development is distinctly different on this score. [251]

Wiles' first example concerns the doctrine of the Trinity. As he sees it, the earliest Fathers followed the Old Testament and Greek philosophical thought by teaching 'an undifferentiated divine unity of an essentially mathematical kind.' [252] By contrast, the Cappadocian Fathers in the fourth century attempted 'to incorporate the new ideas of the full and substantial divinity of the Son and the Spirit into the old

---

[249] Wiles, *Making*, p.140.
[250] Wiles, *Making*, p.143.
[251] Wiles, *Making*, p.144.
[252] Wiles, *Making*, p.145.

pattern of monotheistic faith by a modification of the idea of unity as previously understood.'[253]

Wiles' second example is the failure of the Fathers to make the same kind of modification in the case of the doctrines of the Church and of baptism. With regard to the doctrine of the Church Augustine accepted the validity of baptisms that took place in schismatic groups without modifying Cyprian's teaching that such groups were not part of the Church. Similarly, the penitential system, and ultimately the idea of purgatory, developed as a way of dealing with post baptismal sin without modifying the ideas that baptism only dealt with the sins of the past and was unrepeatable.

According to Wiles, the fundamental problem with the Fathers' treatment of these two issues 'was a tendency to treat earlier convictions as irrevocably fixed, the failure to modify the old pattern of belief into which new ideas were being fitted.' The doctrines of the Trinity and of the person of Christ did undergo modification but only at the cost of the Cappadocians including some 'serious inconsistencies' in their account of the Trinity and the Antiochene Fathers 'having to incorporate directly paradoxical language' into their affirmations about the person of Christ. [254]

In Wiles' view the only way for them to have avoided this would have through a 'complete reorientation 'of their thinking and this fact 'may perhaps provide a glimpse of how drastic and how difficult a process any fruitful development of doctrine in the future is likely to prove.' [255]

Towards a Doctrine of Development
In his final chapter, 'Towards a Doctrine of Development,' Wiles notes that his survey of the development of doctrine in the Early Church'

---

[253] Wiles, *Making*, p.146.
[254] Wiles, *Making,* pp.157-158.
[255] Wiles, *Making*, p.158.

has noted 'a number of points at which the Fathers' reasoning 'seems to me to be open to serious criticism.' [256] However, he says:

> Even if the reasoning of the Fathers be judged to have serious weaknesses in the form in which it was first put forward, we must not conclude too hastily that it is altogether worthless, and its conclusions completely discredited.[257]

In the light of these considerations, he goes on to look at 'the central Christian doctrine of the divinity of Christ' and specifically what he calls the 'three great grounds of appeal, Scripture, worship and soteriology.' [258]

According to Wiles the 'outstanding characteristic of the witness of Scripture in the matter is its ambiguity'. Thus, John 10:30 'I and my Father are one' points one way, and Mark 10:18 'Why callest thou me good? There is none good but one, that is God' points in the other. Furthermore, texts such as Philippians 1:5 'being in the form of God' do not support the teaching of the Father's as directly as they thought.' [259]

With regard to worship, Wiles claims that:

> At the point where the worship of Christ was of decisive significant doctrine, it was a question of popular devotion rather than formal liturgical worship. Popular devotion is not without significance but it is no infallible guide. Its history is full of examples of confusion between the medium and the ultimate object of worship, between the image and the reality. It is not clear that we are in a position to rule out the possibility of something of the same kind having happened in this case also.[260]

---

[256] Wiles, *Making*, p.159.
[257] Wiles, *Making*, p.162.
[258] Wiles, *Making*, p.162.
[259] Wiles, *Making*, p.163.
[260] Wiles, *Making*, p.164.

Finally in the case of soteriology, writes Wiles, we cannot presume to say how God must have acted, the appeal to Scripture suffers from the problems he has already noted and it 'is not easy to see how our present experience could be decisive evidence for the precise nature and manner of God's active presence in Jesus.' [261]

All this means, declares, Wiles, that 'the main lines of patristic argument for the divinity of Jesus are not worthless, but they do not seem to me to be decisive either.' [262]

For Wiles what this conclusion means is that:

> True continuity with the age of the Fathers is to be sought not so much in the repetition of their doctrinal conclusions or even in building upon them, but rather in the continuation of their doctrinal aims. Their doctrinal affirmations are based upon an appeal to the record of Scripture, the activity of worship, and the experience of salvation. Should not true development be seen in the continuation of the attempt to do justice to these three strands of Christian life in the contemporary world? If we accept that development is to be understood in such terms, we cannot rule out in advance the possibility that it could involve shifts in doctrinal affirmation as radical as those embodied for science in the Copernican revolution, or reversals of judgement as drastic as those envisaged in the case of religious liberty or (hypothetically) of contraception. Father Baum quotes contemporary concern, both Christian and secular, with the question Who is man? as the basis for a changed outlook on sexuality calling for a new development in teaching about contraception. Such changes in the understanding of human nature, vividly illustrated but not exclusively delineated by the teaching of Freud, have their relevance for every sphere of Christian doctrine.

---

[261] Wiles, *Making*, p,166.
[262] Wiles, *Making*, p.166.

The idea of doctrinal revolution is therefore not something of which we have cause to be afraid. Indeed, in view of all the contemporary changes in man's understanding of himself and his world, it is something to be expected. Judging from the analogy of the history of science, it need not prove as totally destructive of past ideas as it is likely at first to appear to be. It may be the only, even though painful, path to constructive advance.[263]

Wiles ends the chapter, and the book, by suggesting that the shape that new doctrinal thinking should take is to stop trying to talk about God's being and to talk instead about what God does. Rather than talking about the Triune nature of God and the two natures of Christ we should instead talk about the work God does for us in Christ and the response this elicits from us[264]

In the *Remaking of Christian Doctrine* which we shall look at next, Wiles discusses this idea in more detail.

3. The Remaking of Christian Doctrine

The Remaking of Christian Doctrine is the published version of the Hulsean Lectures given by Wiles at the University of Cambridge in 1973 after he had moved to be Regius Professor of Divinity in Oxford. As he explains in his introduction to this book, the aim of the lectures and of the book was to apply 'the insights gained' from the study of doctrinal development undertaken in *The Making of Christian Doctrine* 'more directly to the work of contemporary Christian Doctrine.'[265]

As he goes on to write, the purpose of his lectures is to apply these insights to: 'the central area of Christian Doctrine – our understanding

---

[263] Wiles, *Making*, pp.173-174.
[264] Wiles, *Making*, pp. 174-179.
[265] Maurice Wiles, *The Remaking of Christian Doctrine* (London: SCM, 1974), p.1

of God and his relation to the world in the spheres of creation, redemption and grace.' [266]

He then further adds that his twin objectives in discussing these matters are 'coherence' and 'economy.' He unpacks these two terms as follows:

> Within the rich field of Christian doctrine as a whole, different themes may be taken up on different occasions and each may properly be developed in relative independence of the other. We do not need to be concerned all the time about the way in which one area of discourse relates to all the others. But coherence remains an important goal. We do need to check whether the different affirmations that we are led to make at various times and for various purposes are consistent with one another. A concern for coherence only becomes objectionable and deserving of the appropriate title of 'rationalism' if the criteria of consistency are regarded as fixed in advance and rigidly applied without adequate sensitivity to the particular nature of the subject matter involved.

> Similarly, there are occasions on which an imaginative expansiveness is the most appropriate path to follow in seeking to give expression to reduce realities. But such imaginative expressiveness requires the doctrinal theologians concern for 'economy' as a kind of dialectical partner in the attempt of the church as a whole to find the most adequate expression of the truth. The tradition in which we live does not stand still. It is constantly changing, and we have a role to play in guiding the direction which those changes shall take. One important contribution to the fulfilling of that role lies in drawing distinctions between what the evidence requires us to say and what the evidence does not disallow us from saying. It is an insistence on

---

[266] Wiles, *Remaking*, p.15.

distinguishing what the evidence requires us to say that I have in mind in speaking of the objective of 'economy.' [267]

In his introduction Wiles also sets out his preferred model for conceiving the nature of doctrinal development. He writes:

> One might call it change through alteration of perspective. Different cultural and philosophical conditions require different understandings and articulation of the Christian faith. The element of identity will be much more difficult to define. It will have to be looked for in the sources to which reference is made, the kinds of concern which direct that reference and the general pattern or character of the affirmations made. [268]

Following the introduction, Wiles' second book consists of four chapters looking at 'God,' 'The Person of Christ,' 'The Work of Christ' and 'Grace and the Holy Spirit.' These chapters are followed by a chapter of 'Final Reflections' and an appendix on 'The Resurrection of the Body' which was not part of the original lectures but was added by Wiles to 'develop the same approach in relation to a more specific item of Christian belief.' [269]

God

In his chapter on God Wiles makes two points about God

First, he says that God must be seen as the transcendent creator. As he puts it:

> ...everything that suggests the validity of belief in God at all points to belief in his transcendence. The 'absoluteness' of Schleiermacher's feeling of absolute dependence and the 'ultimacy' of Tillich's 'ultimate concern' must be taken with full seriousness. However much it might seem to ease the intransigent problem of evil, there is no going back on the Christian conviction of creation

---

[267] Wiles, *Remaking*, pp.17-18.
[268] Wiles, *Remaking*, p.7.
[269] Wiles, *Remaking*, Preface.

ex nihilo. Implicit in awareness of God is awareness of that which is the source and the ground of everything else.[270]

Furthermore, belief in God as creator is linked to a belief that there is 'an overall and ultimate purposiveness' to what happens in creation.[271]

Secondly, he argues that we should believe that God acts 'in a general and universal manner' rather than having a 'special and different relationship' to certain events as Christians have traditionally affirmed. Wiles concedes that 'the idea of some special relationship of God to particular events is not to be excluded in advance as logically absurd' but then adds 'logical possibility is not enough to justify positive affirmation.'[272]

Referring to Jesus' teaching about God clothing the lilies of the field (Matthew 6:28), Wiles declares:

> Certain events happen in the world; the possibility of that happening derives (as with all other events) from the absolute dependence on the world as a whole upon God. But particular events by virtue of their intrinsic character or the results to which they give rise give (like the beauty of the lilies) particular expression to some aspect of God's creative purpose for the world as a whole. They are occasions which arouse in us, either at the time or in retrospect, a sense of divine purpose. But that sense does not necessarily entail any special divine activity in those particular events. Insofar as it is a genuinely rooted sense of purpose to which they give rise, it is by pointing to a purposiveness within the world as a whole.
>
> Talk of God's activity is, then, to be understood as a way of speaking about those events within the natural order or within

---

[270] Wiles, *Remaking*, p.33.
[271] Wiles, *Remaking*, p.34.
[272] Wiles, *Remaking*, pp.36-37.

human history in which God's purpose finds clear expression or special opportunity. [273]

The person and work of Christ

In his chapter on the person of Christ, Wiles insists on our: 'inability to draw firm lines of demarcation between what is true of Jesus himself and what is true of the initial response to him revealed in the New Testament writings' [274] This means that in constructing a Christology we have to consider what it was that drove the first Christians to speak of Jesus in terms of God and to 'associate God's redemptive work so totally with the events of his life, death and resurrection.' [275]

Wiles notes that for some:

> ...it will seem that their accounts run so sharply counter to their monotheistic pre-suppositions that they are only explicable if Jesus was indeed more than a prophet, nothing less than the incarnate Son of God that later orthodoxy has declared him to be.[276]

Wiles, however, declares that his own 'tentative judgement' is that it is not the case that an adequate explanation of the New Testament evidence can only be provided 'by giving a special evaluation to Jesus himself of the unique kind that Christian orthodoxy has in fact given.'[277]

As he sees it, the only way to decide the issue is through: 'reflection on what must be true to make sense of the religious understanding of the world as a whole to which the Christian tradition points.'[278]

---

[273] Wiles, *Remaking*, p.38.
[274] Wiles, *Remaking*, p.50.
[275] Wiles, *Remaking*, p.54.
[276] Wiles, *Remaking*, p.54.
[277] Wiles, *Remaking*, p.54.
[278] Wiles, *Remaking*, p.59.

On this basis Wiles then goes on in his chapter on the work of Christ to consider whether the Chistian belief in the need for human beings to be forgiven and transformed 'shows the necessity of an incarnational doctrine?'[279]

In this chapter he makes three negative points.

First, he argues that the various traditional understandings of the atonement, as a victory over the devil, as a penalty for the human transgression of God's law, as a sacrifice and as a reversal of the sin of Adam, all need to be abandoned today and therefore cannot be appealed to in support of an incarnational Christology.

Secondly, he argues that what is vital for Christian theism is the 'continuing self-identification of God with the sufferings of men and women' and that:

> ...The truth or otherwise of that conviction is not determined by the truth or otherwise of a different order of divine self-identification with suffering in the person of Jesus. There does not seem to be any ground for claiming that the former is either causally dependent on or qualitatively transformed by the latter.[280]

Thirdly, he contends that 'even the hope of resurrection is not logically dependent on invoking 'something beyond history, something transcendent' in the resurrection event of a kind which we would not properly invoke in relation to any other event in history.'[281]

Having made these three points Wiles then gives his own attempt to 'do justice to those things that the earlier doctrinal affirmations had enshrined.' He suggests that there are two things that are required for this purpose, and which are present in all forms of Christian atonement theory:

[279] Wiles, *Remaking*, p.61.
[280] Wiles, *Remaking*, p.72.
[281] Wiles, *Remaking*, pp.76-77.

The first is that Christ's passion is in some way a demonstration of what is true of God's eternal nature. This is clearly true of those who see in it an objective act of God himself. There is no wedge between God's acts and his nature. What he does must be expressive of what he is. Whatever else they may feel needs to be said about the atonement, it will certainly include this affirmation. Those who have criticized such so-called objective theories have usually done so because either they cannot accept, or they cannot attach any meaning to that something more. They have not wished to deny that the death of Christ exemplifies the love of God. That indeed has been the heart of what they do have themselves wanted to affirm.

The second feature is one less often given explicit mention in any discussion of atonement doctrine, but which is normally assumed and should, I think, be made more explicit. That is the recognition that the passion of Christ has been remarkably effective as an historical phenomenon in the transformation of human lives. Christianity is always in a quandary in any apologetic appeal to historical results. They are not negligible, but they are ambiguous, and certainly do not go far in justifying any absolutist or divine claims that the church may want to make. And this applies to the passion as well as to any other aspect of the faith. It has given rise to morbid and masochistic responses as well as to those which we would judge to be spiritually transformations of a profoundly impressive and valuable kind. But we're not using the notion here apologetically so much as simply descriptively. If it is objected that subjective theories of the atonement are inadequate, because for them the passion is merely exhibitive and not performative, because they do not allow that the passion actually does anything - that objection cannot be sustained in any complete way. In the world of historical experience, the passion has done much and continues to do much: nor are there grounds for limiting its potential effectiveness in the future. [282]

Grace and the Holy Spirit

Having argued that our understanding of the work of Christ needs to be re-configured in this way, Wiles undertakes a similar exercise in his chapter on 'Grace and the Holy Spirit.' In this chapter Wiles argues that rather than seeing language about the Holy Spirit and Grace in terms of the third person of the Trinity acting in certain specific ways, whether this is in terms of the inspiration of Scripture, sacramental grace, or bringing people into a right relationship with God more generally, we should instead be content to give a more generalised account of how God is constantly at work in the world by means of human religious experience:

> In outline form the account would go something like this. Man has been created with a capacity for awareness of God and of an ultimate divine purpose for the world. This capacity can become actual through general reflection on the world in which we live. But it is not in fact realised equally and uniformly in all the varied conditions of human existence. Some aspects of human experience give rise to it more frequently and more profoundly than others. In the experience of our culture the records of the Christ event and occasions of worship which focus on that event are particularly powerful agents in giving rise to such awareness…Since it is an awareness which concerns the ultimate character of the world as a whole, it necessarily includes awareness of my own place in and my own relation to the whole. It cannot by its very nature leave me unaffected. It has the power to affect my attitudes and my actions at the deepest level of my being. The particular kinds of attitudes or action to which it gives rise cannot be prescribed in detail in advance. They will be in part dependent on the particular changing circumstances in which I happened to be. They will be the outcome of an interaction between those contingent circumstances and the

[282] Wiles, *Remaking*, pp.79-80.

larger concept of an eternal divine purpose (itself, of course, only imperfectly glimpsed from the restricted standpoint of my own situation).

These, I want to suggest, are the characteristics of religious experience that give rise to talk about grace and about the Holy Spirit. The limits of human experience cannot be fully defined or predicted. Man's imaginative and active faculties can be expanded by the vision of God in ways that continue to excite and to surprise us. It is these features which justify the kind of language that is to be found both in the tradition and on the lips of ordinary religious people. But when we speak of particular occasions - whether the inspiration of Scripture, a eucharistic service, the history of the church, the lives of the Saints or even special experiences of our own - as scenes of the Holy Spirit's activity, we need not (indeed I will be bold enough to say we ought not) imply thereby that they are occasions in which some special supernatural causation is to be looked for. Such a description should rather, I suggest, be understood to mean that here are places where the purpose of God has been apprehended, expressed or put into effect in a particularly profound way. In other words, language about the Holy Spirit is language designed to describe the occasions in which the divine purpose finds effective realization in human life. [283]

Final Reflections

In his concluding chapter, 'Final reflections,' Wiles pulls together the various threads of the argument he wants to present through his lectures by declaring, first of all, that he is not calling on Christian theologians:

> ...to abandon all the old imagery. It is indeed incumbent upon him to continue to draw upon it, for it contains within itself the only available resources of meaning to express vividly the very realities that he desires to express. He may do so with the fullest integrity

[283] Wiles, *Remaking*, pp.101-102.

provided the understanding of that imagery is all the time being modified by its interaction with critical questioning of the kind that I have been trying to pursue here. [284]

Having made this point, he then sets out what he thinks this modified understanding of the meaning of traditional Christian religious imagery would look like. What he says is as follows.

First, concerning God as creator, he declares:

> We speak of the world as God's handiwork. Our knowledge of the evolutionary development of the world means that when we spell out that belief in detail we are bound to do so in ways very different from our forefathers. But that does not evacuate the conviction of its religious importance; nor does it destroy the underlying reality of the world's ontological dependence on God which is the ultimate basis of such pictorial language. We speak of certain events in history as acts of God. Our approach to the understanding of world history means that when we spell out that belief in detail we are most likely to do so in ways very different from our forefathers. But that does not evacuate the language of all religious meaning, or undermine the truth that there are particular events which have embodied and forwarded the purpose of God for the world of his creation.[285]

Secondly, concerning the grace of God he states:

> We speak of God's presence and God's power in the experience of grace. Our approach to understanding of human personality and of human motivation means that when we spell out that belief in more detail we may well be led to do so in ways very different from our forefathers. But that does nothing to detract from the profound importance of those occasions when a man acknowledges and responds with his full self to all that he has

---

[284] Wiles, *Remaking*, p.121.
[285] Wiles, *Remaking*, p.121.

come to know of God and of God's purposes for good; nor does it diminish the transforming power that such experiences can have on all the rest of his life.[286]

Thirdly, concerning the significance of Jesus he writes:

> We speak of God's unique, incarnate presence in the life of Jesus. Within the unity provided by a hallowed formula this has already been understood in a variety of very different ways down the ages. The reflections I have been trying to share lead me to the conclusion that here too our spelling out of that conviction will be increasingly different - moving, it may be, altogether outside the possible bounds of the ancient hallowed formulae. But even here there will be a continuity of religious reality in the conviction that it is supremely through Jesus that the character of these purposes of God and the possibility of this experience of grace has been grasped and made effective in the world. If we speak of him as unique and his claims as universal, the appropriate meaning to be given to such affirmations would seem to be two-fold. They bear witness to the radical nature of the transforming effect in the lives of those who have responded to him; and they express the conviction (which only time can test) that he will continue to fulfil that role in the future, however different the conditions of life may become. [287]

The Resurrection of the Body

In his appendix on 'The resurrection of the body, Wiles continues his radical approach to the re-thinking of traditional Christian belief.

In this appendix he declares, negatively, that the accounts of the bodily resurrection of Jesus are 'irrelevant to the nature of our resurrection' because:

---

[286] Wiles, *Remaking*, pp.121-122.
[287] Wiles, *Remaking*, p.122.

> It seems clear that the bodily aspect to the resurrection stories is directly linked to communication with the still living disciples. In other words, its context is in relation to the physical existence of the disciples. It cannot be extrapolated from that context and used as evidence for the nature of resurrection life itself. [288]

His positive argument is that:

> ...The Christian hope of life after death may not, despite all the obvious difficulties, be an unreasonable belief, if it is closely integrated with belief in God. I have argued that we are equally unable to imagine it, whether we attempt to do so in terms of a disembodied soul - substance, of a spiritual body or as some more fully corporate form of existence, but that this is not necessarily a fatal objection to the belief. I have also argued but there is much less difference between the two formulations in terms of resurrection of the body and immortality of the soul than is usually claimed. I have suggested that there is an advantage from a Christian point of view in resurrection language, but I have expressed serious doubts about the advantages often claimed for body language in his context. All such language has of course to be seen as extremely indirect symbolic language and not as a description of what will be. 'Brethren, we are the children of God; It does not yet appear what we shall be' [1 John 3:2]. The Christian, even or rather especially the Christian theologian, should not be ashamed to express a like agnosticism. [289]

4. Schleiermacher's ghost – assessing Wiles' arguments concerning the development of doctrine

What we can say by way of summary is that *The Making of Christian Doctrine* is a ground clearing exercise which seeks to demonstrate that we cannot in good conscience continue to accept the traditional forms of theology development by the Fathers and reflected in the

---

[288] Wiles, *Remaking*, p.139.
[289] Wiles, *Remaking*, p.146.

Creeds and in the Chalcedonian Confession because both the theological approach taken by the Fathers and the content of their theology are unconvincing in the contemporary world.

The Remaking of Christian Doctrine is a follow up work, which, to continue the construction metaphor, erects a new doctrinal superstructure on the ground that has thus been cleared. In this book Wiles argues that we must abandon the traditional doctrines of revelation, the Trinity, Christology and soteriology along with the doctrine of bodily resurrection. What he offers instead is a unitarian theology, in which God is the transcendent creator who wills the well-being of his creatures and who is known by reflection on human experience of the world. According to Wiles, God never engages in specific forms of activity which differ from his uniform activity in upholding the world that he has made, and Jesus is a human being who exemplifies a proper response to God and thus enables other people to respond rightly to God as well. What we have to look forward to after death is unclear, but in Wiles' view we need not believe that it will include bodily resurrection.

At first reading, these two accounts of the development of Christian doctrine can appear extremely convincing. Wiles writes in a very clear and logical fashion and gives lots of references and examples to back up the case he is making. His work can be recommended to anyone who wants a really good example of why the case for a revolutionary reworking of Christian doctrine appeared to be such an attractive idea to many Anglican theologians, and many ordinary Anglicans as well, in the 1960s and 70s.

However, deeper reflection shows that the case which seem so persuasive at first sight is in fact deeply problematic for two reasons.

The first reason it is deeply problematic is that most of the arguments put forward in his ground clearing exercise in *The Making of Christian Doctrine* simply do not hold water. For example:

a. The Fathers did not 'tame' Paul's teaching about a radical freedom from the curse of the law. Like Paul they held that the law shows us we are sinners, that we are saved from our enslavement to sin by the work of Christ received through faith, but that as saved people we have to live in accordance with the moral law that the Old Testament contains.[290]

b. There is no evidence that it was popular piety that caused the development of belief in the divinity of Christ. Rather this popular piety reflected a belief in the divinity of Christ that had existed from the earliest days of the Church. [291]

c. Although Matthew 28:19 does not imply identity of role between the three persons (as Matthew's Gospel makes clear, they have distinct roles) it does indicate equality of divine status. The 'name' of God, who God is, is the Father, the Son and the Holy Spirit.[292] There is one divine identity which all three persons share.

d. The Fathers of the fourth century did not institute a change in the understanding of the divine unity. Throughout the Patristic period it was understood that there was one divine nature which the Father, Son and Holy Spirit all possessed in common. What the Fathers of the fourth century did was to reaffirm this belief in the face of the denial of it by the Arians and the Macedonians.

---

[290] For this see, for example, Ardel B. Caneday, *The Doctrine of Grace in the theology of Polycarp*, at:
https://www.academia.edu/102400491/The_Doctrine_of_Grace_in_the_Theology_of_Polycarp and Thomas Schreiner, *Faith Alone – The Doctrine of Justification* (Grand Rapids: Zondervan Academic, 2015), Ch.2 'Sola Fide in the Early Fathers.'
[291] See Larry Hurtado, *Lord Jesus Christ – Devotion to Jesus in Earliest Christianity* (Grand Rapids and Cambridge: Eerdmans, 2003).
[292] 'The Father, the Son and the Holy Spirit' names the newly disclosed identity of God, revealed in the story the Gospel has told,' Richard Bauckham, *Jesus and the God of Israel* (Milton Keynes: Authentic, 2008) p.57.

e. Similarly, it is not the case that the ante-Nicene Fathers argued for the Trinity by stressing the differences between the Son and the Father, while the Nicene Fathers then reversed this position and stressed their identity. For example, both the ante-Nicene and Nicene Fathers held that that it was the Son rather than the Father who suffered and died on the cross, and both held that the divine nature of the Son was impassible.

f. Wiles' statement that 'the full divinity of the Holy Spirit could still be doubted more than three and a half centuries after Pentecost' is true in so far as there were people at that time who doubted it, but it is also case that by so doing they fell into heresy by departing from a general acceptance of the divinity of the Spirit alongside the Father and Son that had existed from the earliest days of the Church. The existence of heresy does not rule out the existence (or truthfulness) of orthodoxy. [293]

g. Mark 10:18 does not involve a denial that Jesus is God, rather, this is precisely the claim that is being made. In the words of Simon Gathercole, the point that is being made in Mark 10:17-22 is that 'If God alone is good and able to give commandments, then Jesus does so as well. By implication, then, he is good. And he is good not in the sense implied by the rich man, but in the absolute, divine sense as used by Jesus himself.'[294]

---

[293] For the evidence for what is said in the last three paragraphs see the magisterial study by George Bull, *A Defence of the Nicene Creed* in *Bishop Bull's Works on the Trinity* (London: J H Parker, 1851).

[294] Simon Gathercole, *The Pre-existent Son – Recovering the Christologies of Matthew, Mark and Luke* (Grand Rapids: Eerdmans, 2006), p.74. See also Brant Pitre, *Jesus and divine Christology* (Grand Rapids: Eerdmans, 2024), Kindle edition, pp. 171-182.

h. It is true that salvation involves 'personal knowledge of God which is open to man through divine grace' but it does not follow on from this that the Fathers were wrong to teach that 'the unassumed is the unhealed'. This is because according to Scripture and the Fathers the result of sin is a spiritual darkness that only the assumption and consequent re-creation of human nature by God himself at the incarnation can dispel. That is the significance, for instance, of Jesus's declaration in John 8:12 'I am the light of the word; he who follows me will not walk in darkness but have the light of life.' It is because Jesus is God the Son who has taken human nature upon himself (the meaning of the words 'I am') that those who follow him (in the sense of becoming baptised believers) will not continue in the spiritual darkness that leads to eternal death, but will have the saving knowledge of God that leads to eternal life.

The answer to Wiles' question 'If salvation be understood to be that personal knowledge of God which is open to man through divine grace, can its achievement require as of logical necessity the prior existence of a divine-human meeting of a radically different kind?' is thus 'Yes, it does.' This is because what divine grace does is enable us to receive the new form of human existence that the assumption of human nature by the second person of the Trinity has made possible.

i. The argument that the Cappadocian Fathers failed to uphold the 'full simplicity' of God Is unconvincing because what the simplicity of God means is that each of God's attributes is identical with God's essence. The Cappadocian teaching that God exists as three persons distinguished only by their relationships of origin is not in tension with this truth since it holds that each of the three persons is 'really identical with the divine essence existing in a certain manner' (this is the truth spelled out in the Athanasian Creed).[295]

j. It is true that the Fathers (like the New Testament) held that baptism involves the washing away of the sins of the past, but the orthodox position was not that there was therefore no way of dealing with post-baptismal sin. The idea that the Church's penitential system and its later teaching about purgatory were additions designed to modify this idea is therefore mistaken. [296]

What these examples, and others that could be cited, show is that Wiles' argument that we need a radical re-think of Christian doctrine because the form of doctrine developed by the Fathers lacked an adequate basis in Scripture and its development was self-contradictory falls by the wayside. The evidence he puts forward simply does not support either claim.

The second reason that Wiles' case is deeply problematic is because of the problems involved in the view of God's relationship with the world that he sets out in *The Remaking of Christian Doctrine*.

As we have seen, in this book Wiles argues that while God has created and still upholds the created order, he does not act in specific ways within it. To quote the key section from the book once again:

> Certain events happen in the world; the possibility of that happening derives (as with all other events) from the absolute dependence on the world as a whole upon God. But particular events by virtue of their intrinsic character or the results to which they give rise give (like the beauty of the lilies) particular

---

[295] See Matt Slick, 'Is Divine Simplicity compatible with the Trinity?' CARM, March 29, 2019 at: https://carm.org/doctrine-and-theology/is-divine-simplicity-compatible-with-the-trinity and Steven Duby, *Divine Simplicity – A Dogmatic Account* (London and New York: T&T Clark, 2018), pp.207-233.
[296] See Nathaniel Marshall, *The Penitential Discipline of the Primitive Church* (London: John Henry Parker 1844).

expression to some aspect of God's creative purpose for the world as a whole. They are occasions which arouse in us, either at the time or in retrospect, a sense of divine purpose.

In other words, God does not act in specific events in any way that is different from his maintenance of the world as whole. What makes specific events significant is the human experiences to which they give rise, namely a sense of having grasped God's unchanging purpose for his creation. What is different is not what God does, but the experiences that we have.

This fundamental theological conviction then plays out in what Wiles goes on to say about the person and work of Christ and about grace and the Holy Spirit. For Wiles, talk about these matters is not talk about specific acts of God (since these do not occur) but about different ways in which human beings come to experience the unchanging action and purpose of God as creator and to react appropriately to this experience.

As Vernon White helpfully puts it in his account of Wiles' theology:

> Wiles traces the relationship of God and the world in two ways, both of which are uniform relations. The first is that God is the transcendent ground of all that is (the first starting point). This is a uniform relationship, a relation of creator to creature which remains and continues equally throughout all creation all the time. It is a doctrine of creation which is also a doctrine of the continuing sustaining power of God. The other way of describing God's activity, in terms of purpose - a doctrine of redemption - is also best understood as uniform. The purposive activity of God relates to all events, is within all occurrences equally as a common factor X; it is a transcendent action of God in relation to worldly events which is 'something hidden with all worldly occurrence,'...Thus all appeal to special divine activity is misleading; it should rather be understood as special creaturely activity, the creatures' responsiveness to the final causality of the divine 'aims and motives' for them. God himself does not relate

differently to them except in and through their various responses to him. [297]

There are two key objections to this understanding of the nature of God's activity. To quote White again, the first objection is that:

> If God's purposive activity for the world is uniform and undifferentiated (except through particular creaturely response) then, it is liable to be impersonal, immoral and relatively impotent.[298]

The reason it is impersonal, writes White, is because, according to Wiles, God's activity:

> ...is already there (and everywhere) like a continual pressure in all events, made visible only when a human response embodies it. It is like dropping a log into a river and perceiving its motion in relation to a rock. Those who go with the divine tide reveal its motion in relation to those who resist it. But the tide is there in any case; it does not act in any different way. It is therefore in an impersonal relationship to the particular. [299]

The reason it is amoral is because:

> If there is no differentiation of the divine purpose in relation to the moral diversity of particular creatures and events within the world, then it is hard to see how moral diversity is being properly recognised. It would appear to make God's purpose something indifferent to morality. [300]

The reason it is relatively impotent is because:

---

[297] Vernon White, *The Fall of a Sparrow* (Exeter: Paternoster, 1985), p.67.
[298] White, p.69.
[299] White, p.69
[300] White, p.69

There is an obvious and basic sense in which Wiles' God appears to be severely hampered: if he can only be said to act specifically in and through his creatures' responsiveness then both the scope and efficacy of that action is strictly limited. There is also precious little initiative. Naturally, Wiles has implied something more: God's 'aims and motives.' which would presumably exist prior to and independent from any given response, do exercise some sort of influence as final causality. When a goal is presented to a creature a divine movement (even initiative?) has taken place. Yet it is still a reduced concept of effective action, arguably inferior even to human interpersonal action when we do more than present goals to each other.[301]

The second objection is epistemological. How does Wiles know that God's activity is uniform in the way that he claims? How does he know that God's action is amoral, impersonal and relatively impotent because entirely dependent on a creaturely response?

Obviously, Wiles does not get this idea from the Bible and the consensus teaching of the Christian tradition which maintains that (a) there have been and are numerous specific intentional acts of God in relation to the creation as a whole and to the human beings who inhabit it, alongside God's creation of the world and his subsequently maintaining it in being, and (b) that God's actions are moral, personal and completely effective in achieving those goal that God intends.

Furthermore, he does not get this idea from a study of the natural order itself. As C S Lewis argues in his book *Miracles,* there is nothing that we know about how the world operates that prohibits us from believing that God acts in certain specific ways within it.[302]

To summarise, what we have seen is that Wiles makes two fundamental (and highly problematic) moves. He dismisses the theology of the Fathers and in so doing also dismisses that teaching of

[301] White, pp.69-70.
[302] C S Lewis, *Miracles* (Glasgow: Fontana, 1974).

Scripture, which the Fathers reflect, and the subsequent consensual Christian tradition, which builds on the work of the Fathers. He then 'remakes' Christian theology on the basis of a particular view of how God relates to the world, a view in which the subject matter of theology is the human experience of God's as the transcendent creator, and in which the importance of Jesus is that he models a proper human response to God and therefore makes a similar response possible in others.

If we ask where this theological approach comes from, the answer is the influence of the German theologian Friedrich Schleiermacher (1768-1834), the man who is the Godfather of liberal Protestant theology (the tradition in which Wiles stands) in the same way that John Newman is the Godfather of modern Roman Catholic theology. To put it another way, the ghost of Schleiermacher still haunts contemporary Protestant thought (including its understanding of the development of doctrine).

The words of Stanley Grenz and Roger Olson in their book on twentieth century theology still apply today:

> The influence of this nineteenth-century German theologian on contemporary theology can hardly be overestimated. Although most Christians have never heard of Schleiermacher his ideas about religion in general and Christianity in particular have trickled down to them through the theological education of their pastors, denominational leaders, favourite religious authors and college teachers. His influence is subtle but pervasive in Western Christianity. He is to Christian theology what Newton is to physics what Freud is to psychology and what Darwin is to biology. That is to say, he may not be the absolute authority, but he was the trailblazer and trendsetter, the one thinker subsequent theologians cannot ignore. [303]

---

[303] Stanley Grenz and Roger Olson, *20th Century Theology* (Exeter: Paternoster Press, 1992), p.39.

The two key works by Schleiermacher were his apologetic work *On Religion: Speeches to Its Cultured Despisers,* published in 1799, and his systematic theology, *The Christian Faith*, first published in 1821-22 and revised in 1830.

The reason for Schleiermacher's importance was that in these two, epoch making, works he attempted to fuse German pietist spirituality with its emphasis on religious experience, with the Enlightenment's rejection of traditional Christian doctrine, thus blazing the trail for later generations of theologians (Wiles included) to make the same attempt.

To quote Grenz and Olson again:

> Before Schleiermacher theology was thought of in two major ways. Orthodoxy viewed the discipline as reflection on supernaturally revealed truths and thus practised 'a theology from above.' Enlightenment theology (deism), viewing the enterprise as reflection on rational thoughts about God, engaged in a type of theology 'from below.' According to Schleiermacher (and later liberal theologians) the approach of orthodoxy led to authoritative theology, which stifled human creativity and confused the church's dogmas about God with God himself. The Enlightenment rightly rebelled against this. The deistic approach however, led to sterile, bland natural religion that differed little from religious philosophy. Kant had brought this to a dead end.
>
> In the place of these two alternatives, Schleiermacher sought to reroute theology entirely by considering it as *human* reflection on human experience of God. Thus, not timeless, authoritative propositions but religious experience would become the true source of theological reflection.[304]

As they go on to explain, in *The Christian Faith*:

---

[304] Grenz and Olson, p.44.

Schleiermacher defined theology as the attempt to set forth the Christian religious affections in speech. In essence Christianity is a modification of universal human piety, the consciousness of being absolutely dependent, of being in relation to God. Schleiermacher recognised a specific form of piety that he called Christian God-consciousness or Christian self- consciousness. This is what he meant by 'Christian religious affections' - the feeling of being totally dependent upon the redemptive work of Jesus Christ for one's own relationship to God. The Christian experience of God-consciousness and self-consciousness formed and fulfilled in and through Jesus Christ is the essence of Christianity 'the distinctive essence of Christianity consists in the fact that in it all religious emotions all related to the redemption wrought by Jesus of Nazareth.' Rather than being the project of systematizing some supernaturally revealed set of propositions, Christian theology attempts to set forth a coherent account on to the religious experience of Christians.[305]

The reference to 'the redemptive work of Jesus Christ' sounds very traditionally orthodox, but in fact Schleiermacher's account of Jesus' person and work was anything but traditional. Rejecting the traditional view of Jesus Christ as both divine and human, Schleiermacher viewed Jesus as human being with what he called 'an absolutely potent God-consciousness.' In his words:

> The Redeemer, then, is like all men in virtue of the identity of human nature, but distinguished from them all by the constant potency of his God consciousness which was a veritable existence of God in him.[306]

As this person, Jesus redeems other by enabling others to also share his God-consciousness: 'The Redeemer assumes believers into the

---

[305] Grenz and Olson, pp.45-46, quoting Friedrich Schleiermacher, *The Christian Faith* (Philadelphia: Fortress Press), p.98.
[306] Schleiermacher, p.385.

power of his God-consciousness, and this is his redemptive activity.'[307]

To quote Grenz and Olson once more, Schleiermacher also held that what followed from this understanding of theology was that

> ...theology must continually re-examine the doctrinal formulas of Christianity to determine their adequacy to express the Christian God-consciousness. No doctrine is sacrosanct. Everything is open to revision. Theology's critical task is to hold the church's preaching and doctrinal formulas to strict agreement with the best contemporary analysis of the Christian God - consciousness in order to determine how much of it is to be retained, how much thrown out entirely and how much revised...For him: 'Every doctrinal form is bound to a particular time and no claim can be made for its permanent validity. It is the task of theology in every present age, by critical reflection, to express anew the implications of the living religious consciousness.'[308]

If we compare this account of Schleiermacher's thought with the two works by Wiles that we have looked at in this chapter, we can see that although Wiles does not acknowledge his debt to Schleiermacher, it is nonetheless Schleiermacher's thought that Wiles is echoing. This can be seen in what Wiles says about the experiential basis of theology, his willingness to abandon traditional Christian doctrine, and his account of the person and work of Christ.

In addition, his rejection of specific acts of God also follows Schleiermacher who held that everything that occurs in the world is determined by God as its final cause, but who as a result:

> ...adamantly rejected the reality of miracles. To believe in miracles is to deny that everything that happens is ordained and caused by God. The feeling of absolute dependence requires that all of nature

---

[307] Schleiermacher, p.425.
[308] Grenz and Olson p.46, quoting Schleiermacher, p.390.

in the part and in the whole, is willed, ordained and caused by God. Miracles, in the sense of special acts that abrogate the order of nature would contradict this.[309]

The fundamental problem with the approach to the development of Christian doctrine which was pioneered by Schleiermacher, and which has then been followed by other theologians in the liberal Protestant tradition such as Albrecht Ritschl, Adolf Harnack, Rudolf Bultmann, Paul Tillich and John Robinson as well as Maurice Wiles, is that it starts from the wrong place.

As these theologians would agree, any form of theology that aspires to be Christian has to have the person and work of Jesus Christ at its centre. It is this that makes it a distinctively *Christian* form of theology. However, this raises the question of how we know about Jesus Christ in the first place. If we are going to think about Jesus Christ, we have to first of all determine our source(s) of information about him. Clearly, we cannot determine who Jesus and what he did purely on the basis of our limited contemporary experience. Like Mohammed or the Buddha, Jesus Christ is a historical figure and so the proper starting point for understanding him has to be the historical information we have about him. If we want to know about Alfred the Great, for example, we don't start by considering my own experiences, we begin by looking at the historical sources such as Asser's Life of Alfred.[310] The same is true with regard to Jesus Christ.

There is only one source of comprehensive historical information about Jesus Christ and that is the witness of the New Testament. Even if we wanted to do so, we simply do not have the information that would enable us to uncover the 'real' or 'historical' Jesus whose life underlies what the New Testament says about him. If the New Testament is wrong, then the real Jesus is unrecoverable.

---

[309] Grenz and Olson, summarising Schleiermacher, pp.178-179.
[310] Asser, *Alfred the Great: Asser's Life of King Alfred and Other Contemporary Sources* (London: Penguin Classics, 1983).

There are scattered references to Jesus in the work of the first century Stoic philosopher, Mara bar Sarapion, the first century Jewish historian Flavius Josephus, the collection of Jewish texts known as the *Talmud*, and in the writings of the second century Roman authors Pliny the Younger, Tacitus, Suetonius and Lucian of Samosata. These references make it clear that Jesus existed, and they corroborate certain elements of the New Testament witness, such as, for example, his reputation as a miracle worker, his crucifixion by the Romans at the behest of the Jewish authorities, and the belief of his followers that he came back to life after he died, but they do not give us any information that is not already contained in the New Testament and in themselves they do not give us the information necessary to reconstruct Jesus' life and beliefs in any detail.

This means that we are faced with a simple choice. We either accept the witness of the New Testament about Jesus, or we do not. We believe or we do not. It might be suggested that we could accept some bits of the New Testament witness and not others, but even if it was right in principle to so this, we lack the information to make such a decision, since we cannot get back behind the New Testament witness to a more reliable source of information.

Furthermore, if we attend to the witness of the New Testament what we find is not simply, as liberal Protestant writers such as Schleiermacher and Wiles have suggested, a narrative about a human figure with immensely strong awareness of God and of the mission God had given to him. As Edwyn Hoskyns and Noel Davey write in their classic study *The Riddle of the New Testament*:

> Language descriptive of human heroism is entirely foreign to the New Testament. The event of the life and death of Jesus was not thought of as a human act, but as an act of God wrought out in human flesh and blood, which is a very different matter. The event was conceived of as a descending act of God, not the ascending career of a man who was successful in the sphere of religion. No New Testament writer could think of Jesus in Pelagian terms. The concrete event, which was Jesus of Nazareth, was for them the

sphere in which God had effected a mighty action for the salvation of men. Again, this was no mere piece of theologizing but the very way in which Jesus himself regarded his ministry. Human flesh and blood, words and actions, were, caught up, controlled, energised by the Spirit of God, by the Son of God, so that St. Paul could speak of Christ Jesus as him in whom 'dwelleth all the fullness of the Godhead bodily' (Colossians 2:9) just as the author of the fourth gospel could write of the Word becoming flesh.[311]

To put it another way, what the New Testament gives us is a *theanthropic* theology, a theology centred on a human being who was also the God of Israel. Thus, as Brant Pitre notes, in the New Testament:

> ...When Jesus acts speaks or acts as if he is divine, he does so in such a way that also makes clear that he is truly human. The most obvious example of this is Jesus' repeated use of 'the Son of Man' (*ho huios tou anthropou*) to refer to himself. 'Son of Man' not only identifies Jesus as the heavenly being of Daniel's apocalyptic vision (Daniel 7:13-14), but also as a human being (*anthropos*) (Matthew 9:6, Mark 2:10, Luke 5:24). Likewise, when Jesus responds to John the Baptist's question about his identity, he identifies himself not only with the one God who is to come (Isaiah 35:4-6; 40:9-10) but also with the human figure who was anointed to preach good news to the poor (Isaiah 61:1). Finally, as we saw above when, when Jesus poses his riddle about 'the Messiah' he does not deny that the Messiah is David's 'son' (i.e. human); he only insists that he is also the super-davidic 'lord' (*kyrios*) (i.e. divine) (Mark 12:35-37). Even the account of Jesus' walking on the sea and declaring 'I am' begins with him going away by himself to pray to God like any other human being (Mark 6:46)...in other words, the earliest Christology

---

[311] Edwyn Hoskyns and Noel Davey, *The Riddle of the New Testament* (London: Faber& Faber, 1936), p.220. In a footnote Hoskyns and Davey explain that the word 'Pelagian' refers to 'The doctrine that the human will is of itself capable of good.'

was *theoanthropic Christology*, it not only identified Jesus with God (Greek *theos*) it also radically identified him with human beings (Greek *anthropos*). [312]

It is equally important to understand, however, that according to witness of the New Testament, while the man Jesus is God, he is not the totality of God. The New Testament witness to the mighty acts of God that took place in the life, death and resurrection of Jesus also tell us that these acts were wrought by the God who is Father, Son and Holy Spirit. In the words of the Church of England's Doctrine Commission report *The Mystery of Salvation,* the New Testament declares:

> In the incarnation and death of Jesus the Son, God gave himself *for us* in the once for all historical event which constitutes our salvation, and as the indwelling presence of the Spirit in our lives God continually *gives* himself *to us* in our present experience of salvation. To use the fully trinitarian terms, the Father gave his Son for us (e.g. John 3:1 Romans 8:32; Ephesians 1:22), the Son gave himself for us (e.g. Mark 10:45; John 6:51; Galatians 1:4; 2:20; Ephesians 5:25; Titus 2:14). The Father has given us the Spirit (e.g. Acts 5:32; 1 Thessalonians 4:8; 1 John 3:24), and the Son has given us the Spirit (cf. Acts 2:33). With this divine self- giving all other specific aspects of salvation can be taken for granted 'He who did not withhold his own Son, but gave himself up for all of us, will he not with him also give us everything else? (Romans 8:32). [313]

As the report goes on to say, this New Testament witness leads to the doctrine of the Trinity because:

> If God really gives himself, then who God is in the story of God's self-giving is who God really is. In God's own eternity God is none other than who he is for us in the story of our salvation. In this way

---

[312] Pitre, pp.467-468
[313] The Church of England Doctrine Commission, *The Mystery of Salvation* (London: CHP, 1995), pp.40-41.

the doctrine of the Trinity is an understanding of God's being derived from the narrative, while at the same time it serves to safeguard the theological reality of the narrative as the story of God's self-giving. Because God is Father, Son and Holy Spirit, because the Son and the Spirit are as truly God as the Father is, therefore the self-giving which the story narrates is a real giving of God's own self for us and to us. [314]

Finally, according to the New Testament, the action of the Triune God in the life, death and resurrection of Jesus Christ cannot be reduced to saying that Jesus provides a supreme example of what it means to live rightly in awareness of God's existence and purposes. Rather it tells us that through the life, death and resurrection of Jesus Christ God himself objectively changed the human situation by terminating the old pattern of human existence dominated by sin and leading to death, and replaced it by a new form of human existence in which the risen life of Jesus Christ mediated to human being by the Holy Spirit enables people to live the life he has always intended for his human creatures. As Paul puts it in Romans 6:6-11:

> We know that our old self was crucified with him so that the sinful body might be destroyed, and we might no longer be enslaved to sin. For he who has died is freed from sin. But if we have died with Christ, we believe that we shall also live with him. For we know that Christ being raised from the dead will never die again; death no longer has dominion over him. The death he died he died to sin, once for all, but the life he lives he lives to God. So you also must consider yourselves dead to sin and alive to God in Christ Jesus.

Pulling the threads together, we can say that the liberal Protestant approach exemplified by Wiles, and shaped by the continuing influence of Schleiermacher, is not a legitimate approach to the development of doctrine. It assumes that the proper starting point for doctrine is our own experience interpreted in the light of a particular

---

[314] *The Mystery of Salvation,* p.42.

understanding of the demands of contemporary thought. On this basis, it further holds that we can correct the witness of the Fathers, and the Christian tradition based on the Fathers, and, more fundamentally, correct the apostolic witness contained in the New Testament to who Jesus Christ was and is, and to the mighty acts of God for our salvation wrought through him by the God who is Father, Son and Holy Spirit.

To put the matter at its starkest, it assumes that we today have the right to correct what God has revealed on the basis of our own superior, post Enlightenment, wisdom. In biblical terms this amounts to listening to the voice of the tempter asking 'Did God say?' (Genesis 3:1). As we know, listening to the tempter did not end well.

Chapter 6
The development of doctrine and the Church of England debate about marriage and sexuality

1. What we have learned so far

In chapter 1 of this study, we noted that, in the words of J I Packer: 'Doctrine is the revealed truth of God as defined and taught in the church, by the church, for the church, and for the world.'

We then further noted that the basis of doctrine is the truth concerning the nature, will and action of God revealed by Jesus Christ and made known to us by the record of the Spirit inspired witness of the apostles contained in the books of the New Testament, a witness which supplements and completes the previous witness to Jesus borne by the writers of the Old Testament. It is this truth 'as defined and taught in the church, by the church, for the church, and for the world,' that constitutes Christian doctrine.

In addition, we discovered in this chapter five additional points about the nature of doctrine.

1.Doctrine involves the verbal communication of Christian truth, and the words used must be as adequate as possible in order to ensure that the truth is properly communicated.

2.Tradition has a key place in Christian doctrine because the Christian tradition is the way that Christian truth, normatively taught in Scripture, has been handed on from one generation of Christians to the next.

The most important forms of the Christian tradition have been recognised to be the teaching of the Fathers of the Church, the four great creedal statements produced during the early centuries, the Apostles,' Nicene, and Athanasian Creeds and the Chalcedonian Confession, the decisions of what are known as the six General, or Ecumenical, Councils of the first seven centuries, the Confessions of Faith produced by specific churches at the Reformation and subsequently, the writings of those theologians since the time of the Fathers who are regarded either formally or informally as Doctors of the Church, that is to say particularly important teachers of Christian doctrine and finally the liturgies produced by the various churches down the centuries which have both reflected and shaped how people have understood the Christian faith.

To understand and appreciate the Christian tradition, it is important, as C S Lewis argued, to 'read old books' (i.e., books from the Christian past). Reading such books helps us to understand and assess Christian writings from the present, helps prevent us from being trapped by the particular errors of contemporary thought, and shows us that the orthodox Christian tradition has had a definite and distinctive content over the centuries. 'Christianity' has historically meant something specific.

3.The passage of time does not affect the relevance of truthful statements of doctrine. This is because doctrine is concerned with how God relates to those who possess human nature, God himself does not change and neither does human nature, and therefore what doctrine teaches, providing it is said truthfully, will never become outdated.

4.Although doctrine and ethics developed into two different areas of academic study in the post-Reformation period, it is nonetheless the case that teaching about ethics, how God wishes his human creatures to behave, has in fact always formed part of Christian doctrine.

5.Christian doctrine and the Church's traditional threefold structure of ordained ministry consisting of the three orders of bishops, priests (also called presbyters or elders) and deacons go together in two ways. First, historically most Christians have most Christians have regarded a belief in the God given nature of the three orders of ministry, bishops, priests and deacons, as an integral part of orthodox Christian doctrine. Part of what has traditionally been taught is that the existence of these three orders since the time of the apostles has been something ordained by God himself. Secondly, it has also historically been held that a particular responsibility of bishops and priests is to instruct God's people' both by teaching orthodox doctrine derived from the teaching of Scripture, and by refuting heresy.

In chapter 2 we noted that some Christian theologians such as the seventeenth century Roman Catholic theologian Jacques Bossuet and modern Orthodox writers such as Georges Florovsky, Vladimir Lossky, and Andrew Louth have rejected the idea of doctrinal development.

However, we also saw that it is very difficult, if not impossible, to maintain the principle that every new form of doctrine is necessarily false simply because what it teaches has not been said before (or at least not in the same way). This is because to maintain this principle consistently we would have to say that everything said by every Christian theologian that differs in any way from what was said by Peter on the Day of Pentecost, the day the Church was founded (Acts 2:14-36), including both the doctrine taught by the writers of New Testament, and historic statements of doctrine that have received widespread, if not universal, acceptance by Christians down the ages and across the world, are necessarily wrong simply because at the time they were produced they said something that had not been said before, and this is a position that no Christian has ever wanted to take.

What we also saw is that it would be equally wrong to go to the opposite extreme and say that all new developments of doctrine are to be accepted. While many new forms of teaching have been accepted, it has been held from New Testament times onwards that there are forms of teaching that are heretical because they deny rather than uphold Christian truth.

This last point raises the issue of how we should decide which are positive developments of doctrine and which are heretical? To put it another way, what is the mark of a legitimate as opposed to an illegitimate development of Christian doctrine?

In chapters 3, 4 and 5 we considered the three different answers that have been given to this question by looking at the works of three writers on the development of doctrine, Vincent of Lerins, John Newman and Maurice Wiles.

In chapter 3 we saw that Vincent of Lerins, writing in the fifth century in his work *The Commonitory*, held that Christian doctrine was based on the teaching of Scripture, and that what distinguished an orthodox reading of Scripture from a heretical one was that on orthodox reading was one that reflected the 'faith which has been believed everywhere, always, by all' (*ubique, semper et ab omnibus creditum est*').

In Vincent's own words:

> ...all possible care must be taken, that we hold that faith which has been believed everywhere, always, by all. For that is truly and in the strictest sense 'Catholic,' which, as the name itself and the reason of the thing declare, comprehends all universally. This rule we shall observe if we follow universality, antiquity, consent. We shall follow universality if we confess that one faith to be true, which the whole Church throughout the world confesses; antiquity, if we in no wise depart from those interpretations which it is manifest were notoriously held by our holy ancestors and fathers; consent, in like manner, if in antiquity itself we adhere to the consentient definitions and determinations of all, or at the least of almost all priests and doctors.

However, Vincent also insisted that the necessity of holding the faith which has been believed everywhere, always and by all does not preclude the possibility of doctrinal development. As he puts it:

> ...whatever has been sown by the fidelity of the Fathers in this husbandry of God's Church, the same ought to be cultivated and taken care of by the industry of their children, the same ought to flourish and ripen, the same ought to advance and go forward to perfection. For it is right that those ancient doctrines of heavenly

philosophy should, as time goes on, be cared for, smoothed, polished; but not that they should be changed, not that they should be maimed, not that they should be mutilated. They may receive proof, illustration, definiteness; but they must retain withal their completeness, their integrity, their characteristic properties.

What we also saw is that according to Vincent such development does not involve saying new things (*nova*) but saying old things in new ways (*noviter*) in order to make the truths taught by the apostles more clearly understood.

In chapter 4 we saw that the nineteenth century theologian John Newman, having previously accepted the position taken by Vincent in *The Commonitory,* changed his position as part of his conversion from Anglicanism to Roman Catholicism, and put forward a new approach to the development of doctrine in his *Essay on the Development of Christian Doctrine*, an approach which has subsequently been very influential in Roman Catholic theology.

Newman, like Vincent before him, held that Christian doctrine should not be seen as something that should remain static. He held that Christianity is an idea and like all ideas it is right that it should find constantly new expression. In the most famous passage in his essay Newman uses the image of the growth of a river to explain why doctrinal development should be viewed in a positive light:

> It is indeed sometimes said that the stream is clearest near the spring. Whatever use may fairly be made of this image, it does not apply to the history of a philosophy or belief, which on the contrary is more equable, and purer, and stronger, when its bed has become deep, and broad, and full. It necessarily rises out of an existing state of things, and for a time savours of the soil. Its vital element needs disengaging from what is foreign and temporary, and is employed in efforts after freedom which become more vigorous and hopeful as its years increase. Its beginnings are no measure of its capabilities, nor of its scope. At first no one knows what it is, or what it is worth. It remains perhaps for a time

quiescent; it tries, as it were, its limbs, and proves the ground under it, and feels its way. From time to time, it makes essays which fail, and are in consequence abandoned. It seems in suspense which way to go; it wavers, and at length strikes out in one definite direction. In time it enters upon strange territory; points of controversy alter their bearing; parties rise and fall around it; dangers and hopes appear in new relations; and old principles reappear under new forms. It changes with them in order to remain the same. In a higher world it is otherwise, but here below to live is to change, and to be perfect is to have changed often.

While both Vincent and Newman agree on the need for doctrinal development, what we saw in chapter 4 was that Newman's view of the development of doctrine differs from that of Vincent in two crucial respects.

The first difference is that while Vincent holds that the basis of Christian doctrine is the explicit teaching of the apostles as recorded in the New Testament and handed on in the Church's subsequent teaching, for Newman the apostles knew of the Christian idea (i.e. the fulness of Christian truth), but were not consciously aware of, and therefore did not make explicit, all of the contents of the Christian idea.

However, because the Church (and here Newman means especially the Roman Catholic Church) has had the Christian idea transmitted to it by the apostles it has had the ability over time to become conscious of, and to make explicit, truths which the apostles knew, but of which they were not consciously aware. That is why beliefs such as the existence of purgatory, the transubstantiation of the elements at the Eucharist and the immaculate conception and bodily assumption of the Virgin Mary which can be seen to be part of the corpus of Christian doctrine, even though they are not explicitly taught in the New Testament and were not an explicit part of Christian doctrine in the earliest centuries of the Church's existence.

The second difference is that according to Newman God has provided the office of the Papacy to oversee the development of the Church's doctrine. It is the Pope, working together with the other bishops who has both the responsibility, and the infallible power, to decide whether proposed new developments of Christian belief are legitimate expressions of the Christian idea and to define these developments in new doctrinal formulae.

In summary, what Newman proposes is that Christian doctrine is made up of two parts. There is the explicit teaching of the apostles witnessed to by the New Testament and handed down in the Church from New Testament times onwards, and there are also implicit aspects of the Christian idea which are gradually apprehended by the Church in a gradual process of doctrinal development that is overseen and infallibly guaranteed by the office of the Papacy.

In chapter 5 we noted that the approach to the development of doctrine taken by the Anglican theologian Maurice Wiles reflected the continuing influence of the great liberal German Protestant theologian Friedrich Schleiermacher.

Like Schleiermacher and other theologians influenced by his theological approach, Wiles' view is that the proper starting point for doctrine, and thus for doctrinal development, is not the teaching of the New Testament, or the Fathers, or the subsequent orthodox Christian tradition building on the work of the Fathers. Rather, the proper starting point is our own awareness of God as the creator and sustainer of the world and the continuing influence of Jesus' exemplary relationship with God as witnessed to by the Bible and in Christian worship, which enables us to develop a similar relationship with God for ourselves and thus be 'saved' by allowing the 'divine purpose' to find 'effective realization' in our lives.

From this starting point Wiles argues that we should feel free to correct the teaching of the New Testament, the Fathers and the subsequent orthodox Christian tradition and should feel free to develop a new form of doctrine in the light of our understanding of the demands of contemporary thought.

According to Wiles, Christians should not be afraid of 'doctrinal revolution' even if this means dispensing with key elements of doctrine such as the Triune nature of God, the divinity of Christ or the hope of bodily resurrection. For him doctrinal continuity with previous generations of Christian consists 'not in not so much in the repetition of their doctrinal conclusions or even in building upon them' but in having the same 'doctrinal aims,' namely to do justice to 'the record of Scripture, the activity of worship, and the experience of salvation' in terms which make sense to us today.

2. Assessing the approaches of Newman, Wiles and Vincent of Lerins

What we also learned in chapters 4 and 5 is that there are insurmountable objections to the approach taken to the development of Christian doctrine put forward by Newman and Wiles. The fundamental problem is that they transgress the biblical teaching that it is impermissible to either add to, or subtract from, what God has revealed. (Deuteronomy 4:2, 12:32, Revelation 22:17-18).

Newman's argument, as we have seen, is that there are truths which were revealed to the apostles, but of which they were not consciously aware. However, later generations of the Church, guided by the infallible authority of the Pope and the bishops in communion with him, have become aware of these truths and have rightly included them as part of Christian doctrine

The problem with this argument is that Newman never proves (because it is impossible to prove) that the apostles were possessed of truths of which they were not consciously aware or that later generations of Christians attained knowledge of these truths. The argument that the teaching authority of the Pope guarantees the correctness of belief in these truths fails to work because one of the truths in question is precisely the Pope's infallible teaching authority and so the argument is circular.

This being the case, Newman's argument that the development of Christian doctrine can include new truths which cannot be shown to have their origin in the apostolic witness needs to be rejected. To go back to the notion of the maintenance of historic ships which we considered in the introduction to this study, it is like someone adding new pieces of superstructure to a historic vessel on the basis that this is something of which the original builders of the vessel would have approved, when we have absolutely no evidence to confirm this fact.

Whereas Newman seeks to add new pieces of doctrine that do not have a basis in the apostolic witness, Wiles holds, as we have seen, that we should feel free to remake Christian doctrine in ways which exclude key parts of the apostolic witness such as the divinity of Christ, the trinitarian nature of God, God performing specific acts within the world, and the hope of bodily resurrection. As we have also seen, what we end up with as a result is a unitarian view of God which sees God's relation to the world as uniform and undifferentiated and as a result impersonal, amoral and relatively impotent. God is more like an impersonal force than the moral, active, involved, loving and self-sacrificing God witnessed to by Holy Scripture.

In terms of the analogy of the maintenance of historic ships, what Wiles proposes is deconstructing the existing ship almost entirely and then re-building it according to a radically new design. To use another analogy, Wiles' concept of the development of Christian doctrine is reminiscent of the re-development of many British town centres in the 1960s and '70s with historic structures being bulldozed out of the way to allow the implementation of a radical, modern, architectural vision.

Wiles argument in the *Making* and the *Remaking of Christian Doctrine* seems to be that the sort of doctrinal reconstruction he proposes is legitimate because if the Fathers and the biblical writers before them felt free to construct Christian doctrine according to their own ideas we should feel free to do the same. What he fails to engage with is the evidence that Jesus claimed to be God incarnate[315] an issue which is absolutely crucial to the issue of the origin of Christian doctrine. If, as the Bible teaches, and the Christian faith has always claimed, Jesus is God incarnate, then the teaching that he gave to the apostles, teaching which then became the foundation of subsequent Christian doctrine, has the authority of God himself and is therefore something that theologians are not free to set aside in favour of their own ideas about what God is like and how God acts in the world.

To go back to our nautical analogy, if God has designed a ship in a certain way, who are we to think that we have the right to rebuild it in a different way?

The approach taken by Vincent of Lerins which we looked at in chapter 3 avoids the difficulties which we have noted with the approaches of Newman and Wiles. For him the faith held *ubique, semper et ab omnibus* is the faith taught by Jesus Christ to the apostles which they then passed on to the succeeding generation of orthodox Christian bishops and teachers, who in turn passed it on to their successors and so on down the ages.

As we saw in chapter 3, the historical evidence we have supports his claim. To repeat what was said in that chapter:

> '...not only can it be shown that there is a direct line of theological succession between the teaching of the earliest days of the Church and the teaching of the orthodox Fathers and Councils of the third and fourth centuries, but it can also be shown that this line of theological succession has continued in the Christian Church over the succeeding centuries despite the divisions that have opened up

---

[315] In his famous essay 'Does Christology rest on a mistake?' for example, Wiles deliberately chooses not to engage in an exploration of the biblical evidence concerning Jesus, contenting himself with declaring 'that that evidence by itself seems to be to be ambiguous and inconclusive' (in S W Sykes and J P. Clayton (eds) *Christ, Faith and History* (Cambridge: CUP, 1972), p.13.

between Roman Catholicism, Eastern Orthodoxy and the various forms of Protestantism.'

This historic Christian doctrinal consensus, what Thomas Oden calls 'classic Christianity' provides the plumbline against which we can measure any proposed new development of doctrine. We cannot legitimately add anything new to the consensus because we do not have a new revelation from Jesus Christ that would make this possible. Christ has ascended into heaven having passed on what he wants to say to us to the apostles who have passed it on to us through the succeeding generations of the Church. To echo Paul's words to Timothy (1 Timothy 1:14), the deposit of faith has already been given to the apostles and handed on to us. Conversely, we cannot legitimately remove anything from the consensus because we do not have the authority to do so, and because, as we noted in chapter 1, truthful doctrine never becomes outdated because it deals with the relationship between God and humanity and God and human nature do not change.

3. How we should understand the development of doctrine

If it is the case that there is a deposit of faith passed on from Jesus to the apostles, and from the apostles to the bishops and teachers who succeeded them and from them to all subsequent generations down to the present day, the question that inevitably arises is how we are to understand the kind of historic development of Christian doctrine that we surveyed in chapter 2? What does it mean to say that there is a development of an unchanging deposit of faith?

A helpful answer to this question is provided in the response to John Newman by Jacob Mozley to which we have already referred in chapter 4.

In his response Mozley explains that the term 'development' is used in in two different ways.

The first way that it is used is to refer to the process of explanation. In Mozley's words:

One sense of development makes it a simply explanatory process. Development is explanation; explanation is development. A man in conversation makes an assertion, which another misapprehends; in reply, he explains the meaning, or develops the meaning of his assertion. His meaning is exactly the same with what it was before; it is in order to show what it was before that the explanation is given; the meaning before the explanation or development of it, and the meaning after, are by the very nature and aim of the process the same. It so happens that language, or the medium by which we convey our ideas to one another, is capable of misinterpretation; we have therefore often to alter or add to the language in which we expressed an idea, and express it anew, — not because our idea itself was imperfect, or was different at all from what it is, but because some person has construed our language in a way in which we did not intend it to be construed. This explanation again, inasmuch as language still continues our medium, may be misinterpreted, and a second explanation become necessary for the benefit of some second objector. A third, a fourth, a fifth, an indefinite number of explanations may succeed on the same principle which produced the first. An idea may thus, in course of discussion, be said to be developed; i.e. may go through fresh successional stages of language, according as preceding stages are found not adequate to prevent it from being mistaken and confused with some other idea, different from, or short of it. Each misconstruction, as it shows itself, makes a fresh defence necessary: when three or four defensive explanations have been made, these again have to be reconciled to each other: and the creation of language becomes larger and larger. The case is not unfrequent of a single arguer having to maintain in conversation a particular point against a whole circle of opponents. He adheres firmly, consistently, and with all unity and simplicity, to the one point which he defends, and is only bent on defending it. But, with that one object in view, what a vast formation of language does he raise as he goes on! what distinctions accumulate, and what protests and safeguards grow up out of, and surround the original statement! He would be surprised at the end of the argument to see the edifice he had built. And yet nobody would say that his idea had altered, and was not just the same as it was when he began. It was for the very purpose of so maintaining it, that he explained it again and again anew, as misconstruction threatened it, and so formed all that body of expression around it; and a bystander will make the special remark on such an occasion, that the arguer has kept to his own point, amidst a varied and complex opposition. Cases of legal amplification illustrate the same principle. What a testator or seller of an estate wants to do, is able to be expressed in two words for any fair man's understanding; but the law has the responsibility of guarding against all the possible constructions which may be put upon a statement, and not only that of satisfying an ordinary and simple construction. The case, in short, is a common every day one, in which the idea in a person's mind is exactly the same, whether more shortly and simply, or more fully and guardedly expressed. It is not meant that it may not become clearer by such a process; but the additional clearness is an external argumentative one; not affecting its substance, or making it, as regards natural straightforward thinking, any other than the identical idea which it was before. Such is simply explanatory development.[316]

When used in this sense the development of doctrine takes place when an individual Christian or a group of Christians gives a fresh explanation of the deposit of faith. The content of what is explained remains the same, what changes is how it is expressed at a particular point in the history of the Church.

The second way it is used is to refer to a substantial change in the thing developed. As Mozley puts it:

> On the other hand, there is a kind of development which is a positive increase of the substance of the thing developed, — a fresh formation not contained in, though growing out of, some

---

[316] Mozley, pp.144-146.

original matter. The developed substance here is not the same actual one with the original, but a very different one. Growth-out-of is a wholly different thing from identity-with. The development of a seed into a plant is one of growth, for example, and it does not carry with it identity. It is a pure metaphor by which we say the acorn is the oak; it is so, if by saying so be meant that the acorn is the thing in consequence of which (coupled with other causes) an oak will exist, but it is not identical with it actually. As things actual, things cognisable, an acorn is one thing, an oak is another: the one is a - smooth oval piece of vegetable matter, about an inch long, and of that consistency and appearance of which it is; and the other is a large, wide-spreading tree, with rough bark, and thick branches bearing leaves. When one of these phenomena exists, indeed, the other does not, and this succession in two things is able to be called the existence of one and the same thing in different stages; but it is self-evident that they are not actually one and the same thing, and that, however intimate may be the relation of growth in the two, they have not the relation of identity. This is, perhaps, the most common and natural sense of development; the word, either from etymological or from conventional reasons, is suggestive of an actual enlargement of substance in the thing developed. Power develops, i.e. becomes actually larger; there is more of it. Rome was a small power at first; it developed into a larger one. The 'march of mind' development is of this kind; it consists of new ideas and forms of thoughts, new discoveries in science, new social comforts and conveniences arising. Philosophical development may be partly explanatory only, partly an actually enlarging one. Such are two sorts of development: that of explanation simply, and that of substantial growth. The one begins with what the other ends in; explanation starts with its substance, growth arrives at its substance gradually. In growth it is the ultimate formation of all which is the substance of the thing growing; the substance before that point only existing on a kind of antedating view. The oak is the grown oak, not the acorn; the Roman empire is Augustan and not Romulan Rome. The original thing is not the real, the substantial thing, in this kind of development; it is only the imperfect, half-existing, ambiguous, and struggling element of future reality and proper being.[317]

According to Mozley, the legitimacy of development in the first sense is universally accepted in the Church:

> Now, of these two kinds of development, the former is of course conceded in the case before us. All allow that Christian fundamental truth has been explained. The whole of scientific theology is an explanatory development of it.

Mozley illustrates this last point by referring to the explanatory development of the doctrine of the incarnation:

> To take the doctrine of the Incarnation, the truth that God became man. A whole body of Christian theology, from the short decrees of the earliest councils to the full volumes of the Schoolmen, explain this truth.

> The former guarded it from misconstruction; the latter, besides this, brought out, in detail, the logical contents of the truth. There are inexhaustible logical contents in it. God comprehends all that God is; man comprehends all that man is. All that was logically comprehended under these two terms was brought out; and all that was logically comprehended in the idea of the union of the two was brought out...[318]

---

[317] Mozley, pp.146-147.

[318] To illustrate this point Mozley notes the range of questions explored by Thomas Aquinas with regard to the doctrine of the incarnation in the *Summa Theologica* such as: '(1) Whether the union of the Word Incarnate took place in the nature? (2) Whether it took place in the Person? (3) Whether it took place in the suppositum or hypostasis? (4) Whether the Person or hypostasis of Christ is composite after the Incarnation? (5) Whether any union of body and soul took place in Christ? (6) Whether the human nature was united to the Word accidentally? (7) Whether the union itself is something created? (8) Whether it is the same as assumption? (9) Whether the union of the two natures is the greatest union? (10) Whether the union of the two natures in Christ was brought

> Here, in short, is a field of explanatory theology, which takes the idea of the Incarnation, and brings out all the possible inferences and aspects which can be elicited from it, some nearer and more obvious, others remoter and minuter, till the subject multiplies into a whole world of subtle, and, so to call it, microscopic theological science. But such manifold evolutions do not profess to add anything to the substantial idea of the Incarnation, — the truth that God became man. There is a great difference between the clearness, accuracy, and circumstantiality in the intellectual image of the doctrine, which such an explanatory development as this produces, and the intellectual image in an ordinary Christian mind unversed in scholastic divinity; but the doctrine entertained is the same identical one.[319]

What is at question, argues Mozley, is whether there can be a development of the second sort in which there is a substantial addition to the deposit of faith. Mozley notes that Newman claims that the Nicene Creed was an example of this kind of substantial development in the same way as development of the ideas of purgatory and Papal infallibility.

However, as we saw in chapter 4, according to Mozley this claim is unjustified. To repeat the words of Mozley already given in chapter 4:

> Now a development of this kind the Nicene Creed was not. The Nicene Creed only asserted and guarded a doctrine which had been held from the first, viz., that of Christ's true and proper Divinity. The original Christian Revelation declared that Christ was God. If Christ was God, He was true God; He had true and proper Godhead. The Nicene Creed asserted this of Him, and no more; it expressed this truth, and no more, by the word *Homoousion*. The word *Homoousion* declared that Christ was very God with God the

---

about by grace? (11) Whether any merits preceded it? (12) Whether the grace of union was natural to the man Christ? (*Summa Theologica*, part 3, question 2, 'Of the Mode of Union of the Word Incarnate).
[319] Mozley, pp.147-149.

Father. His oneness of substance with the Father was the term by which the Nicene Fathers declared His true Godhead with the Father. And this true Godhead was attributed to Christ by the original Christian Revelation, which declared Him to be God, and commanded Him to be worshipped as God.

As Mozley goes on to say, the reason the Fathers at Nicaea employed the word Homoousion to explain the deity of Christ afresh in the face of the Arian heresy:

> The Apostles and first Christian preachers were Jews then, and came to the new truth of Christ's Godhead with the Jewish doctrine of the unity of God in their minds. And Christianity gave its own strict sense to the word God by the fact of its speaking to minds who understood it in such a sense. In this true sense, then, the Divinity of Christ, along with the Divinity of God the Father, and consistently with the unity of the Divine Nature (Christianity retaining all the truth of Judaism while it added to it), was handed down to the succeeding Church. But in course of time a heresy arose, denying that Christ was God, and asserting Him to be a creature. The Nicene Fathers met this heresy at the Council of Nice, and framed a test to exclude it. That test was the 'Homoousion.' The Arians used the word God in their own sense, and therefore the word God did not exclude in their case the wrong sense, and was not a test. But the 'Homoousion' was a test, and did as a fact answer in excluding their sense, and therefore the orthodox adopted it. And the Nicene Creed was an explanation, and not a growth, of the doctrine of our Lord's Divinity.[320]

As Mozley further notes, should a 'modern theorist' have gone back in time and suggested to the orthodox Fathers at Nicaea that they were developing doctrine in the sense of making a new addition to Christian theology:

---

[320] Mozley, pp.164-165.

The Fathers would have been utterly astonished at his audacity; and they would have told him to communicate his assistance to heretics, for that they wanted none of it. To have called them developers would have been to take away, in their opinion, the very ground from under them, and to falsify their whole position. The hypothesis would have come into direct collision with the special declared ground on which the whole of their doctrinal teaching went, and would have just interfered with the very essence of their argument. Their argument, on every occasion of heresy arising, was one and the same thing, viz., that they had received a certain doctrine from the first, and that this heresy was contrary to it. They said, This is the old doctrine that we have, the old doctrine which the Apostles delivered, which has been the doctrine of the Church ever since, which we received from our predecessors as they received it from theirs, and which we now here maintain as we received it. The same, the very same, they repeated; they professed to hold it because it was the same, and for that reason only.[321]

To summarise, according to Mozley, there are two possible forms that the development of doctrine can take. The first form is the explanation of existing Christian doctrine in new ways. The second form is a process by means of which there is substantial change in the content of Christian doctrine. According to Mozley, it is the first form of development which has been universally accepted in the history of the Church, and which is illustrated by the development of the doctrine of the incarnation and by the action of the Fathers at the Council of Nicaea.

The first form of development set out by Mozley, what we may call the explanatory understanding of the development of doctrine has three great advantages.

First, an explanatory understanding of the development of doctrine helps to us make sense of Vincent's claim that doctrine can be 'novel

---

[321] Mozley, p.166.

but not new' (*noviter non nova*). If the development of doctrine means explaining the old truths of the Christian revelation in new ways, then it makes perfect sense to say with Vincent that to develop doctrine means to 'designate by new and appropriate words some article of faith, which is, of itself. traditional.' To explain something means precisely to designate something by the use of 'new and appropriate words.' That is what explanation is. Explanation does not involve novelty in the sense of changing an accepted truth. Rather, on involves clarifying through the use of new language what that truth is (which is what the Fathers did at Nicaea).

Secondly, an explanatory understanding of the development of doctrine make sense in terms of the nature of doctrine. What we noted in chapter 1 of this study is that doctrine 'is the revealed truth of God as defined and taught in the church, by the church, for the church, and for the world.' If we think about what it means to define and teach revealed truth, what we find is that it involves explanation. This is because to define something necessarily involves explaining what something is. For example, if I define a triangle as a plane shape with three straight sides and three angles then what I am doing is explaining to someone what a triangle is. Likewise, to teach something also means to explain something. If I teach a class of students that a triangle is a plane shape with three straight sides and three angles, I am likewise explaining what a triangle is. In similar fashion, to define and teach revealed truth means to explain what that revealed truth is, not to change it, or add to it, but to explain it. To develop doctrine therefore cannot mean changing, or adding to, the revealed truth of God. It can only mean, as Vincent says, using new words to explain what that truth is.

Thirdly, an explanatory understanding of doctrine makes sense of the history of the development of Christian doctrine. For instance if we consider the examples of the development of doctrine that we surveyed in chapter of this study, the New Testament writings, the Creeds and the Chalcedonian Confession, confessions of faith produced during the Reformation period and doctrinal statements from the twentieth and twenty first centuries, what we find is that they are all, without exception, attempts to explain and apply the apostolic faith in new ways in new situations.

Now obviously Protestants would not accept what the *Creed of the Council of Trent* says about the seven sacraments, the Mass, purgatory, and the authority of the Roman Catholic Church and of the Papacy as being explanations of the apostolic faith. In similar fashion Orthodox Christians would not accept the filioque clause in the Western version of the Nicene Creed as a proper explanation of the apostolic witness to the procession of the Holy Spirit and both Roman Catholic and Orthodox Christians would reject the doctrine of double predestination as set out in chapter III of the Reformed *Westminster Confession* of 1646 ('By the decree of God, for the manifestation of his glory, some men and angels are predestined to everlasting life, and other foreordained to everlasting death'[322]). However, in each of these three cases the doctrinal disagreement involved reflects a shared belief that doctrine should be an exposition of the apostolic faith. In each case one side believes that the material in question does state what the apostolic faith teaches, and the other side does not. In none of these cases is a claim being made that something can legitimately be added to the apostolic faith as taught in the New Testament and witnessed to by the Fathers.

These examples of doctrinal disagreement, and innumerable similar examples that could be cited, thus serve to emphasise the fact that there has been a generally held conviction in the history of the Church that doctrinal development cannot legitimately mean a departure from the apostolic faith, but can only rightly be a restatement, or further explanation, of it. What have been viewed as departures from the apostolic faith have been viewed as problematic precisely because it has been held that such departure is illegitimate.

---

[322] Text in Leith, p.198.

If we ask when Christians first started to hold that it that it was necessary to adhere to the apostolic faith the answer is that this belief is as old as the Church itself, going all the way back to the teaching of the apostles and those associated with them. Thus in 2 Thessalonians 2:15 Paul tells the Christians in Thessalonica to 'stand firm and hold the traditions which you were taught by us, either by word of mouth or by letter,' in Titus 1:9 Titus is instructed that a bishop must 'hold firm to the sure word as taught [by the apostles], so that he may be able to give instruction in sound doctrine and also to confute those who contradict it' and in 1 John 2:24 John tells his readers 'let what you have heard from the beginning abide in you' which in context is a reference to the apostolic witness referred to 1 John 1:1-3. Similarly in Luke's gospel and in the first chapter of Acts we are told that Jesus instructs the apostles and from then onwards it is the apostles and those associated with them who give instruction to those who subsequently become Christians. It is this 'teaching of the apostles' (Acts 2:42) that is the standard of faith for the Church.

In addition, it has traditionally been held that departure from the apostolic faith is a very serious matter. To use the words of the *Athanasian Creed* which we noted in chapter 2, it has been held that 'Whosoever will be saved: before all things it is necessary that he hold the Catholick Faith' and what has been meant by the 'Catholick Faith' is the faith taught by the apostles, to reject which is to disbelieve the teaching of Christ himself and so make oneself liable to damnation.

4. What happened at the Reformation

A common misconception about the Reformation is that the sixteenth century reformers were revolutionaries who were seeking to introduce a new version of the Christian faith. Nothing could be further from the truth. Just as the Fathers at Nicaea would have been horrified at the suggestion that they were introducing new version of the Christian faith, so also the reformers would have been equally horrified at the same suggestion.

The reformers were in fact conservatives. What they were seeking to do was to return the Church to the pattern of faith and practice which had been taught by the apostles and maintained by the Church of the early centuries, and which had then been corrupted by a subsequent series of ungodly innovations. To put it in Vincentian terms, they were seeking return to the form of faith and practice that in the earliest centuries of the Church had been accepted *ubique, semper et ab omnibus*.

As we have already noted at the end of chapter 3, what was true of the reformers in general was also true of the English reformers in particular. Their argument against their Roman Catholic critics, who accused them of resurrecting ancient heresies, was that far from being heretical the reformed Church of England was upholding the faith of the apostles and the Fathers. This argument is made, for example by John Jewel in his work *An Apology of the Church of England* which was published in 1562 and has been described as the first methodical statement of the position of the Church of England against the Roman Catholic Church.

In the *Apology* Jewel summarises the position taken by the Church of England on a range of matters of faith and practice and then declares rhetorically:

> Behold these are the horrible heresies, for the which, a good part of the world is at this day condemned by the Bishop of Rome; and yet were never heard to plead their cause. He should have commenced his suit rather against Christ, against the Apostles, and against the holy fathers. For these things did not only proceed from them, but were also appointed by them: except perhaps these men will say (as I think they will indeed), that Christ never instituted the Holy Communion to be divided amongst the faithful; or that Christ's Apostles and the ancient fathers said private masses in every corner of the temples, now ten, now twenty together in one day: or that Christ and His Apostles banished all the common people from the Sacrament of His blood: or that the thing, which they themselves do at this day everywhere, and do it so as they condemn him for a heretic which doth otherwise, is not called of Gelasius, their own doctor, plain sacrilege: or that these

be not the very words of Ambrose, Augustine, Gelasius, Theodoret, Chrysostom, and Origen: 'The bread and wine in the Sacraments remain still the same they were before:' 'The thing which is seen upon the Holy Table is bread;' 'There ceaseth not to be still the substance of bread, and nature of wine;' 'The substance and nature of bread are not changed;' 'The self-same bread, as touching the material substance, goeth into the belly, and is cast out into the privy:' or that Christ, the Apostles, and holy fathers prayed not in that tongue which the people might understand: or that Christ hath not performed all things by that one offering which He once offered: or that the same sacrifice was unperfect, and so now we have need of another. All these things must they of necessity say, unless perchance they had rather say thus, that 'all law and right is locked up in the treasury of the Pope's breast,' and that, as once one of his soothing pages and claw-backs did not stick to say, 'The Pope is able to dispense against the Apostles;' against a council, and against the canons and rules of the Apostles: and that he is not bound to stand neither to the examples, nor to the ordinances, nor to the laws of Christ. We, for our part, have learned these things of Christ, of the Apostles, of the devout fathers: and do sincerely, with good faith, teach the people of God the same. Which thing is the only cause why we at this day are called heretics of the chief prelates (no doubt) of religion. O immortal God! hath Christ Himself, then, the Apostles, and so many fathers all at once gone astray? Were then Origen, Ambrose, Augustine, Chrysostom, Gelasius, Theodoret, forsakers of the Catholic faith? was so notable a consent of so many ancient bishops and learned men nothing else but a conspiracy of heretics? or is that now condemned in us, which was then commended in them? or is the thing now, by alteration only of men's affections, suddenly become schismatic, which in them was counted Catholic? or shall that which in times past was true, now by-and-by, because it liketh not these men, be judged false? let them then bring forth another Gospel, and let them show the causes why these things, which so long have openly been observed and well-allowed in the Church of God, ought now in the end to be called in again. We know well enough that the same word which was opened by Christ, and spread abroad by the Apostles, is sufficient both, our salvation and all truth, to uphold and maintain; and also to confound all manner of heresy. By that word only do we condemn all sorts of the old heretics, whom these men say we have called out of hell again. As for the Arians, the Eutychians, the Marcionites, the Ebionites, the Valentinians, the Carpocratians, the Tatians, the Novatians, and shortly all them which have a wicked opinion, either of God the Father, or of Christ, or of the Holy Ghost, or of any other point of Christian religion, forsomuch as they be confuted by the Gospel of Christ, we plainly pronounce them for detestable and castaway persons, and defy them even unto the devil. [323]

As noted in chapter 2, The purpose of *The Thirty-nine Articles*, the confession of faith of the newly reformed Church of England, was to establish 'consent touching true religion' by embodying the faith and practice of the apostles and the Fathers in the life of the Church and the way they do this is to explain in specific terms the nature of that faith and practice on a variety of topics including predestination and election and the authority of the civil magistrate. As we said in chapter 2, the *Articles* constitute a development of doctrine in that what they say is new, but what they say is also old since it is deliberately designed to reflect what has already been said by the apostles and the Fathers.

The *Book of Common Prayer* and the *Ordinal* which were also produced by the English reformers were intended to reflect the faith taught by the apostles and the Fathers in the Church of England's liturgy. As in the case of the *Articles* what we find in them is new content used to reflect old ideas.

The *Articles*, the *Book of Common Prayer* and the *Ordinal* thus fit the explanatory understanding of the development of doctrine for which

---

[323] Ayre (ed), *The Works of John Jewel,* pp. 66-67.

we have argued in this chapter. They are an attempt to set forth anew the Church's unchanging faith.

5. The doctrine of the Church of England today

Today the Church of England has the same basis for its doctrine as the Church of England had in the sixteenth century. We can see this if we look at what is said in Canons A5 and C15 of the current Canon of the Church of England:

As we saw in chapter 3 Canon A5 declares:

> The doctrine of the Church of England is grounded in the Holy Scriptures, and in such teachings of the ancient Fathers and Councils as are agreeable to the said Scriptures.
>
> In particular such doctrine is to be found in the Thirty-nine Articles of Religion, the Book of Common Prayer and the Ordinal.

Likewise, the Preface to the Declaration of Assent in Canon C15 states:

> The Church of England is part of the One, Holy, Catholic and Apostolic Church worshipping the one true God, Father, Son and Holy Spirit. It professes the faith uniquely revealed in the Holy Scriptures and set forth in the catholic creeds, which faith the Church is called upon to proclaim afresh in each generation. Led by the Holy Spirit, it has borne witness to Christian truth in its historic formularies, the Thirty-nine Articles of Religion, The Book of Common Prayer and the Ordering of Bishops, Priests and Deacons.

What these Canons tell us is that the answer to the question 'Where do we find the doctrine of the Church of England?' the answer is that the Church of England has a threefold hierarchy of doctrinal sources.

- The primary source of doctrine is the Holy Scriptures, that is to say, the apostolic witness contained in the New Testament writings and the writings of the Old Testament understood in the light of this apostolic witness.

- The secondary source of doctrine is the teaching of the orthodox Fathers, Councils and Creeds, of early centuries, which reflects the apostolic witness contained in Holy Scripture.

- The tertiary source of doctrine is the three historic formularies which bear witness to the doctrine taught in the Holy Scriptures and by the orthodox Fathers, Councils and Creeds.

What this entails in terms of the development of doctrine is therefore that the development of the Church of England's doctrine must mean the further explanation of the doctrine contained in these three sets of sources. What would not be legitimate would be to either add to what is said in these sources or to decide to set aside what is said in these sources (the errors respectively of Newman and Wiles)

6. The Church of England's doctrine with regard to marriage and sexual activity

As Darrin Belousek notes in his study *Marriage, Scripture and the Church*, the consensual teaching of the Church about marriage, from New Testament times onwards, is absolutely clear:

> Scripture, consistently, presents a single picture of marriage and approves a single pattern of sexual relations: male- female union. Jesus summarizes this witness: 'the two' of 'male and female' joined into 'one flesh.' The Holy Spirit has woven this pattern of holy union throughout Scripture, from Genesis to Revelation, in the form, function, and figure of marriage. Tradition, East and West, also has consistently taught a single standard of sex and marriage: marriage is man-woman monogamy; all sex outside man-woman monogamy is sin. This doctrine has been taught always by the church, beginning with the apostles' testimony to Jesus teaching; It has been proclaimed throughout the worldwide church, among all people in every place and epoch, as God's will for sex and marriage; it has been articulated by apologetic writings and theological treatises, transmitted through baptismal catechesis and

canonical discipline, celebrated in monastic vows and nuptial rites.[324]

This biblical and Catholic consensus about the nature of marriage and the sinfulness of sex outside marriage, is reflected in the Church of England's most authoritative statement about marriage, and about the relationship between marriage and sexual activity, which is to be found in the service for the 'Solemnization of Matrimony' in the *Book of Common Prayer,* a service which reflects the teaching about marriage contained in Holy Scripture and the consensus teaching of the Fathers about how that teaching should be understood.

Solemnization means marking something with a formal ceremony and the form of service for the 'solemnization of matrimony' in the Book of Common Prayer is a formal Church rite to mark the entry of a man and a woman into matrimony (or marriage, for the terms holy matrimony, matrimony marriage and holy wedlock are used as synonyms).

The rite begins by stating positively the status of marriage given that according to the teaching of the reformed Church of England it is no longer to be regarded as a sacrament. It declares that marriage is:

> An honourable estate instituted by God in the time of man's innocency, signifying unto us the mystical union that is betwixt Christ and his Church: which holy estate Christ adorned and beautified with his presence, and the first miracle that he wrought, in Cana of Galilee; and is commended of St. Paul to be honourable among all men.

The words 'in the time of man's innocency' are intended to counter any idea that marriage is a second-class way of life brought in by God simply as a way of harnessing people's undisciplined sexual appetites

---

[324] Darrin Belousek, *Marriage, Scripture and the Church* (Grand Rapids: Baker Academic, 2021), Kindle Edition, p.284.

after the fall. On the contrary, the service says, marriage is something that is 'honourable' and 'holy.'

This is for four reasons given to us in Scripture.

First, as Genesis 1 and 2 tell us, marriage is an ordinance of God in creation and therefore shares in creation's original goodness prior to the Fall. Like everything else created by God it is 'very good.'

Secondly, as Ephesians 5:32 tells us, marriage is a God given sign pointing us to the relationship between Christ and His people, a relationship that has begun on earth and which will finally and fully consummated in the unity between God and his people in the world to come.

Thirdly, as John 2:1-12 tells us, Christ gave his own stamp of approval to marriage when he attended a marriage at Cana in Galilee and made it the occasion of his first miracle. Christ may not have instituted marriage as a sacrament, but he dignified it by his presence and action at Cana.

Fourthly, as Hebrews 13:4 (here attributed to Paul) says, marriage is therefore something that should be held in honour by everyone.

The service then goes on to warn that because marriage is honourable and holy it is therefore:

> ...not by any to be enterprised, nor taken in hand, unadvisedly, lightly, or wantonly, to satisfy men's carnal lusts and appetites, like brute beasts that have no understanding; but reverently, discreetly, advisedly, soberly, and in the fear of God; duly considering the causes for which Matrimony was ordained.

The service lists three causes for which marriage was ordained:

> First, It was ordained for the procreation of children, to be brought up in the fear and nurture of the Lord, and to the praise of his holy Name.

Secondly, It was ordained for a remedy against sin, and to avoid fornication; that such persons as have not the gift of continency might marry, and keep themselves undefiled members of Christ's body.

Thirdly, It was ordained for the mutual society, help, and comfort, that the one ought to have of the other, both in prosperity and adversity.

These three causes are Archbishop Thomas Cranmer's re-working of the traditional medieval list of the three 'goods' of marriage. This list goes back to Augustine's reading of Scripture in his treatise *On the Good of Marriage*[325] and in line with the commitment of the English Reformers to Holy Scripture as the primary theological authority for the Church,[326] Cranmer's re-working of this traditional list of the causes for marriage is likewise based on biblical teaching.

The first of these causes links Gods command to his human creatures 'be fruitful and multiply' in Genesis 1:28 to the building up of the Christian community in accordance with the promise of numerous godly descendants made by God to Abraham in Genesis 12:2-3.

As the homily 'Of the State of Matrimony' in the *Second Book of Homilies* puts it, marriage was ordained:

> ...that the Church of God and his kingdom, might by this kind of life, be conserved and enlarged, not only in that God giveth children, by his blessing, but also, in that they be brought up by the parents godly, in the knowledge of God's word; that thus the knowledge of God, and true religion, might be delivered in succession, from one

---

[325] Augustine, *On the Good of Marriage,* in *The Nicene and Post Nicene Fathers*, First Series, Vol.III (Edinburgh and Grand Rapids: T&T Clark/Eerdmans, 1998), pp. 399-413.

[326] For this see Martin Davie 'The role of Scripture in the Anglican formularies' in C Hill, M Kaiser, L Nathaniel and C Schwöbel (eds.*), Communion Already Shared and Further Steps – 20 Years After the Meissen Declaration* (Frankfurt am Main: Verlag Otto Lembeck, 2010), 331-358.

to another, that finally, many might enjoy that everlasting immortality.[327]

This means that according to the Church of England, procreation is an integral part of marriage, and the normal expectation is that a married couple who are able to do so will have choose to have children. A married couple that chose not to have children when they were able to do so would need to have a very good reason for their decision not to fulfil this aspect of the God given purpose of marriage, (such as, for example, a medical condition that would make childbirth potentially fatal for the mother or a missionary calling impossible to combine with family life).

Although, since the Lambeth Conference of 1930, the Church of England, like the Anglican tradition as a whole, has accepted that while parenthood is 'the glory of married life' it may be a legitimate Christian choice to use artificial contraception where 'there is...a clearly felt moral obligation to limit or avoid parenthood, and where there is a morally sound reason for avoiding complete abstinence,'[328] the fact that there has to be a morally good reason to avoid or limit parenthood means that it is still accepted that marriage and procreation should normally go together, even if procreation does not have to be the intended end of every act of marital sexual intercourse. To quote the words of Oliver O'Donovan

> As a whole, then, the married love of any couple should (barring serious reasons to the contrary) be both relationship building and procreative; the two ends of marriage are held together in the life

---

[327] 'An Homily of the State of Matrimony' in *The Homilies* (Bishopstone: The Brynmill Press/Preservation Press, 2006), p.363. *The First and Second Books of Homilies* were collections of authorised sermons produced by the Church of England during the reigns of Edward VI and Elizabeth I to give teaching on key issues of Christian faith and behaviour. They provide an authorised commentary on the teaching given in the Articles and the Prayer Book.

[328] Lambeth Conference 1930, Resolutions 14 and 15, in R Coleman (ed), *Resolutions of the Lambeth Conferences, 1867-1988* (Toronto: Anglican Book Centre, 1992), p.72.

of sexual partnership which the couple live together. But it is artificial to insist, as *Humanae Vitae* did, that 'each and every marriage act must express the two goods equally.'[329]

The second cause links the teaching of Paul in 1 Corinthians 7:2 and 7:8-9 about marriage as a remedy for the temptation to sexual immorality with his teaching in 1 Corinthians 6 about the sexual purity required of the members of body of Christ. As the homily 'Of the State of Matrimony' puts it, marriage bridles 'the corrupt inclinations of the flesh, within the limits of honesty; for God hath strictly forbidden all whoredom and uncleanness.'[330]

The phrase 'remedy against sin' used in this second cause is an English translation of the Latin phrase *'remedium peccati'* which again goes back to Augustine. Augustine saw marriage as a remedy against sin because its good of faithfulness (*fides*) turned the roaming disorders of excessive sexual appetite into a settled and exclusive attraction and because the link in marriage between sexual activity and the procreation of children (with the consequent responsibilities and constraints of parenthood) meant that 'carnal or youthful incontinence, which is admittedly a defect, is applied to the honourable task of begetting children, and so intercourse within marriage engenders something good from the evil of lust.'[331] Cranmer and the other English Reformers, on the other hand, had a different

---

[329] Oliver O'Donovan, *Begotten or Made?* (Oxford: OUP, 1984), p.77.
O'Donovan's point meets the argument put forward by Rowan Williams in his lecture *The Body's Grace (*London: Lesbian and Gay Christian Movement, 2003) that it is incoherent to both accept contraception and reject same-sex sexual relationships. One can coherently hold that sexual activity should only take place within a relationship that is in principle open to the gift of children through procreation and also hold that not every act of intercourse needs to be procreative in intent. For a further discussion of this point see Belousek pp.138-142 and Dennis Hollinger, *The Meaning of Sex* (Grand Rapids: Baker Academic, 2009), pp.161-166.
[330] 'An Homily on the State of Matrimony,' p.363.
[331] Augustine, *On the Good of Marriage* 3, in Patrick Walsh (ed), *Augustine: De bono coniugali, De sancta virginitate* (Oxford: OUP, 2001), p.7.

focus. For them the problem for which marriage was a remedy was sexual activity outside marriage ('whoredom or uncleanness') rather than excessive sexual desire within it.

The view held by the English reformers, like that of the Church as a whole from New Testament times, was that all forms of sexual intercourse outside marriage (including what we now call same-sex sexual intimacy) were abominable sins forbidden by the seventh commandment. Thus, the homily 'Against whoredom and uncleanness' declares:

> And that ye may perceive, that fornication and whoredom, are in the sight of God, most abominable sins, ye shall call to remembrance, this commandment of God, Thou shalt not commit adultery. By the which word adultery, though it be properly understood of the unlawful commixtion (or joining together), of a married man with any woman beside his wife, or of a wife, with any man beside her husband: yet thereby is signified also, all unlawful use of those parts which be ordained for generation. And this one commandment forbidding adultery, doth sufficiently paint and set forth before our eyes, the greatness of this sin of whoredom, and manifestly declareth how greatly, it ought to be abhorred, of all honest and faithful persons.[332]

It is this conviction that underlies what is said about the second cause of marriage. Marriage, and marriage alone, provides the setting within which people may engage in sexual activity in a godly way that does not breach the seventh commandment and by so doing 'keep themselves undefiled members of Christ's body.'

The third cause links together the teaching of Genesis 2:18-25 about the origins of marriage and the teaching about the nature of the marriage among Christians by Paul in Colossians 3:18-19 and Ephesians 5:21-33 and by Peter in 1 Peter 3:1-7. To quote the homily

---

[332] 'A sermon against whoredom and uncleanness' in *The Homilies*, pp.88-89.

again, it depicts marriage as 'perpetually friendly fellowship'[333] between a husband and wife.

Consideration of the fact that marriage was ordained by God himself for these three causes reinforces the need for marriage not to be undertaken 'unadvisedly, lightly, or wantonly.' They mean that marriage is not simply a matter of engaging in sexual activity 'like brute beasts that have no understanding,' but a serious Christian vocation that is just as spiritually demanding in its own way as the vocation to celibacy and is therefore to be undertaken 'reverently, discreetly, advisedly, soberly, and in the fear of God.'

It should be noted that it is not that Cranmer disapproves of animal instincts in animals. Cranmer's point is rather that marriage is a thoroughly human activity and as such to be woven in with the considered thoughts and plans for life in obedience to God which are proper to human beings.

Further important details about the understanding of marriage in *The Book of Common Prayer* are provided by the part of the marriage service in which the marriage itself takes place.

This part of the service begins with a warning by the minister taking the service that if either party to the marriage knows of any impediment to it, they should confess it because 'so many as are coupled together otherwise than God's word doth allow are not joined together by God; neither is their Matrimony lawful.'

After this a chance is given for any potential impediment to the marriage to be alleged and investigated and if no impediment is alleged then two sets of promises follow.

In the first set the man answers 'I will' to the question:

---

[333] 'An Homily on the State of Matrimony,' p.363.

> Wilt thou have this woman to thy wedded wife, to live together after God's ordinance in the holy estate of Matrimony? Wilt thou love her, comfort her, honour, and keep her, in sickness and in health; and, forsaking all other, keep thee only unto her, so long as ye both shall live?

The woman likewise answers 'I will' to the question:

> Wilt thou have this man to thy wedded husband, to live together after God's ordinance in the holy estate of Matrimony? Wilt thou obey him, and serve him, love, honour, and keep him, in sickness and in health; and, forsaking all other, keep thee only unto him, so long as ye both shall live?

In the second set the man and woman declare in turn:

> I N. take thee N. to my wedded wife, to have and to hold from this day forward, for better for worse, for richer for poorer, in sickness and in health, to love and to cherish, till death us do part, according to God's holy ordinance; and thereto I plight thee my troth.

> I N. take thee N. to my wedded husband, to have and to hold from this day forward, for better for worse, for richer for poorer, in sickness and in health, to love, cherish, and to obey, till death us do part, according to God's holy ordinance; and thereto I give thee my troth.

The man next places a ring on the woman's left hand with the words: 'With this ring I thee wed, with my body I thee worship, and with all my worldly goods I thee endow: In the Name of the Father, and of the Son, and of the Holy Ghost. Amen.'

The minster then prays:

> O eternal God, Creator and Preserver of all mankind, Giver of all spiritual grace, the Author of everlasting life: Send thy blessing upon these thy servants, this man and this woman, whom we bless in thy Name; that, as Isaac and Rebecca lived faithfully together, so

these persons may surely perform and keep the vow and covenant betwixt them made, (whereof this ring given and received is a token and pledge,) and may ever remain in perfect love and peace together, and live according to thy laws; through Jesus Christ our Lord. Amen.

He then joins their right hands together and says:

Those whom God hath joined together let no man put asunder.

After that he tells the congregation:

Forasmuch as N. and N. have consented together in holy wedlock, and have witnessed the same before God and this company, and thereto have given and pledged their troth either to other, and have declared the same by giving and receiving of a ring, and by joining of hands; I pronounce that they be man and wife together, In the Name of the Father, and of the Son, and of the Holy Ghost. Amen.

Finally, he pronounces a further blessing on the newly married couple:

God the Father, God the Son, God the Holy Ghost, bless, preserve, and keep you; the Lord mercifully with his favour look upon you, and so fill you with all spiritual benediction and grace, that ye may so live together in this life, that in the world to come ye may have life everlasting. Amen.

After this the service concludes with the recitation of Psalms 128 or 67, prayers, a concluding blessing and either a sermon or a reading of the teaching on marriage from Ephesians 5, Colossians 3 and 1 Peter 3.

An examination of this part of the marriage service reveals seven key points concerning marriage.

- The opening prayer by the minister holds together creation and grace. Cranmer and the other English Reformers did not see marriage as a sacrament, but they did not see it as a purely secular matter, but as a means of grace through which people might receive God's blessing.

- Although in the sixteenth century a church service was not regarded as a necessary part of marriage,[334] the *Book of Common Prayer* is clear that a wedding is a religious ceremony which is undertaken before God and God's people and blessed in God's name.

- For a marriage to be valid and lawful (under the laws of both Church and state) it cannot take place in any way that is not permitted by Scripture, 'other than God's word doth allow'. That is why the *Book of Common Prayer* contains a table of 'kindred and affinity' listing those relationships that are an impediment to marriage according to Leviticus 18:6-18 and 20:17-21.

- A marriage is a covenant freely entered into by one man and one woman, enacted by a mutual exchange of promises and the giving and receiving of a ring. It is 'vow and covenant betwixt them made' that makes them man and wife. When the minister says 'I pronounce that they be man and wife together' this is the public announcement of an existing reality, not the creation of a new one.

- The character of the covenant that a husband and wife have entered into is a commitment to a life-long exclusive relationship of mutual love between one man and one woman.

- The fact that the bride promises to obey her husband is an indication that the teaching of Ephesians 5:22-24, Colossians 3:18 and 1 Peter 3:1-6, about wives submitting to their

---

[334] See The Church of England, *An Honourable Estate* (London: CHP, 1988), pp.20-21 and more generally Lawrence Stone *The Family, Sex and marriage in England 1500-1800* (Harmondsworth: Penguin, 1979).

husbands is seen as still applicable to Christian marriage in subsequent times and not just in the first century.[335] However, this does not justify a husband exercising arbitrary or tyrannical authority over his wife. Rather, to quote the homily 'Of Matrimony' once again, the husband 'ought to be the leader and author of love, in cherishing and increasing concord'[336] thus fulfilling the apostle's exhortation 'husbands, love your wives as Christ loved the church and gave himself up for her' (Ephesians 5:25).

- The use of the words 'those whom God hath joined together let no man put asunder' taken from Matthew 19:6/Mark 10:9 acts as a solemn warning about the sanctity and therefore permanence of marriage, making clear that human beings should not break apart through divorce those whom God has joined together in marriage.

A final point that is worth noting is that the rubric at the end of the marriage service states that 'it is convenient that the new-married persons should receive the Holy Communion at the time of their Marriage, or at the first opportunity after their Marriage.' This rubric once again underlines the specifically Christian character of the form of marriage envisaged in the marriage service of the *Book of Common Prayer*. The vision is of a newly married couple entering as a couple into the life of the Christian community and symbolizing this by receiving Holy Communion together at the first opportunity.

The doctrine of marriage contained in the *Book of Common Prayer* is reflected in the Church of England's Canon law in Canon B.30, 'Of Holy Matrimony,' which was promulgated in 1969, Like the other Canons, it sets the legal parameters for the corporate life of the Church of

---

[335] This point is also made clear in the exhortation to the newly married couple provided for use at the end of a service where there is no sermon. This exhortation instructs the wife to obey her husband on the basis of the teaching of Ephesians, Colossians and 1 Peter.

[336] 'An Homily on the State of Matrimony,' p.365.

England. In this connection it consciously and deliberately underlines the doctrine of marriage contained in the marriage service in the *Book of Common Prayer* and in the consensual teaching of the Bible and the Christian tradition as a whole.

The Canon specifically affirms that the Church of England's understanding of marriage is set forth in the B*ook of Common Prayer* marriage service:

> The teaching of our Lord affirmed by the Church of England is expressed and maintained in the Form of Solemnization of Matrimony contained in The Book of Common Prayer.[337]

The Canon also summarises the teaching on marriage of the *Book of Common Prayer* and deliberately echoes its language. It declares:

> The Church of England affirms, according to our Lord's teaching, that marriage is in its nature a union permanent and lifelong, for better for worse, till death them do part, of one man with one woman, to the exclusion of all others on either side, for the procreation and nurture of children, for the hallowing and right direction of the natural instincts and affections, and for the mutual society, help and comfort which the one ought to have of the other, both in prosperity and adversity.[338]

'Our Lord's teaching' referred to here, is the teaching of Jesus about marriage in Matthew 19:3-12 and Mark 10:2-12 (which in turn refers to the creation narratives in Genesis 1 and 2). The reference to marriage being 'in its nature a union permanent and lifelong' is an addition to the language of the Prayer Book and was intended to underscore the permanent nature of marriage at a time when this was felt to be under threat in British society. The words 'in its nature' indicate that permanence is an essential feature of marriage as a created ordinance and therefore something that applies to all

---

[337] Canon B30.2
[338] Canon B30.1

marriages, in contrast to the Augustinian and medieval view that permanence is a feature only of sacramental, that is Christian, marriages.

Building on this last point it is important to recognise that the term 'Holy Matrimony' in the title of the Canon, which is taken from the language of the Prayer Book, does not refer to a specific Church of England type of marriage which is different from other marriages. There is not 'holy matrimony' as opposed to 'unholy matrimony.' In this Canon, as in the theology of the Church of England in general, there is only one type of marriage which is the form of marriage affirmed by Jesus outlined in the Prayer Book marriage service, referred to in the marriage service and summarised in the Canon.

The words 'for the hallowing and right direction of the natural instincts and affections' (which are taken from the marriage service in the 1928 Prayer Book) are the Canon's gloss on the second cause of matrimony in the *Book of Common Prayer.* The point made by this gloss is that marriage allows natural human instincts and affections (including the natural human desire for a sexual relationship) to find expression in a way that is holy and that is accord with the way that God has created his human creatures to live. The Canon expresses this point in a positive way, but by implication it highlights the truth made explicitly in the *Book of Common Prayer* and the *Homilies* that that the expression of human desires and instincts outside of marriage can be unholy and not in accordance with God's will (as in the case of sexual activity outside marriage).

7. What would a development of doctrine mean in relation to the Church of England's doctrine concerning marriage and sexual activity?

There are three ideas currently supported by those in the Church of England who take a liberal approach to marriage and sexual activity (including members of the House of Bishops) and which are being pushed as part of the *Prayers of Love and Faith* process that cannot rightly be seen as a development of the Church of England's doctrine with regard to these matters that we have noted in the previous section of this chapter if we accept an explanatory view of the nature of the development of doctrine.

The first idea is that it would be right to bless same-sex couples who are in a sexually active relationship either in normal church services or in special 'standalone' or 'bespoke' services.

The reason that this would not be a development of doctrine is that the doctrine of the Church of England, as we have seen, is that all forms of sexual activity outside heterosexual marriage are forms of the sin of fornication which all Christians are called to avoid committing (and for which those Christians who have committed it are called to repent, confess and receive absolution as they would with all other forms of sin). It is not an explanation of the Church's doctrine on this matter to say that those who continue to be in a relationship involving the sin of fornication should be able to have this relationship blessed by the Church. Rather, saying this would contradict the Church's doctrine in one of two ways. It would involve saying either (a) that fornication is not a sin or (b) that sin does not need to be met with a call to repentance, confession, absolution and amendment of life but can instead be the object of prayers of blessing.[339]

The second idea is that those who are in same-sex sexual relationships should be admitted to, or allowed to continue to exercise, ordained ministry.

The reason that this would not be a development of doctrine is that the Church of England's doctrine, as set out in the 1662 *Ordinal* is that it is an integral part of the calling of those who are ordained to be: 'diligent to frame and fashion your own selves, and your families, according to the doctrine of Christ; and to make both yourselves and

---

[339] For more details on why the blessing of same-sex couples is theologically illegitimate see Martin Davie, *With God's Approval? - A theological exploration of blessing same-sex couples in dialogue with Walter Moberly and Isabelle Hamley* (Oxford, Dictum Press, 2023).

them, as much as in you lieth, wholesome examples and patterns to the flock of Christ.'[340] It is not an explanation of the Church's doctrine to say that being in a same-sex sexual relationship is compatible with providing a wholesome example and pattern to the flock of Christ. As in the previous example, it would instead contradict the Church's doctrine by in this case suggesting either (a) that being in a same-sex sexual relationship is in accordance with 'the doctrine of Christ' or (b) that the requirements for ministerial conduct set out in the *Ordinal* no longer matter.

The third idea is that the Church of England should accept that marriage can rightly be between two people of the same sex as well as two people of the opposite sex. This again would not be an explanation of the Church's doctrine, but rather a contradiction of it. One cannot say both that 'The Church of England affirms, according to our Lord's teaching, that marriage is in its nature a union permanent and life-long, for better or worse, till death do them part of one man and one woman' and also say that a relationship between two people of the same-sex is a marriage. The only way one can consistently say that a relationship between two-people of the same-sex is a marriage is if one has a different understanding of the nature of marriage. The idea that a doctrine of marriage that teaches that marriage is between two people of the opposite sex could be 'spacious' enough (as the bishops put it) to include same-sex relationships simply does not make sense.

What all this means is that the development of doctrine, rightly understood, rules out rather than permits these innovations which liberals wish to introduce, and which members of the House of Bishops are proposing.

The only theologically coherent reasons for saying that the Church's doctrine could include the affirmation of same-sex sexual relationships and the recognition of same-sex relationships as

---

[340] 1662 *Ordinal,* 'The Ordering of Priests.'

marriage (and thus the ordination of those in such relationships or marriages) would be either:

a) To follow the approach taken on other matters by Newman and say that the faith of the apostles had an implicit caveat which said that same-sexual relationships are morally acceptable if they are consensual and loving and that marriages could be between two people of the same sex as well as two people of the opposite sex.

or

b) To follow the approach taken by Wiles (and liberal Protestantism more widely) and set aside the apostolic teaching forbidding fornication and restricting marriage to people of the opposite sex on the grounds that it no longer makes sense in terms of the thought of our day.

However, as we have noted in this study (a) does not work because we simply cannot know that such a caveat was ever an implicit part of the apostolic faith and (b) is unacceptable because setting aside the teaching of the apostles means rejecting the teaching authority of Christ and therefore of God himself.

If one really wants to engage in a development of the Church of England's doctrine with regard to marriage and sexual ethics, the only legitimate way to do this would be to produce fresh doctrinal material setting out anew the Church's *existing* doctrine on marriage and sexual activity in a way that engages with the current debates about these matters, just as Paul set out his apostolic doctrine in engagement with the issue facing the Church in Rome and as the Fathers at Nicaea set out their understanding of the apostolic doctrine concerning the nature of God in engagement with the debate about these matters caused by the heretical teaching of Arius.

In its statement *Gospel Church and Marriage* the Church of England Evangelical Council has produced a statement which gives a good example of what this kind of doctrinal development, *noviter*, but not *nova* would look like. I conclude this study by including this statement as a model for the Church of England as a whole to follow.

Gospel, Church & Marriage

Preserving Apostolic Faith and Life

As members of the Church of England Evangelical Council ("CEEC") within the Church of England and the one, holy, catholic and apostolic Church, we offer this reflection out of our deep love for the Church of England, the wider Anglican Communion, and the world we want to serve.

As we face many changes in British society and forceful challenges within the Church of England on matters of human sexuality and marriage, we believe it is important not simply to focus on these contentious areas of disagreement but to set them within a wider and deeper theological vision. Our desire is for the Church's teaching and practice to offer a vision of human flourishing which is faithful to Scripture.

This vision begins with God's good purposes for us all as human beings and His plan to bring these purposes to birth in His world through the gospel of His forgiveness and grace, revealed in Jesus Christ and proclaimed in the power of the Spirit by Christ's apostles. This good news creates and shapes a holy people who are called to believe it, live it, guard it, and share it with others. Together, we are called to worship the Triune God, the source of grace who 'has created all things, and us in His own image' and from whom comes 'all life, truth, holiness and beauty'.1

Scripture reveals that the Creator's passionate longing is for human flourishing and the good of all. He works to bless all nations through His people (Gen. 12:3). The laws God gave to Israel were His gracious gift ('for your good': Deut. 10:13) designed to create a healthy society that would reflect God's holiness and goodness, His justice and compassion. The prophets called Israel back to this way of life in obedience to God and away from idolatry, injustice and immorality so that she could be 'a light to the nations' (Isa. 42:1-6). Likewise the Church, rooted in the apostles' teaching, is called by Jesus to be 'salt and light' in the world (Matt. 5:13-16). The Gospel shines into the darkness of our fallen hearts and cultures, and gives us the transforming knowledge of God's mercy and grace in the face of Jesus Christ.

We long for all to hear and believe this message—of God's unmerited grace and mercy shown to us all as sinful people through the atoning death and resurrection of Jesus Christ, our Lord (1 John 4:10; Eph. 2:1-10) – and, in particular, for the people of England to come under the loving rule of Christ and so to discover the life-changing goodness of this 'amazing grace' for themselves.

The presenting divisive issues in the Church surrounding marriage and sex, and our society's movement away from Christian teaching in this area, must not distract us from working towards that goal. Yet neither can they be ignored or treated as having no bearing on how this is achieved. In order to discern how to respond to these specific matters, we must first recall and re-commit ourselves to the gospel and its purpose as revealed in Scripture:

i. Through His Son and by His Spirit, God is working within human history and across all cultures to rescue His creation from sin and to transform the lives of Jesus' followers so that we embody His positive, life-enhancing purposes for all people.

ii. The Church is God's gift, sign and instrument of the restoration of His creation, and is the foretaste of His new creation that is breaking in. This in turn requires us to consider what it means for the Church to have integrity as the body of Christ by remaining rooted in God's grace and being shaped by the biblical story of creation, fall, redemption and future hope.

iii. In awaiting the final judgment and the fulfilment of God's good purposes, the Church must – at all times and in all places – faithfully obey the apostles' teaching on the pattern of faith and life that we are called to in Christ. This includes their teaching on marriage and singleness. Only when we have received what the apostles have to say to us in each of these three areas and uncovered the deeper biblical truths that are at stake in this debate can we draw conclusions as to the necessary shape of apostolic faith and life today and what that means for our way forward as Anglicans within the one, holy, catholic and apostolic Church.

A. Apostolic Insistence on the Gospel's Purpose

As God's grace and truth prepare us for Christ's return as the triumph of grace over all the effects of sin, His will is that all who come under Christ's rule should turn from sin and be sanctified (1 Thess. 4:3). In this way, the true nature of God's holy purposes in the gospel are revealed to the world.

The apostolic gospel proclaimed the *work of grace*: that God, revealing His glory in human form, demonstrated His holy love and His opposition to all sin by redeeming His creation and rescuing humanity through Christ and His atoning death and glorious resurrection (Gal. 1:4; 1 John 4:10; Rom 3:21-26). Christ had thus 'given himself' in dying on the cross with the express purpose 'to purify for himself a people, eager to do what is good' (Titus 2:14, cf. Rom 7:4). The gospel, as proclaimed by the apostles, had the goal and purpose—as well as the power—to transform people's lives into the likeness of Christ (Eph. 2:8-10; 1 Jn. 3:2-10; Rom. 8:29).

In establishing Christian communities the apostles therefore did not teach doctrine without discipleship, faith without formation, or grace without godliness. Rather, they called believers to 'live lives worthy of the gospel', insisting 'in the Lord' that they abandon their 'former way of life' and embrace 'the new humanity', 'putting on Christ' and living His new life (Eph. 4:17-24; cf. Rom. 6:1-14;1 Pet. 1:14-15; 2:11).

Moreover, the apostles consistently taught that the baptised were, by the Spirit, to pursue godliness and combat sin by putting to death the 'works of the flesh' (e.g. Gal. 5:16-21; 1 John 2:15-17). And teaching communities of disciples who would offer this good news of God's grace to all, the apostles therefore repeatedly issued a serious call to holiness which embraced all areas of human life including sexual conduct (1 Cor. 6:9-11; 1 Tim. 1:8-10; Heb. 12:14-16; Jude 1:4; Rev. 2:14).

B. Apostolic Commitment to the Church's Integrity
In its ministry of stewarding God's grace so as to offer it to the world, the Church, being 'built on the foundation of the apostles and prophets' (Eph. 2:20) must in every age follow the apostles' example. Its teaching and discipline must remain centred on Christ and within the boundaries of essential apostolic teaching.

The apostles' preaching established *communities of grace* who confessed 'Jesus is Lord'. These 'apostolic congregations' were marked by believers' devoted submission to apostolic teaching (Acts 2:42; Rom. 6:17; Eph. 4:20). Building on the one foundation of Jesus himself (1 Cor. 3:11; Eph. 2:20), who had 'loved the Church' as His bride and had 'given himself up for her to make her holy' (Eph. 5:25-26), the apostles could not compromise the holiness of the Church. Instead they saw that, as God had called Israel to be 'holy', 'set apart' as distinct 'amongst the nations', so now the Church was to be a 'holy temple' and a 'holy nation' (Eph. 2:19-22; 1 Pet. 2:4-9; cf. Exod. 19:3-6; Lev. 18:3-5; 19:2; Deut. 4:5-8; Isa. 42:6-7). They thus sought to build a united body drawn from the nations ('one' and 'catholic') which was the 'pillar and foundation of the truth' (1 Tim. 3.15) and which, through obedience to apostolic teaching (Rom. 15:18; Phil. 2:12-13; 1 Pet. 1:22), conveyed and embodied that teaching in the wider world with clarity and consistency (Eph. 3:10; 4:4-17).

In order, then, for the Church to witness to the gospel with integrity and to embody the gospel's purpose, the apostles had to guard the Church's distinctive boundaries on matters of both doctrine and ethics, including sexual morality. This is evident in their use of appropriate loving discipline to ensure obedience to apostolic teaching (1 Cor. 4:14-5:5; 2 Cor. 2:5-11; Rev. 2:20), their appointment of local teachers to teach the truth (Tit. 1:9; 2 Tim. 2:2), and their warnings against harmful false teachers (e.g. Acts 20:29-31; 2 Pet. 2:1-3; 1 John 2:18-23).

This is why, as part of the 'one, holy, catholic and apostolic' church, the Church of England rightly orders its common life so that there are 'shepherds of Christ's flock and guardians of the faith of the apostles' who, in 'proclaiming the gospel of God's kingdom and leading His people in mission', vow to 'refute error' (Common Worship: Ordination & and Consecration of a Bishop) and are called to 'banish and drive away all erroneous and strange opinions' (Canon C18).

C. Apostolic Teaching about Marriage and Singleness

The Bible as the *revelation of grace* clearly teaches that God made humanity in His image and likeness—embodied as male and female—and gave the gifts of marriage and singleness for our benefit. This apostolic teaching about marriage and singleness is part of God's gracious call and purposes for human flourishing and is good news for all.

On Jesus' authority (e.g. Matt. 19:4-6, based on Gen. 2:24), the Church of England bears witness to this teaching by affirming that 'marriage is in its nature a union permanent and lifelong, for better for worse, till death them do part, of one man with one woman, to the exclusion of all others on either side' (Canon B30). Moreover, like the sacraments, marriage is a gift of God and a sign of grace in which His faithful and sacrificial covenant-love for us is made visible in and through our created human bodies (Eph. 5:31-2). As 'a gift of God in creation', marriage enables human flourishing and serves the common good by being 'the foundation of family life in which children are [born and] nurtured and in which each member of the family, in good times and in bad, may find strength, companionship and comfort, and grow to maturity in love' (Preface to Marriage Service).

Jesus' own understanding of the importance of marriage is underlined by His radical teaching on adultery and divorce (Matt. 5:27-32), which went to the heart of the Old Testament prohibitions in these areas. His reputation as a 'friend of sinners' was never won at the cost of watering down such ethical teachings or advocating 'cheap grace'. He rather held together grace and truth (John 1:14) in His teaching and pastoral practice — a model which the Church should always aim to follow.

Jesus, in His own experience and express teaching (Matt. 19:12), also affirmed singleness, equally, as a gracious gift from God—as did Paul (1 Cor. 7:7, 32-35); it is an opportunity for faithful and sacrificial dedication to 'the Lord's affairs' and for demonstrating an embodied longing for the ultimate marital union of Christ to His Church (Rev. 19:6-9).

In keeping with this understanding, rooted in the teaching of the Old Testament (e.g. Exod. 20:14; Prov. 5:15-23) and reaffirmed by Jesus himself, the apostles taught that any sex outside marriage has the character of sin (e.g. Matt. 5:27-29; 1 Thess. 4:3-8; Heb. 13:4). Thus, as the House of Bishops recently reaffirmed, sexual relations are 'properly conducted only within heterosexual marriage' (GS 2055, para 54). Sex is not a personal 'right' to be grasped or demanded. It is a gracious gift ordained by our Creator—tied to His gift of marriage—which is to be 'received with thanksgiving' (1 Tim. 4:4), but only within the limits He has laid down.

Application: Apostolic Faith and Life Today
In the light of this wider theological vision and apostolic teaching on the gospel's purpose, the church's integrity, and marriage and singleness, we therefore commit ourselves to the following five conclusions and commend them to the Church of England as it considers these complex issues of human sexuality and marriage:

1. We, in the church of Jesus Christ, are called to welcome, and offer God's saving grace to, everyone—whatever their sexual history, identity or behaviour—thus manifesting the radical inclusivity of the gospel by which 'God our Saviour wants all people to be saved' (1 Tim. 2:3).

- Knowing that God's created intent for human sexuality has been spoilt by sin in all people and all societies, we acknowledge our own need, following conversion, to keep turning to God for forgiveness and transformation.

- We confess that to be the community of grace the Church itself needs forgiveness and transformation. We long for all to hear and receive the gospel message of grace and truth, rather than to fear that we, as Christians, will cast the first stone. So we receive Jesus' words as also applying to us and to all: 'Neither do I condemn you ...Go now and leave your life of sin' (John 8:11). We want the church to be a community of love, warmth, hospitality, vulnerability, covenant friendship, appropriate touch, mutual support, and to be a family unit which is far bigger than some small, inward-looking heterosexual pairing.

- We therefore repent of our many failures in this area, seeking God's grace afresh to welcome, listen to, and provide pastoral support and care for all.

- Together, we will seek to honour the gift of our embodied sexual differentiation; to express life-long faithful love in marriage; and to nurture love and intimacy while abstaining from sex in all our relationships other than marriage.

2. We recognise that some fellow Christians no longer accept the Church's teaching on marriage, singleness and sex but, because it is an integral part of our calling to be holy, we cannot treat this teaching as an 'optional extra' (or adiaphora).

- We believe this teaching is both apostolic and essential to the gospel's transforming purpose and thus must be compassionately and clearly proclaimed and explained in and by the Church.

- This area is therefore of a higher order than other divisive matters, often viewed as 'secondary' (for example, the ordination of women), because it calls for faithful obedience to the unambiguous and authoritative teaching of Scripture concerning godly living and human flourishing.

- Thus, the upholding of this teaching, rooted in our creedal confession of God as Creator, and the enabling of Christians to live it with joy and confidence, is an essential aspect of biblical faithfulness—especially when, as in our day, these matters are being so hotly contested.

3. We believe that the Church of England, being defined by adherence to essential apostolic truth, should not accept teaching or affirm behaviour—whether implicitly or explicitly—which contradicts or undermines the boundaries laid down by apostolic teaching and practice.

- Although other actions may also amount to such affirmation, we hold, on the basis of our Anglican understanding of our prayers expressing what we believe ('*lex orandi, lex credendi*') and of a Church that is ordered by its liturgy, formularies and legal provisions, that any changes in our liturgy or canons which seek to express, authorise or commend a divergence from these distinctive boundaries would be seen as a departure from the apostolic faith.

4. We further believe that, as we have sadly witnessed in recent years among Anglicans, the affirmation of non-apostolic teaching and behaviour necessarily 'tears the fabric of our Communion at its deepest level' (Primates' Communiqué, Oct. 2003) and creates 'significant distance' (Primates' Communiqué, Jan. 2016) between those who are following the apostles' teaching and those departing from it. Such affirmation by the Church of England would have a

similar distancing effect on our ecumenical relationships with the Roman Catholic, Orthodox and most Protestant and Pentecostal churches, which have not changed their doctrine in this vital area.

- These consequences inevitably arise because—for those who wish to follow the apostles' practice—such significant departure from apostolic teaching regrettably requires in response some degree of visible differentiation, in order formally to acknowledge and mark this distance. Moving away from 'apostolic' and 'catholic' teaching concerning what it means to be 'holy' will tragically mean we are less visibly 'one'.

- The potential forms and extent of such differentiation are varied and they must never lose sight of the goal of restored unity in apostolic truth. Nevertheless, such acts of differentiation become a necessary component of biblical faithfulness if they are the only means to ensure the continued preservation of a cohesive 'apostolic' community, clearly defined and publicly distinguished by apostolic truth and thus able to offer a faithful and coherent witness to a confused and needy world.

5. We do not wish for this differentiation, but recognise that it may become a tragic necessity. Our submission to apostolic teaching and practice means that, as apostolic Anglicans, we are deeply committed to being members of Church of England provinces which are similarly submissive and so communicating and clearly upholding—both de facto and de jure—the pattern of teaching and discipline handed down to us by the apostles.

- We therefore pray that the Church of England does not turn away from its teaching on marriage, singleness and sex—entrusted to it by Christ and His apostles—or abandon its goal of empowering Christians to live lives worthy of the gospel of grace.

- We believe this teaching remains good news for society today, where many struggle to form wholesome and life-giving intimate friendships, lack good models of loving, faithful marriage and parenting, and face confusing choices of identity and gender.

• And so we commit ourselves to working within our local congregations and networks in order that they too may walk compassionately in obedience to the apostles' teaching. We also commit to praying for the people of England that these biblical truths will increasingly come to be recognized for their long-established and proven benefit.

Conclusion

In offering this reflection we place ourselves afresh under the grace of God and the authority of Scripture, and we consecrate ourselves to Jesus as Lord, rededicating ourselves to obey the teaching of His apostles. And we do so in a spirit of repentance for the ways we daily fail to practise the grace and truth that Jesus both preached and lived.

Our hope and prayer is that it will provide clarity in a time of confusion, encourage and bring together those who share its vision, and enable those with a different vision to understand the nature and depth of our concerns and disagreement. Going forward, we need to consider together the implications of our differences for our life together. We do this with the positive hope that in due course we might come again as Anglicans to 'experience that unity in truth and love we have in Christ especially through confession of the apostolic faith'.

'Now to Him who is able to do immeasurably more than all we ask or imagine, to Him be glory in the Church and in Christ Jesus for ever and ever' (Eph. 3:20-21).

Almighty God, who built your Church upon the foundation of the apostles and prophets, with Jesus Christ himself as the chief cornerstone: so join us together in unity of spirit by their doctrine, that we may be made a holy temple acceptable to you; through Jesus Christ your Son our Lord, who is alive and reigns with you, in the unity of the Holy Spirit, one God, now and for ever.[341]

---

[341] Church of England Evangelical Council, *Gospel Church and Marriage,* at: https://ceec.info/wp-content/uploads/2022/10/gospel_church___marriage_-_preserving_apostolic_faith_and_life.pdf

Bibliography

Primary Sources

'A fruitful exhortation to the reading and knowledge of Holy Scripture,' in Ian Robinson (ed), The Homilies (Bishopstone: The Brynmill Press/Preservation Press, 2006.

Walter Abbott, *The Documents of Vatican II* (London: Geoffrey Chapman, 1967).

'An Homily of the State of Matrimony' in *The Homilies* (Bishopstone: The Brynmill Press/Preservation Press, 2006),

'A sermon against whoredom and uncleanness' in Ian Robinson (ed) *The Homilies* (Press/Preservation Press, 2006),

Asser, *Alfred the Great: Asser's Life of King Alfred and Other Contemporary Sources* (London: Penguin Classics, 1983).

Augustine, *On the Good of Marriage,* in *The Nicene and Post Nicene Fathers*, First Series, Vol.III (Edinburgh and Grand Rapids: T&T Clark/Eerdmans, 1998).

Augustine, *On the Good of Marriage* 3, in Patrick Walsh (ed), *Augustine: De bono coniugali, De sancta virginitate* (Oxford: OUP, 2001),

David Baggett and Jerry Walls, *Good God – The theistic foundations of morality* (Oxford: OUP, 2011).

Karl Barth, *Church Dogmatics* 1.2 (London and New York; T&T Clark International, 2004).

George Bull, *A Defence of the Nicene Creed* in *Bishop Bull's Works on the Trinity* (London: J H Parker, 1851).

William Butler, *Lectures on Romanism* (London: Macmillan, 1854)

The Canons of 1571 in English and Latin (London: SPCK, 1899),

Stephen Charnock, *The Existence and Attributes of God* (New York: Robert Carter and Brothers, 1874

The Church of England, *Canons of the Church of England*, Canon A5 at: https://www.churchofengland.org/about/leadership-and-governance/legal-services/canons-church-england/section.

The Church of England, GS 2358, *LLF: Moving Forward as One Church* at: https://www.churchofengland.org/sites/default/files/2024-06/gs-2358-living-in-love-and-faith.pdf.

The Church of England, GS Misc 1407, *A part report of the Episcopal Reference Group of the Faith and Order Commission Living in Love and Faith and the Doctrine of Marriage,* at: https://www.churchofengland.org/sites/default/files/2025-01/gs-misc-1407-part-report-from-episcopal-reference-group.pdf.

The Church of England, 'Prayers for God's blessing for same-sex couples take step forward after Synod Debate' at https://www.churchofengland.org/media/press-releases/prayers-gods-blessing-same-sex-couples-take-step-forward-after-synod-debate.

The Church of England, 'The Ordering of Priests' in the *Ordinal*.

The Church of England, 'The Form of Solemnization of Marriage' in *The Book of Common Prayer*.

The Church of England, *Prayers of Love and Faith* at: https://www.churchofengland.org/sites/default/files/2023-12/prayers-of-love-and-faith.pdf.

Church of England Evangelical Council, *Gospel Church and Marriage,* at: https://ceec.info/wp-content/uploads/2022/10/gospel_church__marriage_preserving_apostolic_faith_and_life.pdf.

R Coleman (ed), *Resolutions of the Lambeth Conferences, 1867-1988* (Toronto: Anglican Book Centre, 1992

The Creed of Nicaea' at *Early Church Texts*: https://www.earlychurchtexts.com/public/creed_of_nicaea_325.htm.

Martin Davie, *With God's Approval? - A theological exploration of blessing same-sex couples in dialogue with Walter Moberly and Isabelle Hamley* (oxford: Dictum Press, 2023).

The Doctrine Commission of the Church of England, *The Mystery of Salvation* (London: CHP, 1995)

Evangelische Kirche in Deutschland, 'The Barmen Declaration' at: https://www.ekd.de/en/The-Barmen-Declaration-303.html.

Mark Fischetti & Jen Christiansen, 'Our Bodies Replace Billions of Cells Every Day', *Scientific American*, April 1, 2021, at: https://www.scientificamerican.com/article/our-bodies-replace-billions-of-cells-every-day/https://www.scientificamerican.com/article/our-bodies-replace-billions-of-cells-every-day/.

GAFCON,' Jerusalem Declaration – June 2008' at: https://civicrm.gafcon.org/about/jerusalem-Declaration.

Gennadius, *Lives of Illustrious Men,* in *The Nicene and Post-Nicene Fathers*, 2nd series (Edinburgh and Grand Rapids: T&T Clark: Eerdmans 1996)

Thomas Gornall (eds*) John Newman, Letters and Diaries*, vol 25 (Oxford: Clarendon Press, 1973).

G D Henderson and John Bulloch, *The Scots Confession of 1560* (Edinburgh: The St Andrew Press, 1960).

HMS Victory – Conservation Log, at https://www.nmrn.org.uk/hms-victory-conservation-log.

Irenaeus, *Against Heresies* in *The Ante-Nice Fathers*, Vol I (Edinburgh and Grand Rapids: T&T Clark/Eerdmans 1996).

John Jewel, 'An apology of the Church of England' in John Ayre (ed) *The Works of John Jewel, The Third Portion* (Cambridge: Parker Society/CUP, 1848).

Ian Ker, Foreword, in *John Henry Cardinal Newman, An Essay on the Development of Christian Doctrine* (Notre Dame: University of Notre Dame Prees, 1989).

John Leith, *Creeds of the Churches* revd ed (Oxford: Blackwells, 1973).

C S Lewis, 'Introduction,' in *St Athanasius, The Incarnation of the World of God* (London: Geoffrey Bless, 1944).

C S Lewis, *Miracles* (Glasgow: Fontana, 1974).

Andrew Louth, 'Is Development of Doctrine a Valid Category for Orthodox Theology?' in Valerie Hotchkiss and Patrick Henry (eds), *Orthodoxy and Western Culture: A Collection of Essays Honoring Jaroslav Pelikan on His Eightieth Birthday* (Crestwood: SVS Press, 2005).

Martin Luther's Small Catechism, 1529' in Mark Noll (ed), *Confessions and Catechisms of the Reformation* (Vancouver: Regent College Publishing 2004).

Martin Luther, *Three Treatises* (Philadelphia, Fortress Press, 1978).

Justin Martyr, *First Apology*, in *The Ante-Nicene Fathers*, Vol.1 (Edinburgh and Grand Rapids T&T Clark/Eerdmans, 1996).

Alister McGrath, *The Nature of Christian Doctrine* (Oxford: OUP, 2024).

Jacob Mozley, *The theory of development* (Oxford: Rivingtons, 1848).

John Newman, *An Essay on the Development of Christian Doctrine* (London: Longmans Green and co, 1909)

John Newman *Records of the Church*, XXIV, p. 3. in *Tracts for the Times* (London: J H Rivington, 1840).

John Newman, *Tract XC* at https://www.anglicanhistory.org/tracts/tract90/

Mark Noll (ed), *Confessions and Catechisms of the Reformation* (Vancouver: Regent College Publishing, 2004),

J I Packer, *Taking God Seriously* ((Wheaton: Crossway, 2013).

Plutarch, *Plutarch's Lives,* Vol I (Harvard and London: Harvard University Press/William Heinemann, 1917).

The Principles of Canon Law Common to the Churches of the Anglican Communion (London: Anglican Communion Office, 2008)

Edward Pusey, *The Rule of Faith as Maintained by the Fathers and the Church of England* (Oxford: John Henry Parker, 1851).

John Robinson, Honest to God (London: SCM, 1963

Dumitru Staniloae, 'The Orthodox Conception of Tradition and The Development of Doctrine,' *Sobornost* 5 (1969), pp.658-659.

John Richardson, *What God has made clean* (Epsom: Good Book Company, 2013).

Rufinus, *A Commentary on the Apostles' Creed* in *The Nicene and Post-Nicene Fathers*, 2nd series, Vol. III (Edinburgh and Grand Rapids: T&T Clark/Eerdmans 1996).

Tertullian, *The Prescription against Heretics in The Ante-Nice Fathers*, Vol III (Edinburgh and Grand Rapids: T&T Clark/Eerdmans 1997).

Carl Trueman, *Crisis of Confidence* (Wheaton: Crossway, 2024).

Vincent of Lerins, *The Commonitory*, in *The Nicene and Post-Nicene Fathers*, 2nd series, Vol. XI (Edinburgh and Grand Rapids: T&T Clark: Eerdmans 1998).

Maurice Wiles, 'Does Christology rest on a mistake?' in S W Sykes and J P. Clayton (eds) *Christ, Faith and History* (Cambridge: CUP, 1972).

Maurice Wiles, *The Making of Christian Doctrine* (Cambridge: CUP, 1967).

Maurice Wiles, *The Remaking of Christian Doctrine* (London: SCM, 1974),

World Council of Churches, 'New Dehli Statement on Unity' at: https://www.oikoumene.org/resources/documents/new-delhi-statement-on-unity.

Secondary Sources

Richard Bauckham, *Jesus and the Eyewitnesses* (Grand Rapids: Eerdmans, 2006).

Richard Bauckham, *Jesus and the God of Israel* (Milton Keynes: Authentic, 2008).

Walter Bauer, *Orthodoxy and Heresy in Earliest Christianity* (Philadelphia: Fortress Press, 1971).

Darrin Belousek, *Marriage, Scripture and the Church* (Grand Rapids: Baker Academic, 2021).

Gerald Bray, *Ancient Christian Doctrine 1, We Believe in One God* (Downers Grove: Inter-Varsity Press, 2009).

Gerald Bray, *The faith we confess* (London: Latimer Trust, 2009).

Richard Burridge, *Four Gospels, one Jesus?* (London: SPCK, 1994).

George Caird, *The Revelation of St John the Divine* (London A&C Black 1984).

J M Cameron (ed), John Henry Newman, *An Essay on the Development of Doctrine* (Harmondsworth: Penguin, 1974), Introduction.

Ardel B. Caneday, *The Doctrine of Grace in the theology of Polycarp*, at: https://www.academia.edu/102400491/The_Doctrine_of_Grace_in_t he_Theology_of_Polycarp.

Owen Chadwick, *From Bossuet to Newman*, 2ed (Cambridge: CUP, 1987).

The Church of England, *An Honourable Estate* (London: CHP, 1988)

Charles Cranfield, *The Apostles' Creed – A faith to live by (*Edinburgh: T&T Clark, 1993).

F L Cross *The Early Christian Fathers (*London: Duckworth, 1960).

Peter Davids, 'The Gospels and Jewish Tradition' in R T France and David Wenham (eds), *Studies of History and Tradition in the Four Gospels* (Sheffield: JSOT, 1980

Martin Davie, *Bishops Past, Present and Future* (Malton: Gilead Books, 2022).

Martin Davie 'The role of Scripture in the Anglican formularies' in C Hill, M Kaiser, L Nathaniel and C Schwöbel (eds*.), Communion Already Shared and Further Steps – 20 Years After the Meissen Declaration* (Frankfurt am Main: Verlag Otto Lembeck, 2010).

Steven Duby, *Divine Simplicity – A Dogmatic Account* (London and New York: T&T Clark, 2018).

Avery Dulles, *John Henry Newman* (London: Continuum, 2002).

Bart Ehrman, *Lost Christianities: The Battles for Scripture and the Faiths we never knew* (Oxford: OUP, 2003).

Georges Florovsky, *Bible, Church, Tradition: An Eastern Orthodox View* (Belmont: Nordland, 1972),

GAFCON Global Anglicans, 'The history of GAFCON at a glance' at: https://www.gafcon.org/about/.

Stanley Grenz and Roger Olson, *20th Century Theology* (Exeter: Paternoster Press, 1992).

Thomas Guarino, *Vincent of Lerins and the Development of Christian Doctrine* (Grand Rapids: Baker Academic, 2013).

Donald Guthrie, *New Testament Introduction* (Leicester: Inter-Varsity Press, 1970).

Adrian Hastings, *A History of English Christianity 1920-1985* (London: Fount, 1987).

Richard Hays, *Reading Backwards* (London: SPCK, 2014).

A I C Heron, 'Homoousios with the Father' in Thomas F Torrance (ed), *The incarnation – Ecumenical Studies in the Nicene-Constantinoplian Creed A.D. 381* (Edinburgh: The Handsel Press, 1981).

Susanna Heschel, *The Aryan Jesus: Christian Theologians and the Bible in Nazi* Germany (Princeton: Princeton University Press, 2008).

Justin Holcomb, *Know the Creeds and Councils* (Grand Rapids: Zondervan 2014).

Dennis Hollinger, The Meaning of Sex (Grand Rapids: Baker Academic, 2009).

J Derek Holmes (ed), *The Theological Papers of John Henry Newman on Biblical Inspiration and on Infallibility (*Oxford: Clarendon Press, 1979).

Stephen Holmes, *Listening to the Past* (Carlisle and Grand Rapids: Paternoster/Baker Academic,2002).

Edwyn Hoskyns and Noel Davey, *The Riddle of the New Testament* (London: Faber& Faber, 1936),

Edith Humphrey, *Scripture and Tradition (*Grand Rapids: Baker Academic, 2013).

Larry Hurtado, *Lord Jesus Christ – Devotion to Jesus in Earliest Christianity* (Grand Rapids and Cambridge: Eerdmans, 2003).

Jacob Jervell, The Problem of Traditions in Acts in *Luke and the People of God* (Minneapolis: Augsburg, 1972).

Timothy Paul Jones, 'Martin Luther on Beards and Human Depravity' *Proof* 31 October 2014 at: https://www.timothypauljones.com/proof-what-we-did-and-what-we- deserve/.

Eberhard Jungel *The Freedom of a Christian: Luther's Significance for Contemporary Theology* (Minneapolis: Augsburg Press, 1988).

John Kelly, *Early Christian Creeds,* 3ed (Harlow: Longmans, 1972),

John Kelly, *Early Christian Doctrines* 5th ed (London: A&C Black, 1977).

Craig Keener, *Christobiography* (Grand Rapids: Eerdmans, 2019).

Andreas Kostenberger and Michael Kruger, *The Heresy of Orthodoxy* (Nottingham: Apollos, 2010).

Tony Lane, *The Lion Book of Christian Thought* (Oxford: Lion, 1984).

Daniel Lattier, 'The Orthodox Rejection of Doctrinal Development,' *The Holy Catholic Religion*, 7 May 2016 at https://holycatholicreligion.blogspot.com/2016/05/the-orthodox-rejection-of-doctrinal.html2016.

Sean Lau, 'The Distinction between Theology and Ethics: A critical history,' *The Journal of Religious Ethics,* Vol.52, Issue 2, June 2024, p,215 at: https://onlinelibrary.wiley.com/doi/epdf/10.1111/jore.12468.

Peter Leithart, *The Four – A Survey of the Gospels* (Moscow: Canon Press, 2010).

Nathaniel Marshall, *The Penitential Discipline of the Primitive Church* (London: John Henry Parker, 1844),

Bruce Metzger, *The Canon of the New Testament* (Oxford: Clarendon Press, 1997).

Reginald Moxon, *The Commonitorium of Vincent of Lerins* (Cambridge: CUP, 1915).

Oliver O'Donovan, *Begotten or Made?* (Oxford: OUP, 1984).

Thomas Oden, *Classic Christianity* (London: Harper Collins, 2009).

Roger Olson, *The Story of Christian Theology* (Leicester: Apollos 1999).

James Orr, The Progress of Dogma (Cambridge: James Clarke 2002).

Ian Paul, *Revelation – An introduction and commentary* (London, Inter-Varsity Press, 2018).

Jaroslav Pelikan, *The Christian Tradition: A History of the Development of Doctrine, Volume 2: The Spirit of Eastern Christendom (600-1700)* (Chicago: Chicago University Press, 1977).

Brant Pitre, *Jesus and divine Christology* (Grand Rapids: Eerdmans, 2024),

Thomas Schreiner, *Faith Alone – The Doctrine of Justification* (Grand Rapids: Zondervan Academic, 2015).

Matt Slick, 'Is Divine Simplicity compatible with the Trinity?' CARM, March 29, 2019 at: https://carm.org/doctrine-and-theology/is-divine-simplicity-compatible-with-the-trinity.

Lawrence Stone *The Family, Sex and marriage in England 1500-1800* (Harmondsworth: Penguin, 1979).

John Stott, *The Message of Acts* (Leicester: Inter-Varsity Press, 1990).

Michael Thompson, 'Arianism: Is Jesus Christ divine and eternal or was he created?' in Ben Quash and Michael Ward (eds), *Heresies and how to avoid them* (London: SPCK, 2007).

Peter Toon *The Development of Doctrine in the Church* (Grand Rapids: Eerdmans 1979).

H E W Turner, *The Pattern of Christian Truth* (London: Mowbray 1954).

Kallistos Ware, 'Christian Theology in the East' in Hubert Cunliffe Jones and Benjamin Drewery (eds), *A History of Christian Doctrine* (Edinburgh: T&T Clark 1980).

John Wenham, *Redating Matthew, Mark and Luke* (London: Hodder and Stoughton, 1991).

Vernon White, *The Fall of a Sparrow* (Exeter: Paternoster, 1985).

Rowan Williams, *The Body's Grace* (2ed, London: Lesbian and Gay Christian Movement, 2003).

Subject index

Page numbers with 'n' refer to a footnote. For example, 125n149 means footnote 149 on page 125.

adultery 259, 275
'Against whoredom and uncleanness,' *The Homilies* (Church of England) 259
Anabaptist beliefs 75
Anglican Church of Canada 84
Anglican Communion 84–87, 128, 270, 277
Anglicanism
    Newman's career 129, 132
    Newman's writing on 132, 134–136, 162, 164–166
    'Vincentian Canon' 127, 162
    Wiles' career 178
Antiochenes 189, 195
antiquity *see* '*ubique, semper et ab omnibus*' ('everywhere, always, and by all'/universality, antiquity, consent)
Apollinarian heresy 64, 101
Apostles' Creed 55–59, 68, 134, 145, 164, 228
apostles/apostolic faith
    Christ's revelation continued by 14–15, 52, 56, 238
    Creed of the Council of Trent (1564) 75, 77, 116, 247
    creeds/confessions/declarations 65, 83, 85
    explanatory understanding of doctrinal development 247–248
    Gospel Church and Marriage (CEEC) 269–280
    New Testament writings 50, 52–53, 164, 166, 169
    Newman 131–132, 134–135, 145, 157, 162, 166–169, 175, 236
    Reformation sought return to 249–251
    as source of doctrine 21, 127, 252–253
    sufficiency of/no additions permitted 121, 123, 124
    threefold order of ministry 41, 229
    tradition, role of 18–19
    Vincent of Lerins 126
    Wiles 193, 227
Arianism
    Athanasius 65
    heresy 64, 90, 244
    Newman 130, 156
    Nicene Creed 64, 244
    Vincent of Lerins 99, 130
    Wiles 187, 188, 211
ascension
    Christ's revelation continued by apostles 14–15, 52, 56, 238
    creeds and confessions refer to 58, 60, 61, 66, 68, 70–72
Athanasian Creed 65–66, 135, 164, 214, 228, 248
Athanasius 23, 65, 162, 185, 189
atonement theory 203–205
Augsburg Confession (1530) 67–70, 176
Augustine of Hippo
    creeds influenced by 62, 66
    on marriage 256, 258
    Newman's mention of 156
    Thirty-Nine Articles influenced by 73
    and Wiles' position 185, 195

Bancroft, Richard 127
baptism
    Newman 150, 159
    rebaptism controversy 99, 118
    Wiles 186, 187, 188, 195, 214

Barmen Declaration (1934) 78–82
Barth, Karl 78, 114–115, 116–117
Bauer, Walter 120, 122
Baum, Gregory 197
Belousek, Darrin 253–254
Bible *see* Scripture
bishops
    The Commonitory (Vincent of Lerins) 117–118, 119, 126
    House of Bishops 6–8, 266, 268, 275
    threefold order of ministry 41–44, 86, 229–230, 252
Book of Common Prayer (1662)
    Apostles' Creed included in 58
    Jerusalem Declaration (2008) refers to 86
    Nicene Creed version in 60–61, 62
    'Solemnization of Matrimony' 254–256, 260–266
    as source of doctrine 9, 86, 128, 251–253
    Ten Commandments exposition in 35, 38–40
Bossuet, Jacques 46, 47, 88, 230
Bray, Gerald 122, 165–166
Butler, Joseph 173
Butler, William 170

Cameron, J M 163
Canada 84, 87
Canons of the Church of England
    Canon A5 128, 252
    Canon B30 'Of Holy Matrimony' 9, 264–266, 274
    Canon C15 252
    Canon C18 274
Cappadocian Fathers 193, 194–195, 213
catechisms 35–38
Chadwick, Owen 88, 179
Chalcedon, Council of (451 AD) 59, 63, 66, 188
Chalcedonian Confession (451 AD) 63–64, 68, 228
Charles V, Emperor 67

Charnock, Stephen 28–31
Chillingworth, William 148
Church of England
    The Homilies 44, 256–257, 258–260, 264, 266
    House of Bishops 6–8, 266, 268, 275
    Living in Love and Faith documents 6–9
    Prayers of Love and Faith (PLF) 6–7, 9, 10, 266
    sources of doctrine for 252–253
Church of England Evangelical Council (CEEC), *Gospel Church and Marriage* 269–280
civil partnerships 7–8
College of Bishops 6–7
commonitory, definition 95–96
The Commonitory (Vincent of Lerins) 93–128
    authorship and composition of 93–95
    consensus/consent 108–109, 118–126, 127, 131, 218, 238
    critiqued via Mozley 245–246
    doctrinal progress shown to be possible 104–106, 112–114, 126–127
    on General Councils 98, 109–110, 111–113, 117, 119, 126
    heresy, identification of 96, 99, 101–103, 106–107, 109, 111, 120, 125–126
    Newman on 129–134, 136
    Scripture 97, 99–100, 107–108, 114–117, 119, 126
    summary 231–232, 233–234, 237–238
    'Vincentian Canon' 97–98, 119, 120, 125n149, 127, 136
confessions of faith 21–22, 67–78, 228, 247
consensus/consent 108–109, 118–126, 127, 131, 218, 238
    doctrine of marriage 253–254

Constantinople, First Council of (381 AD) 59, 64, 66
continuity
   Newman 152–153, 155–157, 161–162
   overview 5–6, 10, 19
   Wiles 197
contraception 257
Council of Chalcedon (451 AD) 59, 63, 66, 188; see also Chalcedonian Confession (451 AD)
Council of Ephesus (431 AD) 94, 95–96, 109–110, 111, 113, 117
Council of Trent (1545–1563) 75, 77–78, 115; see also *Creed of the Council of Trent* (1564)
Councils *see* General (Ecumenical) Councils
Cranfield, Charles 57, 59
Cranmer, Thomas 256, 258–259, 260, 262–263
creation
   God's immutability 30, 32
   New Testament writings 49
   Newman 159
   Wiles 200–201, 207, 210, 215, 218
Creed of Nicaea 59–60, 61
Creed of the Council of Trent (1564) 75–78, 88, 115–116, 135, 143–144, 247
creeds
   doctrinal development 55–63, 65–66, 88, 181
   as source of doctrine 21, 44, 72, 128, 253
   see also Apostles' Creed; Athanasian Creed; Nicene Creed
Cyprian 184–185, 191, 195
Cyril of Alexandria 111

Davey, Noel 223–224
Davids, Peter 50
deacons 41–42, 86, 229, 252
Decalogue (Ten Commandments) 35–41, 259

'Decree Concerning the Canonical Scriptures' (1546) 115
discipleship, definition 13
Docetism 64, 89
Doctors of the Church
   The Commonitory (Vincent of Lerins) 119
   consensus 123, 124
   Newman 129, 163
   tradition and doctrine 22, 44–45, 229
doctrinal development 46–92
   Eastern Orthodox Churches 90–92, 230
   explanatory understanding of (Mozley) 238–240, 242–243, 245–248
   explanatory understanding of (wider discussion) 251, 253
   New Testament writings 48–55
   'noviter, non nova' (newly but not new) 113, 126, 128, 232, 245–246, 269–280
   overview 46–48, 88–90
   pre-Reformation period 55–66
   Reformation period 67–78
   as substantive change (Mozley) 240–242, 243–245
   twentieth/twenty-first centuries 78–87
   see also The Commonitory (Vincent of Lerins); *Essay on the Development of Christian Doctrine* (Newman, 1845, 1878); *The Making of Christian Doctrine* (Wiles, 1967); *Remaking of Christian Doctrine* (Wiles, 1973)
doctrine
   definition of 12–15, 35, 47, 228
   sources of 21, 85, 228–229, 251–253
Doctrine Commission (Church of England) 225–226
doctrine of marriage
   current doctrine 254–266

Gospel Church and Marriage
  (CEEC) 269–280
Jerusalem Declaration (2008) 86
  proposals for 7–10, 266–269
dynamic monarchianism 186–187

Eastern Orthodox Churches 90–92,
  123, 143, 166, 175, 230
Ecumenical Councils *see* General
  (Ecumenical) Councils
ecumenical movement 82–84, 86,
  278
Ehrman, Bart 120, 121, 122
election/predestination 72–74
Enlightenment theology (deism) 219
Ephesus, Council of (431 AD) 94, 95–
  96, 109–110, 111, 113, 117
Episcopal Church, USA 84
Episcopal Reference Group (ERG) 8–
  9
*Essay on the Development of Christian
  Doctrine* (Newman, 1845, 1878)
  132–177
  argument summary 162–163,
    232–234, 243
  assessment of argument 163–177,
    235–236, 243
  Christianity as 'idea' over time
    142–143, 166–169
  historical pattern of development
    145–151, 162
  ideas develop over time 138–142,
    162
  illustrations 149–151
  introduction 133–138
  prominence and permanence
    143–144
  seven tests of healthy doctrinal
    development 152–162, 176
  Wiles' discussion of 179–181
ethics (moral theology) 33–41, 229
Eucharistic theology 76, 191–192;
  see also Holy Communion; Mass
Eunomians 156
Eutychianism 64, 90

explanatory understanding of
  doctrinal development
  doctrine of marriage 267, 269
  Mozley 238–240, 242–243, 245–
    248, 251, 253
eyewitness testimony 49, 50

Faith and Order Commission (FAOC)
  8–9
false doctrine *see* heresy and false
  doctrine
false prophets 101, 107
Fathers of the Church
  apostolic authority 121
  historical sources on early church
    122
  Newman 131, 135–136
  as source of doctrine 21, 64, 128,
    228, 253, 254
  Thirty-Nine Articles influenced by
    72
  threefold order of ministry 41, 44
  Wiles 194, 211–212, 217–218,
    227
  see also The Commonitory (Vincent
    of Lerins)
Faustus the Manichee 156
filioque clause, Nicene Creed 62, 77,
  247
First Council of Constantinople (381
  AD) 59, 64, 66
First Council of Nicaea (325 AD) 59,
  64, 66, 113, 117, 245
First Vatican Council (1870) 77, 78,
  129
Flavius Josephus 223
Florovsky, George 119, 230
'A fruitful exhortation to the reading
  and knowledge of Holy Scripture,'
  The Homilies (Church of England)
  44

GAFCON (Global Anglican Future
  Conference), *Jerusalem Declaration*
  (2008) 84–87
Gathercole, Simon 212

General (Ecumenical) Councils
  consensus 123, 124
  Newman refers to 145
  as source of doctrine 21, 44, 72, 85, 128, 164, 253
  Vincent of Lerins on 98, 109–110, 111–113, 117, 119, 126
  see also Council of Chalcedon (451 AD); Council of Ephesus (431 AD); Council of Trent (1545–1563); First Council of Constantinople (381 AD); First Council of Nicaea (325 AD); Vatican Councils
General Synod (GS) 6–7
German Evangelical Church 78, 81
Germany 78, 81–82
Gnosticism 90, 122, 156, 157, 186, 188
God
  immutability 27–33, 204, 229
  Wiles' chapter in *Remaking of Christian Doctrine* (Wiles) 200–202, 207, 210
  Wiles critiqued 214–217, 218, 225
God-consciousness 220–221
Gospel Church and Marriage (CEEC) 269–280
Greek language 13, 17, 57, 59
Grenz, Stanley 218, 219–220, 221–222
Guarino, Thomas
  on *The Commonitory* (Vincent of Lerins) 110–114, 117–118
  on Newman 132, 163
Guthrie, Donald 51

Harding, Thomas 120
Hastings, Adrian 178
heresy and false doctrine
  bishops'/priests' responsibility to banish 43, 44, 230
  and consensus 108–109, 118–126
  creeds/confessions/declarations refer to 64, 77, 79–81
  English reformers view of Roman Catholicism 249–251
  Newman critiqued by Mozley 173, 174–175, 243–245
  Newman on Vincent of Lerins 129–131, 136
  Newman's seven tests 152–162
  signs of 13, 19, 46, 47–48
  Vincent of Lerins 96, 99, 101–103, 106–109, 111, 120–122, 125–126
  Wiles 182, 212
  see also Arianism; Docetism; Eunomians; Eutychianism; Faustus the Manichee; Gnosticism; Nestorianism; Vigilantius
Hilary of Poitiers 62
history of Christianity
  Gospels as biographies/historical information about Christ 19, 49, 50–51, 222–224
  Newman 133–134, 145–151, 162, 163
  see also tradition
HMS Belfast 5, 10
HMS Victory 4–5, 10
Holcomb, Justin 62
Holy Communion 136, 150, 249–250, 264; see also Eucharistic theology; Mass
'Holy Matrimony,' terminology 266
Holy Roman Empire 67
Holy Spirit
  apostles empowered with 14–15, 228
  creeds/confessions/declarations 61–63, 68–69, 83, 85, 87
  doctrine of marriage 253
  Eastern Orthodox Churches 92
  General (Ecumenical) Councils 124
  Thirty-Nine Articles 73
  Wiles 187, 205, 211–212, 215, 226

'An Homily on the State of Matrimony,' *The Homilies* (Church of England) 256–257, 258, 260, 264
homoiousios/homoousios debate 17, 62, 150, 165, 243–244
Horton, Michael 18
Hoskyns, Edwyn 223–224
House of Bishops 6–8, 266, 268, 275
human nature 32–33

identity 5, 6, 33, 87, 200, 279
image of God 32–33
immutability
  of God 27–33, 204, 229
  of the Gospel 46–47
  of human nature 32–33
incarnation, doctrine of 155–156, 242–243
indulgences 76–77, 132
infallibility
  of Christianity 134, 142
  of God's word/Scripture 70, 180–181
  see also Papal infallibility
interpretation 19, 108, 114, 116–118
Irenaeus 121
Issues in Human Sexuality (Church of England) 6, 7, 8

Jerusalem Declaration (2008) 84–87
Jervell, Jacob 52
Jesus Christ
  Gospels as biographies/historical information 19, 49, 50–51, 222–224
  head of Church 41
  Newman 150, 159–160
  Schleiermacher 220, 222–223
  theoanthropic Christology 224–225
  Wiles 190, 196, 202–205, 208, 210
  Wiles' position critiqued 211–213, 222–227
  see also ascension; resurrection; salvation

Jewel, John
  An Apology of the Church of England (1562) 41–42, 249–251
  'The Defence of the Apology of the Church of England' 120
John Chrysostom 151
justification 70, 73, 76, 79, 89

Kelly, John 55, 56
Ker, Ian 166–169
Knox, John 70, 72
Kostenberger, Andreas 120–122
Kruger, Michael 120–122

Lambeth Conference (1930) 257
Lane, Tony 164
language and words
  doctrine communication 16–18, 19–20, 47, 92, 113, 155–156, 228
  explanatory understanding of doctrinal development 239, 246
Latin language 13, 18, 57, 77; see also *'noviter, non nova'* (newly but not new); *'ubique, semper et ab omnibus'* ('everywhere, always, and by all'/universality, antiquity, consent)
Lattier, Daniel 90
Lau, Sean 33–34
law, Old Testament 30, 31–32; see also Ten Commandments (Decalogue)
Lérins 65, 93
Lewis, C S 22–27, 125, 217, 229
LGBTQI+ people 6
liberal Protestantism *see* Schleiermacher, Friedrich; Wiles, Maurice
Liturgical Commission 9
liturgical practice
  Gospel Church and Marriage (CEEC) 277
  tradition and doctrine 22, 229
  Wiles 185–188, 196, 197
Living in Love and Faith and the Doctrine of Marriage (GS Misc 1407) 8–9

Living in Love and Faith (GS 2289) 6
LLF: Moving Forward as One Church (GS 2358) 7–8
Lossky, Vladimir 90, 230
Louth, Andrew 90–91, 230
Lucian of Samosata 223
Luther, Martin
   Augsburg Confession (1530) 67
   The Freedom of a Christian 89
   Small Catechism 35–38

Macdonald, George 25
Macedonianism 61, 211
McGrath, Alister 12
The Making of Christian Doctrine (Wiles, 1967) 179–198
   conclusions 195–198
   critique of 210–214
   Early Church forms of argument 190–194, 209
   introduction and context 178–179
   liturgical practice 185–188, 196, 197
   new ideas, assimilation of 194–195
   salvation 188–190, 197
   Scripture 180–181, 182–185, 193, 196, 197
Manichees 156–157
Mara bar Sarapion 223
Marcellus of Ancyra 57
Marcionism 89
marriage *see* doctrine of marriage; same-sex marriages
Mass 69–70, 76, 88, 132, 150; see also Eucharistic theology; Holy Communion
Melanchthon, Philip 67, 73
ministry *see* ordained ministry
miracles 221–222, 223, 254, 255
monasticism 93, 152, 153, 159
monogamy 253
moral theology (ethics) 33–41, 229
Moxon, Reginald 94
Mozley, Jacob
   critique of Newman 165, 170–175

explanatory understanding of doctrinal development 238–240, 242–243, 245–248
substantive change as doctrinal development 240–242, 243–245
The Mystery of Salvation (Church of England Doctrine Commission) 225–226

Nazism 78, 82
Nestorianism 64, 90, 101, 109, 111, 156
New Delhi Statement on Unity (1961) 82–84
New Testament
   creeds/confessions/declarations based on 58–59, 61, 65, 67–69, 88
   doctrine definition 13, 15, 228
   historical information about Christ 19, 49, 50–51, 222–224
   Newman 150–151, 164–166, 169
   as source of doctrine 48–55, 230, 252
   Thirty-Nine Articles based on 72
   Vincent of Lerins 126
   Wiles 183–184, 202, 222–227
Newman, John Henry
   Anglican to Roman Catholic conversion 129, 132–133, 177
   Lectures on the Prophetical Office of the Church (1837) 131–132
   'Vincentius of Lerins on the Tests of Heresy and Error' (*Records of the Church*, 1834) 129–131
   Tracts for The Times, Remarks on Certain Passages in the Thirty-Nine Articles 132
   see also *Essay on the Development of Christian Doctrine* (Newman, 1845, 1878)
Nicaea, First Council of (325 AD) 59, 64, 66, 113, 117, 245
Nicene Creed 59–63, 122, 164–166, 243–245
   filioque clause 62, 77, 247

Noll, Mark 67
'noviter, non nova' (newly but not new) 113, 126, 128, 232, 245–246, 269–280
Nowell, Alexander 39

Oden, Thomas 123–125, 238
O'Donovan, Oliver 257–258
Old Roman Creed 57
Old Testament
   law 30, 31–32; *see also* Ten Commandments (Decalogue)
   as source of doctrine 252
   Wiles 183–185, 194, 211
Olson, Roger 218, 219–220, 221
oral transmission of Gospel 16, 181, 183
ordained ministry
   inclusion of those in same-sex relationships 7, 8, 84, 267–269
   threefold order of 41–44, 86, 229–230, 252
Ordinal (1662) 42–44, 86, 128, 251, 252–253, 267–268
Origen 102, 185, 186
original sin 68, 69, 76, 136, 150, 151
Orthodox Churches *see* Eastern Orthodox Churches

Packer, J I 12–14, 16, 35, 47, 228
Papal infallibility
   Creed of the Council of Trent (1564) 77
   First Vatican Council (1870) 78, 129
   Newman shows link to doctrinal development 132, 144–145, 168–169, 234, 235
   Newman's link critiqued 170–172, 175, 243
Papal jurisdiction 74–75, 77
Papal supremacy 135, 150
A part report of the Episcopal Reference Group of the Faith and Order Commission: Living in Love and Faith and the Doctrine of Marriage (GS Misc 1407) 8–9
Paul VI, Pope 164
   Humanae vitae 258
Pecock, Reginald 56
Pitrie, Brant 224–225
Pius IV, Pope 75, 135
Pius IX, Pope 78
Pliny the Younger 223
Prayers of Love and Faith (PLF) 6–7, 9, 10, 266
predestination/election 72–74
priests (presbyters/elders) 41–44, 86, 229–230, 252
Primates' Communiqué (Jan. 2016) 277
Primates' Communiqué (Oct. 2003) 277
The Principles of Canon Law Common to the Churches of the Anglican Communion (2008), Principle 49 128
procreation 257–258, 274
Prosper of Aquitaine 73
Protestantism
   Barmen Declaration (1934) 78
   ethics 33–34
   Newman on 135, 143–145, 151–152, 157, 158
   Newman's *Essay* controversial within 163
   sources of doctrine for 44, 46, 67, 89, 175, 247
   Thirty-Nine Articles influenced by 72
   tradition 18
   Vincent of Lerins' influence on 93, 116
   see also Reformation; Schleiermacher, Friedrich; Wiles, Maurice
purgatory
   Creed of the Council of Trent (1564) 76
   Newman 132, 135, 159, 165–166
   Wiles 195, 214
Pusey, Edward 20

Quicunque vult see Athanasian Creed

Ratzinger, Joseph 110
Reformation
    confessions of faith 67–75, 124, 228
    Roman Catholic Church response 67, 75–78
    sources of doctrine for reformers 44, 175–176, 248–252, 256
Remaking of Christian Doctrine (Wiles, 1973) 198–209
    Christ's person and work 202–205, 208, 210
    critique of 214–227
    God 200–202, 207–208, 210
    Grace and the Holy Spirit 205–206, 207–208
    introduction 178–179, 198–200
    resurrection 208–209, 210
resurrection
    creeds and confessions refer to 58, 61, 62, 66, 68, 70–72
    Eastern Orthodox Churches 92
    Jerusalem Declaration (2008) refers to 86
    Newman 160
    Wiles 186, 203, 208–209, 210
Robinson, Gene 84
Robinson, John 179
Roman Catholic Church
    Counter-Reformation 67, 75–78
    Doctors of the Church, formal list 22n22
    moral theology 33–34
    Newman's conversion from Anglicanism 129, 132–133, 177
    Newman's discussion of 130–132, 135–137, 143, 151–152, 163–167, 175–176
    Newman's seven tests of healthy doctrinal development are met by 154–167, 176
    Vincent of Lerins' discussion of 101–102, 108–109, 114–117
    Vincent of Lerins' influence on 93

see also Papal infallibility

salvation
    creeds and declarations refer to 65–66, 76, 85
    Gospels as good news of 46, 49
    heresies about 90
    Ordinal refers to 42–43
    Thirty-Nine Articles refer to 72–73
    tradition passes on news of 19
    Wiles 188–190, 197, 212–213, 225–227
same-sex marriages 7–8, 9–10, 84, 268
same-sex relationships
    blessings 84, 267
    ordained ministry 7, 8, 84, 267–269
    sexual activity 7, 258n329, 259, 267
Schleiermacher, Friedrich 200, 218–223, 234
    The Christian Faith (1821-22, 1830) 218–219
    On Religion: Speeches to Its Cultured Despisers (1799) 218
Scots Confession (1560) 70–72
Scripture
    authority of 15, 19–20, 183
    bishops'/priests' responsibility to teach 42–44, 230
    Canons of the Church of England 128
    Church of England marriage service 263
    creeds/confessions/declarations 75, 80, 81, 82, 85, 115
    doctrine of marriage 253–255
    Eastern Orthodox Churches 91–92
    epistles/letters 52–53
    infallibility 70, 180–181
    Newman 147–148, 150–151
    as source of doctrine 252–253
    Thirty-Nine Articles based on 72, 73, 74

Vincent of Lerins 97, 99–100,
107–108, 114–117, 119, 126
Wiles 180–181, 182–185, 193,
196, 197, 202
Wiles' position critiqued 214, 217,
218, 236–237
see also New Testament; Old
Testament
Second Vatican Council (1962-1965)
164
sexual activity
doctrine of marriage 257–260,
266
same-sex relationships 7,
258n329, 259, 267
sexual ethics
Gospel Church and Marriage
(CEEC) 269, 273, 274, 275, 276
Jerusalem Declaration (2008) 86,
87
Ship of Theseus 4–5, 236, 237
'Solemnization of Matrimony' (Book
of Common Prayer, 1662) 254–256,
260–266
Staniloae, Dumitru 91
Stephen, Pope 99, 118
Stott, John 52
Suetonius 223

Tacitus 223
Talmud 223
Ten Commandments (Decalogue)
35–41, 259
Tertullian 102, 121, 156
theoanthropic Christology 224–225
Theseus Paradox 4–5, 236, 237
*Thirty-Nine Articles of the Church of
England* (1571)
Article XVII 'Of Predestination and
Election' 72–74
Article XXXVII 'Of the Civil
Magistrate' 74–75
Jerusalem Declaration (2008)
refers to 85
Newman 132, 135

as source of doctrine 72, 85, 127–
128, 176, 251, 252–253
Thomas Aquinas, *Summa Theologiae*
242–243n318
Thompson, Michael 17
threefold order of ministry 41–44,
86, 229–230, 252
Tillich, Paul 200
time/temporality
Newman 138–142, 153, 161–162
Vincent of Lerins 111–113
Toon, Peter 152–154
totalitarianism 78, 81, 82
Tractarian movement 129
tradition
Eastern Orthodox Churches 92
Newman on history of Christianity
133–134, 145–151, 162, 163
overview 18–27, 228–229
Vincent of Lerins 97–98, 108–109,
111, 113, 114–117
Wiles 183
Trent, Council of *see* Council of Trent
(1545-1563)
Trinity
Athanasian Creed refers to 65, 66,
135
doctrinal development 88
heresies about 101–102
Newman 135
theological definition 18
Wiles 186–187, 194–195, 198,
205, 210
Wiles' position critiqued 211–213,
225–227
Trueman, Carl 16, 18–20, 32

'*ubique, semper et ab omnibus*'
('everywhere, always, and by
all'/universality, antiquity, consent)
consensual doctrine of marriage
253–254
consent/consensus 108–109,
118–126, 127, 131, 218, 238
Newman's use of Vincent's test of
doctrine 130–134

Reformation use of Vincent's test of doctrine 249
  Vincent of Lerins' test of doctrine 108–114, 119, 125–126, 129–130, 231, 237
United States of America (USA) 84, 87
universality *see 'ubique, semper et ab omnibus'* ('everywhere, always, and by all'/universality, antiquity, consent)

Valla, Lorenzo 56
Vatican Councils
  First (1870) 77, 78, 129
  Second (1962–1965) 164
Vermigli, Peter Martyr 73
Vigilantius 157
Vincent of Lerins *see The Commonitory* (Vincent of Lerins)

Wenham, John 49
Westminster Confession (1646) 21, 247
White, Vernon 215–217
Wiles, Maurice 178–179, 234–235, 236–237; see also *The Making of Christian Doctrine* (Wiles, 1967); *Remaking of Christian Doctrine* (Wiles, 1973)
Williams, Rowan 258
words *see* language and words
World Council of Churches 82–84

Scripture and ancient sources index

OLD TESTAMENT
Genesis
1-2 255
1:1 61
1:28 256
2:18-25 259
2:24 274
3:1 227
12:2-3 256
12:32 270

Exodus
19:3-6 273
20:1-17 35
20:14 275

Leviticus
18:3-5 273
18:6-18 263
19:2 273
20:17-21 263

Numbers
23:19 29

Deuteronomy
4:2 235
4:5-8 273
5:5 35
10:13 270
12:32 235
13:1-3 101
32:7 95

Psalms
67 262
110:3 185
121:1 61
124:8 61
128 262

Proverbs
3:1 95

5:15-23 275
8:22 185
22:17 95
22:28 103

Ecclesiastes
10:8 103

Isaiah
35:4-6 224
40:9-10 224
42:1-6 271
42:6-7 273
46:11 29
55:11 29
61:1 224

Jeremiah
23:24 29

Daniel
7:13-14 224

Jonah
3:10 30

Zechariah
6:1 29

Malachi
1:11 191
3:6 27

DEUTEROCANONICAL WORKS
Sirach
8:14 103

NEW TESTAMENT
Matthew 49–50, 51
4:1-11 107
5:13-16 271
5:27-32 275
6:28 201

7:13 107
9:6 224
15:1-20 18
19:3-12 265
19:4-6 274
19:6 264
19:12 275
20:25-26 80
28:19 188, 211
28:20 81

Mark 49–50, 51
2:10 224
6:46 224
10:2-12 265
10:9 264
10:17-22 212
10:18 196, 212
10:45 225
12:35-37 224
16:16 65

Luke 49–50, 51, 52
1:2 49
5:24 224
24:26-27 15
24:44-45 15

John 51
1:14 155, 275
2:1-12 255
3:1 225
3:16-18 65
6:51 225
8:11 276
8:12 213
8:40 185
10:1 79
10:9 79
10:30 196
11:50 185
14:6 79
14:9 14

Acts 51–53
1:1-2 52

1:8-11 14
2:14-36 88, 230
2:22-36 71
2:33 225
2:42 248, 273
4:13 50
5:32 225
20:29-31 274

Romans
3:21-26 272
3:28 65
5:12 185
6:1-14 273
6:6-11 226
6:17 273
7:4 272
8:28-30 73
8:29 272
8:32 225
9:23-24 73
13:1-7 75
15:18 273
16:17-18 99

1 Corinthians
1:30 79
2:9 103
3:11 273
4:14-5:5 274
6 258
6:9-11 273
7:2 258
7:7 275
7:8-9 258
7:32-35 275
11:2 19
15:24 61
16:21 186

2 Corinthians
2:5-11 274
5:20 65
8:9 155
11:12 107

Galatians
1:4 225, 272
1:6 99
1:8 100
2:9 107
2:20 155, 225
5:16-21 273

Ephesians
1:4-5 73
1:11-12 73
1:22 225
2:1-10 271
2:8-10 272
2:19-22 273
2:20 273
3:10 273
3:20-21 279
4:4-17 273
4:15-16 79
4:17-24 273
4:20 273
5 262
5:21-33 259
5:22-24 263
5:25 225, 264
5:25-26 273
5:31-32 274
5:32 255

Philippians
1:5 196
2:12-13 273

Colossians
2:9 224
3:1 262
3:18-19 259, 263

1 Thessalonians
4:3-8 275
4:8 225

2 Thessalonians
2:6 19
2:15 19, 248

1 Timothy
1:8-10 273
1:14 238
1:19 100
2:3 276
3:15 273
4:4 275
5:12 99
5:13 100
6:4 100
6:20 103, 106, 126

2 Timothy
1:13 20n16
2:9 81
2:11-12 186
2:16-17 100
2:20 274
3:6 99
3:8 100
3:9 100
4:3-4 99

Titus
1:9 41, 248, 274
1:10 100
2:1 41
2:14 225
2:14-36 272

Hebrews
4:13 28
12:14-16 273
13:4 255, 275
13:8 46

1 Peter
1:14-15 273
1:22 273
2:4-9 273
2:11 273
2:17 80
3 262
3:1-6 263
3:1-7 259

2 Peter
2:1-3 274

1 John
1:1-2 155
1:1-3 248
2:15-17 273
2:18-23 274
2:24 248
3:2 209
3:2-10 272
3:24 225
4:10 271, 272

Jude
1:3 47, 110
1:4 273

Revelation 53–55
1:1-20 53
2:1-3:22 53
2:14 273
2:20 274
4:1-22:21 53
5:1-14 54–55
19:6-9 275
22:17-18 235

EARLY CHRISTIAN WRITING
Augustine of Hippo
De Utilitate Credendi 156
On the Good of Marriage 256, 258

Gennadius of Marseilles
Lives of Illustrious Men 93–95

Hippolytus
Apostolic Tradition 57, 58
Justin Martyr
First Apology 176

Rufinus of Aquileia
A Commentary on the Apostles' Creed 56

Vincent of Lerins
The Commonitory 93–128

CLASSICAL WRITING
Aristotle
Nichomachean Ethics 34

Plutarch
'Life of Theseus' 23:1 in *Lives*, Vol I 4

www.ingramcontent.com/pod-product-compliance
Lightning Source LLC
Chambersburg PA
CBHW052014070526
44584CB00016B/1742